Personnel Management in Local Government

Second edition

Alan Fowler

Institute of Personnel Management

First published 1975
© *Institute of Personnel Management, 1975, 1980*
Second edition published 1980

Printed in Great Britain by Martin's of Berwick

British Library Cataloguing in Publication Data
Fowler, Alan
    Personnel management in local government. – 2nd ed.
    1. Local government – England – Personnel management
    2. Local officials and employees – England
    I.Title   II. Institute of Personnel Management
    325'.005'100942   JS3173

ISBN 0–85292–270 1 ✓

Personnel Management in Local Government

Alan Fowler was born in 1927. He studied personnel management at the London School of Economics. He spent 20 years in industry with Elliott Automation, Clarks Shoes, the Nigerian Sugar Company, and Richard Costain Limited, where he was Head of UK Personnel.

In 1973 he joined the Greater London Council as Assistant Director of Establishments, heading the Industrial Relations Branch. While with the GLC he frequently acted as an employers' side member of various National Joint Councils and Joint Negotiating Committees.

In 1977 he took up his present appointment of Head of Manpower Services for Hampshire County Council – the largest of the shire counties employing some 52,000 people. His work spans both personnel management and management services. Alan Fowler is a member of Industrial Tribunals for England and Wales, a Member of the Society of Chief Personnel Officers in Local Government, and a Fellow of the Institute of Personnel Management.

Contents

p65

Preface to first edition

It is as necessary to know what a book is not as it is to define its objectives. There are four disclaimers for this volume:

It is not intended as a general textbook of personnel management theory and practice. Other books are available to serve this end, and textbook personnel management is discussed here only to the extent that is relevant to the local government setting. For this reason, subjects such as personnel selection and safety, which have few specific local government characteristics, are not treated in any detail, though they are, of course, important personnel management functions. Conversely, certain aspects of work study and job evaluation are discussed at some length because of the existence of specific local government schemes or procedures.

Its excursions into the management services field are limited to areas in which management services techniques serve mainstream personnel management ends.

Its descriptive, historical sections are limited to local government in England and Wales. Scottish local government has its own history; and its re-organization in 1975, while following the broad pattern of its southern counterparts, has had its own characteristics and was too recent to include in any definitive fashion at the time of writing. It is hoped that, in sections other than the historical, it will be as relevant to Scotland as elsewhere.

The views, comments and criticisms in this book are solely the author's in his private capacity as a personnel professional. They are not to be attributed to his current employer (the Greater London Council), to his colleagues there who wittingly or otherwise have helped with the book, or to the Institute of Personnel Management.

What the book does set out to do is to describe and discuss personnel management in its local government setting; this involves a description of that setting in both historical and management terms. Despite the major changes introduced with the 1974 re-organization of local government, many of the current attitudes of councillors, managers, staff and trade unions are influenced by the experience and traditions of the past. Old style establishments work was not changed overnight merely by its re-christening as personnel management. Personnel management, too, can only be effective, can only make sense, if it is placed firmly within its general management setting; here too there are unique local government traditions and patterns. This book attempts to summarize these factors and show their relevance to the nature and style of personnel management in local government.

It is hoped therefore that the book will be of interest to a wider local government readership than merely the denizens of the new personnel departments. Most local government officers in administrative and professional departments find their work affected by personnel matters – by problems of staffing, morale, productivity, industrial relations. The most effective method of tackling these problems is by a partnership between the departmental manager and the personnel officer. This book may help the former to get the best advice and service from the latter.

The role of the councillor has also been given some attention. Inadequate standards of personnel management will inhibit a Council's ability to achieve its public and political objectives, so a lively and informed interest in employment matters by councillors is to be encouraged.

Finally, I must express some trepidation about attempting these objectives within a very short period of entering the local government world. Rationalizing, it is hoped that the 20 years personnel management experience in industries as diverse as shoe manufacture, tropical agriculture and construction which preceded my entry into local government in 1973 have at least developed my awareness of the similarities between apparently totally distinct employment environments. I have therefore consciously introduced a comparative element into this book by contrasting or relating private and public sector personnel management practice. Each sector can learn from the other and, were I to return to the industrial world, I know that my last few years in local government would enable me to write more effectively of personnel management in industry.

Preface to second edition

A good deal has happened in local government and in the general employment scene since the first edition of this book. Bains is receding into history, local government services are under severe strain as a result of the financial recession, case law arising from the massive legislation boom of the mid 1970s has become extensive, a further four years of various pay policies have left more marks on pay levels and differentials, and Whitley pay bargaining is under some strain.

For all these reasons an extensive revision of the book has become necessary. For my own part, too, four more years' experience and a move from the metropolis to a shire county have widened and changed some of my own perceptions of the problems and possibilities facing local government personnel officers.

Apart from general revisions throughout the text I have added a new chapter – on manpower planning looked at from a practical and operational, rather than theoretical, basis – and expanded the original single chapter on employment legislation into two. In these two chapters, in addition to updating comments on unfair dismissal, redundancy and other elements of recent legislation, I have also added new sections on the doctrine of *ultra vires* as this applies to employment matters, and on industrial democracy.

I have resisted a temptation to include comprehensive coverage of management services. Although the trend seems to be for management services to become integrated with personnel work, it is not possible to do full justice to all aspects of this subject and still keep the book within respectable size limits. I have, however, expanded the establishment control chapter somewhat, particularly to include reference to manpower budgeting.

I hope my colleagues in counties and districts will find this revised edition a little more attuned to life outside London. And I have to continue my original apologies to personnel officers in Scotland for not separately describing the Scottish scene.

As the bibliography indicates, more publications are now generally available to personnel officers about the local government aspects of their jobs than was so in 1974 and I have been aided in this new edition by a number of LACSAB and LGTB reports and booklets. LAC-SAB's Employee Relations Handbook has become an invaluable and essential aid to personnel officers and I have not attempted to compete with it.

Finally, as with the first edition, I am glad both to acknowledge the direct and indirect help I have had from colleagues in and outside my own authority and to exonerate them from any blame for any of the book's failings, which are mine alone. Hampshire County Council, too, is now joined with GLC as being wholly exempt from any identification with any of the views expressed herein.

Alan Fowler

1 The local government setting

Management, whether in a general or specialist sense, cannot sensibly be discussed in the abstract. The characteristics of management processes, the types of management structure and the style of managerial action are all inevitably and rightly influenced by the whole setting in which they occur. These influences on the nature of management have many dimensions. There is the influence of time – of tradition, custom and precedent. There are economic influences: is the activity labour or capital intensive? What is the interaction between the two key resources of finance and manpower? There are influences stemming from size and location: is the organization a large or small scale employer? Is it basically local, regional or national? Is it a single or multi-employer activity? There are influences deriving from the nature of work: is there one dominant activity or are the activities diverse and unrelated? Are these activities reliant on high technology? Are they production or service orientated?

Finally, there are the influences of ownership and control. The owner-manager of a small business manages differently from the board of a multi-national corporation. Public accountability generates influences which differ from those which arise from accountability to shareholders. And the extent of government influence, by direct control financial constraints or 'back door' pressure, also generates different management reactions in different situations.

It is an underlying theme of this book that personnel management must be discussed in, and related to, its general management setting. The purpose of this opening chapter is to describe the local government setting to which both its general and personnel management must relate. Local government is a part of our national life and is a national institution which has its own complex history and traditions, plays a unique social and economic role, has a unique pattern of organization and control – and has recently undergone a more fundamental re-organization and restructuring than either it, or most other large institutions, have ever previously experienced. It would be surprising and disturbing if management generally, and personnel

1

management particularly, did not reflect in some unique forms, the specific characteristics and traditions of local government as a whole.

This chapter, therefore, is designed to set the local government scene. It first outlines the historical development of local government, and then examines its present position in terms both of its social and economic acitivites and of its role as an employer. Because size is an important determinant of management character, details are also given of the scale of local government employment.

The historical development of local government

In 1835, a Royal Commission reported on the state of municipal corporations in England and Wales. The Commission's conclusions were direct and unreserved:

> There prevails amongst the inhabitants of a great majority of the incorporated towns a general, and in our opinion, a just dissatisfaction with their Municipal Institutions; a distrust of the self-elected Municipal Councils, whose powers are subject to no popular control, and whose acts and proceedings being secret are unchecked by the influence of public opinion; a distrust of the Municipal Magistracy tainting with suspicion the local administration of justice and often accompanied with contempt of the persons by whom the law is administered; a discontent under the burthens of Local Taxation, while revenues that ought to be applied for the public advantage are diverted from their legitimate use and are sometimes wastefully bestowed for the benefit of individuals, sometimes squandered for purposes injurious to the character and morals of the people. We therefore feel it to be our duty to represent to Your Majesty that the existing Municipal Corporations of England and Wales neither possess nor deserve the confidence or respect of Your Majesty's subjects and that a thorough reform must be effected before they can become, what we humbly submit to Your Majesty they ought to be, useful and efficient instruments of local government.

This reforming report marks the beginning of local government as we know it today and to this extent local government is a 19th century invention, steeped in 19th century traditions. Yet its roots go back as far as documented history. Very broadly, its history falls into two phases – pre 1832 when local institutions derived power from the Crown in the boroughs and from the land-owning class in the counties; and post 1832 when the basis of power and authority was progressively moved to the people through extensions of the local franchise.

By 1830 three types of local authority had developed. In the towns were the borough councils, incorporated by royal charter; in the counties, county magistrates had a range of general and administrative duties in addition to their legal role; only at parish level did the local community have the power of local control by the election of certain designated officials for certain limited purposes, particularly poor relief, local peace-keeping and the upkeep of highways. The whole system (or rather the whole uncoordinated mixture of systems) was under strain. There was growing pressure for more democratic institutions, there were increasing financial difficulties as public standards and expectations grew. Above all, the rapidly expanding cities and towns in the new industrial areas required far more effective social and public health measures than the antiquated boroughs were able or willing to provide. Local government reform was one of the many side effects of the industrial revolution.

Two different types of reform can be followed through the 19th and 20th centuries: first, reform of the nature and structure of local government as a political institution; secondly, almost continual change in the functions over which local government has been given control.

The conflict, or relationship, between these two types of change is not unimportant when considering the type of management structure appropriate to a local authority. Emphasis on the political role of local government results in priority being given to the role of the elected assembly as the focus for community discussion and decision. Emphasis on the functional, or operational, role results in priority being given to effective, industrial-style management. The dichotomy has not yet been resolved.

Political reform
Political reform of local government was closely linked with electoral reform, initiated by the Reform Act of 1832 which removed the parliamentary franchise from the boroughs. The Municipal Corporations Act of 1835 began the more direct process of re-shaping local authorities, though a similar attempt to reform the situation in the counties was defeated in 1836 by the landowning gentry, the most powerful voice in Parliament at that time. A 50 year period of parliamentary skirmishing eventually resulted in the 1888 Local Government Act which established the County Councils and County Borough Councils. Urban and Rural District Councils were formed by another Local Government Act of 1894. The political effect of this series of Acts was a power struggle between the counties and the boroughs – between town and country. A rural district would grow and seek to attain urban district status. Further growth, and it sought incorporation as a municipal borough. Then, to escape county domination, when its population reached 50,000 it would apply for county borough status and so stand at the peak of the local government

3

pyramid. A further Local Government Act in 1926 eventually placed limits on this process.

No further major changes occurred until after the second world war when social and political institutions were again opened to debate and change. Local government commissions set up in 1945 and 1958 proposed a variety of structural changes but encountered bitter and well-organized local and national opposition from particular interest groups. The more intense the political debate about boundaries and structures the less attention seemed to be given to the *functions* of local government, a point referred to by the 1945 Commission's report which commented that discussion about geographical areas for local authorities made little sense without considering local authority functions. But the warning went largely unheeded. Yet another Royal Commission was established by the 1966 Labour Government, and in 1969 it presented its recommendations for sweeping reforms – for 'a new structure and a new map', as the report had it. England should be divided into 62 local government areas and in all but four of them (London, Birmingham, Liverpool and Manchester) there should be a single authority. Only in the four conurbations would two-tier authorities be needed. The Redcliffe-Maud Commission's remedy was thus that of the unitary principle and this view was certainly influenced by considerations of administrative and functional efficiency.

It was attacked – particularly by one of its own members in a long minority report – largely on the grounds that it weakened community involvement and influence over local affairs.

The Conservative Government of 1972 eventually introduced the most recent Local Government Act in which the unitary principle was abandoned in favour of a two-tier approach. This system had been introduced in London in 1965 as a separate piece of local government reform. Theoretically, this seemed a compromise between the need for large units to achieve the economies and efficiencies of size, and the smaller units needed for the continuation of local participation.

The changing funcions of local government
Before outlining the post 1974 system it is necessary to go back to the 19th century to follow the other line of development – the changes in local government functions. Five primary influences on the nature of local government activities can be distinguished:

poor law, leading to social welfare services generally
public health, leading to drainage, medical and housing services
roads and highways construction and maintenance
education
municipal trading, leading to public transport, gas, electricity,
water services and other public services.

4

The responsibility of the parish for the relief of its poor goes back into the origins of English history; 19th century reform included, in 1834, an improvement in parish administration, when parishes were grouped into larger 'unions' for poor law administrative purposes. The government also took responsibility for the oversight of poor law matters through a Poor Law Board, and this soon became concerned with the low standards of public health, particularly in the new industrial conurbations. Urbanization, poverty and insanitary conditions had become coincident.

The first organizational solution by government was a functional one. A central General Board of Health was set up, supported by local boards across the country and while the former was disbanded in 1858, largely as a result of a political battle about the distribution of power, the local boards soon had their powers extended and became known as Local Government Boards.

They were given responsibility for the management of streets and highways, other than the main turnpike routes, largely on the functional grounds that well kept roads and good drainage were both essential to higher standards of public health. Confusion in responsibility for public health and highways between the Local Boards, highway districts (where no local board had been established) and borough councils (which replaced the boards in the boroughs) led to a Royal Sanitary Commission in 1868 taking the view that public health was 'part of the larger subject of the entire system of local government'. The 1872 Public Health Act began to re-organize the system and eventually, in 1895, the urban and rural sanitary districts became the urban and rural district councils which were to be a feature of local government for the next 80 years.

Rooted in this early concern for public health, and in the transfer of functions from specialized bodies (health boards, highway boards etc) to multi-purpose local authorities, lie the origins of local government's involvement in a massive range of welfare services. Two are of particular note – health and housing. The National Health Service is basically founded on services (including hospitals) initially established by local government. The 1936 Public Health Act specifically required County and County Borough Councils to ensure the provision of adequate hospital services. While the provision of new housing was potentially a local government matter from as early as 1890, it was the impact of social and economic change after each of the two world wars which stimulated the expansion of local government activity in this field. That it was a local government function at all originates in the 19th century concern for the sanitary conditions of the poor in the expanding industrial towns and cities.

The involvement of local authorities in education derives formally from the 1902 Education Act which transferred powers from the

School Boards to the local councils. Educational reform, however, was very much a feature of national, and not local, government and the pace and nature of the evolution of a full system of state education was determined first by the Central Board of Education, and later by the Ministries and Departments of Education and Science. Local authorities were expected to apply national policy while providing local control, and the differences in political views between local and national government made this an uneasy role. Friction between local education authorities and central government remains endemic to this duality of direction.

The extension of local government into 'municipal trading' – the running of gas works, tramways, electricity supply, crematoria, slaughter-houses, cold-storage facilities, airports and the like – owes its origins to 19th century political theory. A primary concern of 19th century government was the regulation of the monopoly powers of private undertakings in the public utility field.

Far more attention was paid to the political implications of the growth of towns, and of the power and influence of industrial monopolists, than to the types of organizational structure best suited to the efficient managerial control of the new technologies. Local authorities were, in consequence, given sweeping powers to set up trading organizations to produce and sell gas, water, electricity and public transport, or to take over privately run utilities.

By the end of the 19th century, local authorities were extensively involved in the provision of a whole range of public utilities on a quasi-commercial basis and this situation continued right through to the late 1940s. By then, however, it was becoming clear that the financial and technical demands of high technology functions were not being met by the politically-shaped nature of local government finances and structures.

Electricity supply provides a good example. Technological developments, combined with a rapid growth in demand for electrical power from industry, required both a massive capital investment programme and a national system of power generation and distribution. Local government was not structured or financed to meet these requirements. Electricity undertakings were under-capitalized and electricity supply was uncoordinated. Similar considerations applied to gas undertakings. In the public health field, deficiencies in the hospital services were also revealing small-scale local government's inability to manage large scale technically-based undertakings.

Since the second world war, the main functional trend has been the reverse of that of the 19th century. That century saw a continual addition to local government of functions transferred from specialist boards. In the 20th century we are experiencing the reverse – transfers of major functions from local government to new single-purpose

6

authorities not subject to local political control. And the pressure for such transfers is that of achieving higher standards of managerial and technological control.

In health and welfare, the main transfers of services away from local government were achieved by the National Health Acts of the late 1940s, though the process was extended by the 1974 transfers of many of the remaining functions to the new Health Authorities.

In public transport, the process has not gone quite so far although, from the Transport Act of 1968 onwards, considerable inroads have been made into local government's involvement with bus services: the creation of the British Airports Authority involved similar restrictions on local authority control over the larger airports.

In public utilities, 1948 and 1949 saw the transfer of some 600 electricity and gas undertakings from local control to the new nationalized industries, a process that again was followed in 1974 by the transfer of water, sewerage and sewage treatment functions to the new Water Authorities.

If the main emphases from a central government viewpoint were to remain those of technological efficiency and national uniformity it would be pertinent to wonder how long it will be before the police, the fire service, education and refuse disposal (or solid waste management to use current jargon) come under similar pressure. The conflict between the potential efficiency of national single purpose organizations and the demand for local community control remains as keenly unresolved as it was in the great 'centralization' debates of the 1850s. And in the decentralizing direction, current political pressures for devolution seem stronger than at any time since the 1939-45 war.

Local government today: the councils

The shape and functions of local government today, while influenced by all the developments of the 19th century and by the post second world war transfers, were redefined in 1974 in the most comprehensive reorganization yet attempted. Previous reorganizations dealt, in the main, with only parts of the system – boroughs or counties. The 1974 reorganization rationalized the whole system on the two-tier basis: counties at tier one, districts at tier two. The unitary county boroughs disappeared as did the three tier county, borough, district pattern. Some 1,400 authorities in England and Wales were reduced to just over 450. A similar reorganization in Scotland in 1975 resulted in the establishment of nine regional and 53 district authorities, plus three all-purpose authorites in the Western and Northern Isles.

The division of functions between the first and second tier authorities varies, and counties and districts are therefore grouped into metropolitan and non-metropolitan authorities.

7

Metropolitan counties and districts: England and Wales
There are six metropolitan counties, excluding London, and 36 metropolitan district councils.

Some population statistics are:

total population of metropolitan areas	11,750,000
largest metropolitan county: West Midlands	2,800,000
smallest metropolitan county: Tyne and Wear	1,200,000
largest metropolitan district: Birmingham	1,100,000
smallest metropolitan district: S Tyneside	173,000

The functions of the various types of authorities are set out in tabular form below.

Function	Metropolitan		Non-metropolitan		London	
	County	Dist	County	Dist	Boro	GLC
Clean air	—	√	—	√	√	—
Consumer protection	√	—	√	—	√	—
Education	—	√	√	—	√¹	√
Environmental health	—	√	—	√	√	√²
Fire services	√	—	√	—	—	√
Police	√	—	√	—	—	—
Housing	—	√	—	√	√	√
Libraries	—	√	√	—	√	—
Museums, art galleries	√	√	√	√	√	√
Parks, recreation	√	√	√	√	√	√
Personal social services	—	√	√	—	√	—
Refuse collection	—	√	—	√	√	—
Refuse disposal	√	—	√	—	—	√
Planning	√	√	√	√	√	√
Transport, highways	√	√	√	√	√	√³
Youth employment	—	√	√	—	√	—

1 Outer boroughs only. Inner boroughs covered by Inner London Education Authority (GLC).
2 Includes Thames flood control.
3 Includes oversight of London Transport.

Non-metropolitan counties
There are 47 non-metropolitan counties and 333 district councils. Population details are:

total non-metropolitan population	30,500,000
largest county: Hampshire	1,450,000
smallest county: Isle of Wight	110,000
largest district: Bristol	420,000
smallest district: Scilly Isles	2,000

London, while similar in structure, differs in allocation of functions. It has one regional authority – the Greater London Council (GLC) – 32 boroughs and the traditional exception to almost all the rules, the Corporation of the City of London: 34 authorites in all.

Population details are:

GLC area	7,300,000
largest borough: Croydon	333,000
smallest borough: Kingston	139,000
City of London	5,200

Local authority income amounts to some £15,000,000,000 annually or about 13 per cent of the gross national product. And local government employs some two and a half million people–10 per cent of the working population, costing about £10,000,000,000 in wages or eight per cent of the gross domestic product. This is twice the size of the whole construction industry and as large, in employment terms, as the car, shipbuilding, engineering and metal manufacturing industries put together. In economic terms, local government is big business and labour intensive.

Further political reform

Within a very short period after the 1974 reorganization, agitation for further changes began to re-emerge. This was centred partly on the distribution of services between the counties and districts and partly on the erosion of status, involved in the two-tier authority system, of the old, single status county boroughs. By 1977, the 'Big Nine' of these authorities – Southampton, Portsmouth, Derby, Stoke-on-Trent, Leicester, Nottingham, Hull, Plymouth, Bristol – were being considered by the government as eligible candidates for what a Government White Paper described as 'organic change'. This implied a possible transfer to them, from the first tier counties, of various functions in planning, highways, education and social services. The Labour Party separately produced a new plan for large regional authorities (to replace counties and to take over water and health services) and district councils with more powers than present districts.

Conflicting views on all these proposals were not, however, on wholly party lines. The Conservative dominated Association of District Councils backed organic change: the equally Conservative Association of County Councils opposed it. Some Labour politicians campaigned for the delegation of education services to districts, but some opposition to this was evident from other influential Labour factions.

The Labour Government's plans fell at the 1979 General Election but the new Conservative Government immediately set in train proposals for a redistribution of a variety of planning functions between districts and counties. The overall impact of these proposals was markedly less than organic change would have involved. Transfers of education and social services to the districts would have meant that some 100,000 staff could have had an enforced change of employer. The planning function changes involve far fewer staff, as only some 3,000 staff are employed in the whole planning activity throughout England and Wales. In 1980, the old issue of national control versus local autonomy dominated the scene.

Local government employment

Having sketched the historical background and the current size and functions of local government, we can now move closer to the world of personnel management and examine the scale and nature of employment in this labour intensive sector.

For many years there was a problem in quantifying local government manpower, caused by a variety of differing and sometimes conflicting statistics. The Department of Employment produces a quarterly return: statistics are produced by the various National Joint Councils (NJC) of the numbers of employees within each: the Local Government Training Board (LGTB) has also undertaken manpower surveys.

In 1975, a Joint Manpower Watch was set up between local and national government to monitor the level of local government staffing. This has become the most accurate source of employment data, and a 1979 return produced the following totals:

Activity	Total no employed	Percentage of part-timers
Teachers, lecturers	705,334	23.0
Education – non-teaching employees	717,509	70.1
Construction services	135,909	0.4
Transport services	22,449	1.8
Social services	302,578	55.0
Libraries, museums	41,588	39.1
Recreation, parks, baths	83,943	21.5
Environmental health	22,950	8.9
Refuse collection and disposal	49,729	0.5
Housing services	56,280	21.9
Planning	22,672	2.6
Consumer protection	4,174	8.0
Treasurers' departments	45,101	5.4
Secretarys' Solicitors' departments	53,394	30.9
Architects' departments	25,218	3.2

continued on next page

Activity	Total no employed	Percentage of part-timers
Estates departments	8,170	9.4
Engineering departments	89,167	4.4
Personnel/Management Services	9,928	3.3
Fire services	41,145	4.7
Police: uniformed and traffic wardens	118,428	nil
: civilians	39,301	20.3
Others (incl central admin and computers)	58,463	35.8
Totals	2,653,430	34.4

Source: Joint Manpower Watch Return, March, 1979

Of these totals, about 46 per cent are manual workers, and 54 per cent non-manual. The following table shows a further breakdown of each of these groups into male and female employees.

	Percentage	
	Male	Female
Manual full time	32	11
part time	3	54
Totals	35	65
Non-manual full time	46	41
part time	3	10
Totals	49	51

(This table is based on LGTB figures and does not equate exactly with Joint Manpower Watch figures—which do not show sex analyses).

There are obvious difficulties in collating national statistics of this kind. Some authorities send in late returns. Not all keep their employee records in a form compatible with the categories required. There is evidence that different authorities categorize their staff in different ways so that some of the individual totals for the various services set out in the first of the above tables must be treated with caution. One or two authorities in a revolt against form-filling have failed to make any return, and their totals have had to be estimated from other sources. Any one total includes a wide number of different types of jobs.

These figures are of limited use, therefore, in assessing the types and sizes of occupational groups. For these we need to turn to National Joint Council and Local Government Training Board figures. From these sources, the main occupational groups can be categorized thus:

Administrative, clerical, technical and professional staff	568,700
includes:	
clerical staff	164,900
technicians	112,700
residual social workers	55,900
General manual workers	c. 1,002,700
includes: school meals staff, school caretakers and	
cleaners; roadworkers, parks and garden staff, refuse	
collectors transport workers	
Building and civil engineering workers	87,000
includes: building craftsmen and labourers	
Engineering craftsmen	8,200
includes: fitters, electricians and heating and	
ventilating engineers	
Police	151,000
includes: 62,000 traffic wardens and	
37,000 civilians	
Fire brigades	51,000
Teaching staff	573,600

(*Source:* Employee Relations in Local Government, LACSAB, 1978)

LGTB and LACSAB figures of the approximate numbers employed in other specific groups include:

Accountants/assistants (qualified)	6,000
Administrative officers/assistants	20,000
Caretakers (schools) and cleaners	172,500
Careers officers	2,250
Catering workers	37,000
Civil and municipal engineers (qualified)	8,500
Clerical officers/assistants	87,000
Drivers (HGV)	40,000
Education welfare officers	2,400
Electricians	5,100
Home helps	88,400
Managers	56,500
Management services officers	4,000
Parks and playing fields workers	5,600
Refuse collectors	26,800
Roadmen	45,000
Supervisors of manual workers	50,000
Typists and secretaries	25,700

(Further statistics from Joint Manpower Watch returns are given in Appendix A on page 293).

Local government's massive labour force has a number of important characteristics.

First, the very large number of occupations – certainly totalling several hundred – including a wide range of white-collar professions. In addition to over half a million teachers, there are large numbers of architects, accountants, engineers of most disciplines (civil, mechanical, electrical, structural etc), quantity and land surveyors, valuers, planners, solicitors and administrators.

Secondly, the large number of women employees in professional jobs (particularly teaching and social work), in office work and in the manual worker group. Some 65 per cent of manual workers are women, mainly though not exclusively in the school meals and school cleaning services.

Thirdly, the large number of part-time employees – again particularly among schools' manual workers, though also accounting for over 20 per cent of the white-collar group.

Fourthly, the existence of the two uniformed services of the fire brigades and the police forces with their own highly idiosyncratic styles and traditions and in which many aspects of employment and organization structures are determined as much by Home Office regulation as by the local authorities who employ them.

Fifthly, the wide geographical scatter of employing establishments in most authorities. Manual workers in particular tend to be employed in ones or twos (or in relatively small groups) in a large number of different locations. The tensions and solidarities of large-scale factory employment where 10,000 workers may be on one site do not occur in local government, despite its being a labour-intensive activity. The biggest concentration of staff is usually the white-collar group at the Town Hall.

The diversity in size of local authorities and the differences in function between the two tiers and between metropolitan and non-metropolitan authorities makes it impossible to describe a typical authority. But a theoretical idea of the scale of each authority as an employer can be given by dividing the total work force fairly evenly between the 456 authorities to give one, admittedly non-existent, average. On this basis, the average authority would employ about:

9 chief officers
1500 white collar staff
1000 manual workers

(Police, firemen and education department staff have been excluded as they are not employed by all authorities.) This gives an average work force of around 2,500 – the actual range is from less than 500 to the combined GLC/ILEA total (including teachers) of over 115,000.

A more specific type of average is that obtained by looking at the mean employee totals for each type of authority. These figures demonstrate the very considerable effect of education, social services and police on the manpower totals of the shire counties and metropolitan districts.

Type of Authority	Average no of employees per authority
Non-metropolitan counties	27,850
Non-metropolitan districts	850
Metropolitan counties	5,550
Metropolitan districts	16,410
London boroughs	8,430

The total numbers employed in local government have remained relatively constant in the period 1974 to 1978, following a period in the late 1960s and early 1970s in which they grew by some three to five per cent annually. Changes since reorganization show a small rise to 1976, a decline from 1976 to 1978, a levelling out at that point, and a further rise into 1979, halted and then reversed by the 1979 Conservative Government's cuts in public expenditure. Thus:

March 1975 to March 1976:	+1.5%
March 1976 to March 1977:	−0.8%
March 1977 to March 1978:	−0.6%
March 1978 to March 1979:	+1.6%
March 1979 to March 1980:	−0.6%

Overall totals have hovered around the two and a half million mark; equivalent to about two million when part-timers are converted statistically to full-time equivalents.

This then, is the scale of local authority employment, set against a continuously changing political and functional background and with a wide range of current functions, some of which interlink and some of which are distinct, separate and unique. What kind of setting is this for management generally and for personnel management in particular?

If the management of each local authority is considered as a corporate or unified activity, then the local government setting is a difficult one. Corporate management – the management of the work of an organization as an integrated whole – needs unifying influences which induce individual managers to come together as a working team. The purposes and objects of the organization as a whole need to

14

be felt by its top management to be more important than the achievements of any of its parts.

Local government suffers here from having no one concrete, 'manageable' purpose. Functionally there is little in common between, say, education, road maintenance and the fire service. They compete for resources (particularly finance) but do not contribute to any overriding, common, management objective. For managers (as distinct from councillors) the underlying problem is that the *raison d'être* for local government is not the provision of the particular range of functions or services which it operates. These are little more than a current compromise between technological practicability, administrative convenience and the age-old battle of centralization *v* decentralization. The *raison d'être* of local government lies in its political, rather than functional, role. Local government provides local communities with a means of sharing, supporting, modifying, reducing central government power. It spreads the democratic process more widely throughout the community than can be achieved solely through the parliamentary franchise.

It follows that local government managers will always be faced with potential conflict between the narrow, operational efficiency which might be achieved by autocratic concentration on single services; and the political needs of an elected assembly continually to resist the concentration of power either of central government or of single-purpose authorities not subject to direct elected member control. Local government is a battlefield between high technology and democracy; between economic efficiency and lay management; between the centre and the periphery.

But some unifying factors do exist. Managers surely share with councillors the desire to promote the general well-being and sense of community of their areas – and all the authority's functions serve this end. Managers are concerned too, to explain to the local electorate, through the elected members, the factors that need to be taken into account in assessing priorities between the services.

More directly from a management viewpoint, all managers need to be able to demonstrate that they are managing each service effectively and economically; and there are common techniques and skills involved in this.

Above all, all mangers of all services use the two common resources of finance and manpower and need to develop and apply common skills in the effective procurement, development and use of each.

Moreover, and here we turn towards personnel management, many important occupational groups of employees are common to all or most services. Clerical staff, administrators, financial specialists, many manual worker groups, are employed in all local government functions and can move between them. Common policies and procedures in the recruitment, training and development of such staff are important contributors to manpower effectiveness. And even for the specialist and professional groups employed only in particular services, managers share one common problem – that of achieving a high degree of employee enthusiasm and motivation. All managers of all functions are, or should be, concerned to extend employee consultation, involvement and participation; to ensure that employees are well-informed and can contribute fully to the whole process of operating their council's services. All are involved in the effect on employee attitudes, expectations and aspirations of changes in society at large. All carry responsibility for the application of current employment legislation to promote a higher level of employment protection and industrial democracy. All managers thus have important personnel management responsibilities.

2 Personnel management - definitions

Before examining the nature and development of personnel management in local government, an explanation is necessary of the way in which terms such as 'personnel management' and 'the personnel function' are used in this book; and of the author's particular view of the role of the personnel officer in a modern management setting. Personnel management is a relatively new concept for many local authorities and there may well be officers and elected members who have either a restricted view of the nature of a personnel officer's job, or may be concerned about the possibility of his taking important employment responsibilities and authority away from other senior officers or from the Council's committees.

A summary of some of the most common misconceptions about personnel management illustrates this need for a definition of the function and its terms:

that personnel management is a new element of management which can be added as an extra, as it were, to an existing management system

that personnel management is an activity which can be carried out in its entirety by a specialist – by a personnel manager

that it is made up solely of a set of specialized techniques

that the personnel officer is in a midway position between the employer and the employees – that he is, in effect, an intermediary

that the personnel officer's role is a purely advisory one

that unless management services are directly linked with personnel management, the latter will consist of little more than hiring, firing and welfare.

This list could be extended, but enough has been described to illustrate the confusion which can result from a personnel department being established before all the managers concerned have a common view of its function. The starting point for a clearer understanding of the subject is to look at the duties and activities of *any* manager – that is of anyone in an organization who has a direct responsibility for supervising and organizing the work of subordinate staff. This broad definition of a manager can cover a road foreman, a design project team leader, a senior solicitor in charge of a section, or an assistant treasurer, just as much as a chief executive.

All these jobs, all managers' jobs, include certain common elements concerned with the management of people. Subordinate staff have to be selected, deployed, instructed, directed, consulted, advised, encouraged, motivated. Staff problems can arise in all types of work: employees have grievances, misbehave, disagree with each other, have personal problems. Staff join trade unions and elect representatives and shop stewards. Shop stewards make claims, press managers for improvements, demand consultation and involvement. The law imposes constraints on managers' employment decisions and lays down requirements and minimum standards in the fields of job security, equal opportunity, safety and health.

In the most general sense, 'personnel management' is a term embracing all these managerial activities – all aspects, that is, of man management. In this sense all managers undertake personnel management whether they have thought consciously about it or not. But a growth of awareness of the importance of the human aspects of management has led to the establishment of personnel management as a significant and distinct field of management studies. To an increasing extent it has become evident that the effectiveness of any organization is dependent as much, if not more, on the quality of its staff as on any other single factor; and that this quality, too, is not a static or permanent feature like the quality of plant and equipment. It consists partly of the match of man to job and job to man; partly on the extent to which each employee is interested and involved in his work, on motivation; and partly on the ability of the organization to plan for, and cope with, the changes in its manpower requirements and attitudes necessitated by its own evolution and by the changing nature of standards and expectations in society at large. Personnel management in this sense is a positive, dynamic element in general management.

It involves a view of work as a social activity, and manpower as a major resource. It involves a view of management as having responsibility for the development of this resource as well as its effective use. This may sound an impersonal, mechanistic or exploitive view and, indeed, there is a danger of over-concentration on the economic implications of employment to the exclusion of the human aspects. So the well-rounded view of personnel management is incomplete without the acceptance of the employee as an individual with his own human hopes, fears, needs, ambitions and rights.

In summary, personnel management is that part of management as a whole which is concerned with people at work; with the relationships between man and job, man and man (individually and collectively), and between employer and employee institutions. As with all management, the object of personnel management must be the promotion of effectiveness of the organization – but with the belief that this effectiveness is directly related to the physical and psychological well-being of the employees.

These definitions, however, are all rather generalized. For a clearer view of personnel management as an active, working element in management, a classification of its areas of activity into four broad categories is useful:

employment and deployment
training and development
personnel relations
pay and conditions.

Each category includes a number of activities and these are summarized below.

Employment and deployment

Manpower planning – forecasting demands for manpower and matching these to trends in supply. This can include analysing the age structure, turnover, retirement rates and promotion patterns of existing staff; projecting these forward against changes in external factors (such as a reduction in the number of school leavers); working out the manpower requirements of the organization's future work programmes; comparing these with the likely supply situation and planning any consequently necessary changes in recruitment and training programmes – or in the work programmes themselves. Planning should also include the forecasting of, and preparation for, changes in employee attitudes and expectations.

Two practical aspects of manpower planning are decisions about the number of trainees of various kinds to be recruited each year; and planning for the effects of future retirements.

With a large, complex labour force, operational research techniques can be used to forecast the ebb and flow of labour movements.

Recruitment – the process of generating a required volume of applicants for jobs. This means far more than the insertion of press advertisements. The most important single factor affecting recruitment is the general reputation the organization has as an employer; and a local authority should be able to build up a sufficiently high reputation to generate a steady stream of unsolicited applications. Beyond this, recruitment also means developing links with careers advisory services, with university appointments boards and with local schools and colleges. The advertising of specific vacancies can then be set against a general background of careers promotion. There are also specific skills involved in the drafting of job advertisements and supporting documents (job descriptions, application forms etc) and in selecting the most cost-effective media.

Selection – one of the most important personnel management activities which can vitally affect the quality of an organization's manpower. Conventionally, selection has been based almost wholly on interviews and, in local government, on selection boards. Effective selection can use a whole range of techniques: aptitude and ability tests, group assessments, in-depth individual interviews, project work under observation.

Deployment – the employment aspect concerned with the movement of existing staff between departments and jobs, as work loads change. It involves the assessment of changing manpower requirements in quantity and quality, and the arrangements necessary to transfer employees to meet these changes. Procedures become necessary to deal with transfer applications, the resistance of individuals to make such changes, the discussion and negotiation of changes with the trade unions. It is also within this area of employment that techniques such as work study and O and M (organization and methods) can be applied to ensure economically effective job and organization design and structures. Personnel management, however, is equally concerned with ensuring that jobs are shaped to fit people rather than the reverse, and with trying to create a total work environment in which employees can gain a sense of personal achievement and satisfaction. Re-training may also need to be provided as the requirement for different skills varies.

Redundancy – the more negative end of the employment spectrum, but one requiring skilled and sensitive management treatment.

Training and development

No organization can be fully effective unless it takes positive action to raise the levels of skill and expertise of its employees generally, and to develop individual employees' potential for promotion. The main elements of this work are:

Induction training – introducing new employees to the organization, to their colleagues, to their jobs, in order to reduce the difficulties any new employee experiences in changing his employment.

Skills and job training – although it might by possible to rely entirely on the recruitment of fully-trained craftsmen, typists, computer operators, civil engineers and so on, most organizations of any size accept a responsibility to conduct some training of their own and so to contribute to the local or national pool of skilled manpower. Apprentice training, administrative trainee schemes, training schemes to assist engineering graduates to obtain professional qualifications, the use of short courses for specialist skills such as computer programming – all these and many more may be necessary in the development of a sufficiently highly skilled workforce.

Traditionally, local government has concentrated very much on assisting employees to acquire professional qualifications. It has done much less to promote manual worker training, or to use short single-subject courses to raise the skill and knowledge of its clerical, technical and supervisory staffs.

The planned use of training can involve both internally organized courses and the use of external training facilities provided by colleges and consultants.

Management development – the planned growth and development of individual employees to fill management posts; and the raising of managerial standards of the management group as a whole. This can include not only the use of management training courses, but also a variety of broader activities such as the adoption of a management-by-objectives philosophy or style, the personal coaching of subordinates, the use of a planned variety of job experience and the use of multi-discipline teams of senior managers to study particular problems or projects. In this context, management also extends into the general supervisory area and thus includes the training and development of foremen and office supervisors.

Career development – an extension of the management development approach to the whole workforce. It involves examining the career opportunities open for all types of employees, and where possible structuring the work to ensure that every employee can, if he wishes and has the ability, work towards promotion. Under this heading too may be placed the work incurred in meeting the requirements of equal opportunity legislation – or more positively in the promotion of equal opportunity policies to combat discrimination.

Staff assessment – along with selection, another under-rated activity in many local authorities, yet essential to the effective deployment, development and promotion of staff. It means regular or continuous reviews of each employee's work performance, an assessment of his strengths and weaknesses in this work, action to capitalize on his strengths and correct his weaknesses, and a forecast of his promotability. Effective systems involve the employee himself in making a

21

positive contribution to the assessments, and a concentration on achieving improvements in current work-performance.

Appraisal discussions, and forms of recording progress, are essential parts of the total system.

Personnel relations

This aspect of personnel management is concerned with employees collectively and with employees in conflict with their employer. The sometimes differing interests of employer and employee have resulted in many aspects of the employer/employee relationship becoming institutionalized – through employer's organizations on one side and trade unions on the other. Beyond this, there is in any event a growing trend to involve employee interests as a whole in sharing managerial concerns or responsibilities.

Industrial relations – an important area of personnel management, not always given the attention it merits in local government. The work at local authority level can include contributing to regional or national employer policy deliberations; negotiating local agreements including productivity bargains; resolving disputes and discussing current and future operational or financial problems and plans which have employment implications with shop stewards and other employee representatives.

A particular feature of local government is that all employee groups are unionized up to and including the chief officers and chief executives.

Joint consultation and communication – an activity related to industrial relations though not necessarily directly linked. It includes the design, introduction and maintenance of joint management/employee committee systems to act as an information and discussion channel. The subject matter for these committees may include any matters of joint interest and concern except those reserved for formal negotiation with the trade unions. There is, however, a trend towards eliminating the distinction between negotiation and consultation.

Additionally, effective communications between management and employees can be aided by various other activities such as newssheets, information bulletins and, perhaps more effective, briefing sessions between managers and subordinates in small, informal groups.

Linked in a general sense with this subject can be the assessment of employee morale and attitudes. Management needs to know what employees really think of their employer; what their attitudes are towards their work and towards the aims and objectives of the organization. Behavioural science techniques can be used to assess these factors.

22

Participation – current thinking on industrial democracy is demanding more direct employee involvement in management processes, not merely consultation and information. The design of new management systems which will enable this participation to occur as an integral (rather than additional) process seems likely to be a key element of personnel management over the next few years – and again to require the application of skills and knowledge in the behavioural sciences.

Grievances and discipline – the design and operation of procedures to handle grievances and to apply disciplinary sanctions. This is an area in which the pressure of employment legislation in recent years has resulted in considerable systematization of what had previously been an underdeveloped aspect of personnel management.

Pay and conditions

Pay systems – although the main structure and level of local government pay systems are determined nationally, there is considerable scope for local initiative in the effective local application of these systems and in the development of efficiency or productivity schemes. Two particular techniques can be applied. Job evaluation provides a rational and systematic method of allocating jobs to grades: work study provides a measured basis for incentive bonus schemes.

Other conditions of employment – the application of the various national agreements which lay down employee entitlements to leave, sick pay, various allowances and superannuation, leave individual local authorities with little more than administrative work in recording and authorizing various payments, and with industrial relations work in negotiating more minor matters such as 'conditions money' for manual workers.

Where working hours are concerned, however, there is scope for considerable effort in formulating attendance systems to meet local work and travelling patterns; and the growth in various types of flexible working hours has been a significant feature of personnel management in this field.

Physical working conditions – personnel management includes consideration of the effect of physical features (such as temperature, lighting, office and workshop layout) on employee morale and efficiency. Work study and ergonomics can assist in the design of the workplace and of working equipment. Environmental engineers can contribute to this process and the skill of the office 'landscape designer' is available, particularly for the growing use of open-planned offices.

Employee safety also includes attention to machine design and physical systems; it is too a growing area for joint management/employee consultation and decision-making.

23

Employee health and welfare – the growth of community welfare services and of the National Health Service has reduced the involvement of employers in promoting the personal health and welfare of their staff. But employees still turn to their employer for advice, and morale and personnel relations can be improved by the employer acting as a link between the employee with a problem and the right external welfare agency.

Additionally, the effect of work pressures on employees' physical and mental health can be under-estimated. Absenteeism, lateness, low productivity may all be symptoms of boredom or stress, and there is a role here for sensitive management generally, possibly aided by an employee welfare service, to diagnose the real ills and ameliorate the consequences.

This brief summary of the main working elements of personnel management shows both the wide range of the work and the potential contribution managers and specialists of various kinds can make to effective personnel management.

All managers will undertake some aspects of this work. They will calculate their manpower requirements, serve as interviewers, help to design and implement training courses, assess their subordinates' work and potential, deal with grievances, negotiate with shop stewards, sit on joint consultative committees, help to grade jobs, ensure safe working methods.

Management services experts can contribute the skills of method study, work measurement, operational research and O and M to the planning and design of cost-effective work systems, layouts and jobs. Behavioural scientists can help to identify the causes of employee dissatisfactions, to design work systems to satisfy social psychological needs, and to monitor the effect of changes and decisions on employee attitudes.

What of the personnel manager? How does he best contribute to this complex network of activities and relationships?

The role of the personnel manager

'Personnel manager' and 'personnel officer' have been used interchangeably in this book although the former is used in this chapter in order to emphasize that the role of at least the more senior personnel specialist is primarily one of contributing to the overall management process. The term 'personnel function' is used primarily to cover those activities which are grouped together to form the total range of work for which the personnel manager is responsible: that is, the work of the personnel department. (In a broader sense it can be used to describe the *total* personnel management process as already summarized in this chapter).

24

There is no one agreed or uniform prescription for the work of the personnel manager. The extent of his duties varies in practice from one employer to another and depends on several factors. The nature of employment pressures varies; one employer may give the highest priority to recruitment; another may treat industrial relations as the key employment activity – and the emphases in the jobs of the personnel managers concerned will reflect these differences.

Most personnel managers, however, are involved to some extent in all the activities already summarized in this chapter and the nature of their work falls, broadly, into three categories:

executive action, in which they take full responsibility for particular elements of work and make decisions and take action accordingly

advisory action, when they provide other managers who will take the executive decisions with specialized advice and information about personnel matters

administrative action, involving the maintenance of employment procedures and systems and the keeping of records.

A short, and not necessarily comprehensive, list of duties commonly undertaken by personnel managers shows this variety of work in practice.

In *manpower planning*, personnel managers commonly collate manpower forecasts from other managers, add their own information and ideas about trends in the supply of new recruits, staff turnover and retirement rates and the like, and put forward the resulting match (or mis-match) of demand and supply, with proposals as to action needed. This in itself is a mixture of executive, advisory and administrative action.

In *recruitment*, most personnel managers take full charge of liaison with careers agencies (at universities, schools etc); plan and co-ordinate recruitment advertising and produce the final drafts of job advertisements.

In *selection*, personnel managers administer selection tests and procedures and interview candidates. They do not normally make the final selection; a more normal procedure is for the personnel manager to submit a short-list of candidates for final selection to the manager in whose department the vacancy exists or for the more senior posts in local government, to a members' selection panel.

In *deployment*, the personnel manger normally acts as the agency through which departments with varying manpower demands have these demands balanced by the matching of surpluses and shortages. He will also assist in any necessary employee consultation or negotiation about staff transfers. He is often the co-ordinator of the use of management techniques to improve work methods or systems.

In *redundancy* situations, he will negotiate the necessary agreements with the unions and give such assistance as he can to help redundant employees find alternative work.

In *training*, the personnel manager will normally assist other managers in identifying training needs and in designing training programmes to meet these needs. He may act as a trainer in subjects such as industrial relations: more generally he will co-ordinate training programmes and provide the administrative services necessary to maintain them.

In *management development*, he advises on the procedures and systems which may be appropriate, helps to design and sometimes to run management and supervisory training courses and provide top management with a procedural framework for the planning of management succession (coping with known retirements and likely turnover).

In *career development*, he examines the nature of career and promotion opportunities open to different groups of employees, advises other managers of changes he thinks may achieve improvements, and provides a career counselling service to the staff. He is also likely to be his authority's expert on the practical implications of equal opportunity legislation and on positive methods of preventing racial or sex discrimination.

In *staff assessment*, the personnel manager is normally the manager who designs the whole system of appraisal interviews and records; collates information from the system in order to highlight strengths and weaknesses in the organization's manpower resources, and provides any necessary training in the operation of the system.

In *industrial relations*, he usually plays a treble role: advising other managers on their handling of relationships with shop stewards and the trade unions; providing information about national and local agreements and their interpretation; at times acting as a negotiator with the delegated authority of top management.

He will also be the practical expert on industrial relations legislation, though with the lawyers' advice on the more legal implications.

In *joint consultation and participation*, he is usually responsible for the design of the joint committee structure and will often provide the necessary administrative support to these committees. In the best systems, he does not act as a spokesman for other managers in these committees; they participate directly.

In *participation*, again, he advises on methods and assists with administration, without usurping the role of the line manager. He will advise managers generally on methods of keeping communication open between employees and management: he may produce or edit news sheets or house journals.

In *grievances and disciplinary matters*, he is primarily a designer and monitor of procedures, though it may be necessary for him sometimes to act with delegated authority. He should certainly help to ensure that all legal requirements are met when dealing with potential dismissals. (As with other legal matters, a partnership between the solicitor and the personnel manager is usually the best arrangement.)

In *payment matters*, the personnel manager provides the expert knowledge of national and local systems, and may have authority to authorize or veto other managers' proposals or applications for special payments or for changes in the systems. More constructively, he should be able to advise on the applicability of various productivity techniques and payment systems, and to assist in their negotiation. He will often operate a job evaluation scheme.

In *other conditions of employment*, he will also act as the guardian and interpreter of the rules; he should also take the initiative in proposing changes where he considers these necessary to the promotion of organizational efficiency and employee morale.

Physical working conditions are usually kept under review by the personnel manager, if necessary with technical assistance, and he advises on the general organization of the safety function and on joint safety committees.

In *welfare*, he may provide a confidential counselling service for employees, and usually acts as their link with the external medical and other welfare and social services.

This is not an exhaustive list though it covers as wide a spectrum as most personnel managers are involved in. Large personnel departments often have to divide their activities into several units or branches, so that some personnel officers may concentrate entirely on just one aspect of personnel management. Employment, training, and industrial relations are the three most common specialisms. To an increasing extent in local government, the most senior personnel manager in an authority is likely also to be responsible for management services with its two primary activities of work study and O and M.

One most important element has been omitted from the preceding lists: it is less easy to categorize, and it depends as much on the intellectual capacity and personality of the personnel manager as on his specialist knowledge. It is his role in acting as his organization's general adviser on the personnel (the human) implications of *all* major policy and operational decisions. When an important policy matter is under discussion – say, a switch in emphasis from council house building to the purchase of existing private properties – it is the personnel manager who should think of the effect of this change on the attitudes and morale of existing employees, on the nature and volume of manpower, on the trade unions; and who should advise the management team as a whole of action in the personnel field which they and he will need to take if the policy is to be effectively introduced. At lower levels, every personnel officer should be capable of helping the managers at his level and with whom he works to think through the effects on employees of management actions and decisions, and the steps they can take to maintain an informed and enthusiastic workforce.

There is another way of categorizing the personnel manager's work by examining the variety of roles he has to play. To illustrate how wide this variety is, even for a personnel officer who does not span the whole spectrum of activities discussed above, we can take the job of an industrial relations officer.

His general responsibility will be to ensure that industrial relations decisions are informed, relevant to the needs of the organization, and compatible with employee, management and union attitudes. In carrying out this responsibility he will frequently find himself occupying the middle ground between extremes of opinion or position, not only between management and trade unions, but within the management team. There are the extremes, within management of:

extreme legalism ('sticking to the book'), against extreme expediency
authoritarianism against a surrender of managerial authority.

It is not the industrial relations officer's job merely to reinforce instinctive management reactions, or merely to reflect and repeat trade union views. He has to search out the most effective meeting ground between these positions. He is an intermediary not between people, or between employer and employee, but between opinions and attitudes.

Eight types of role can be identified in his work:

The intelligence role: he acts as an information centre about relevant legislation, trade union agreements, trends in government, employer and union policies on employment issues. He collects information within the organization about the nature and causes of employee unrest, about precedents and solutions.

The interpretative role: having built up this information he can produce alternative lines of action to deal with different situations. He can answer the question 'what is the relevance to the organization of this or that law or agreement?' He can interpret and apply the rules and precedents to the various problems that arise.

The policy formulation role: having established the facts, the alternatives and the pros and cons, the industrial relations officer can advise when and which new policies are required to establish new guidelines for management action. (For example, he may advise a need for a policy about the closed shop; or about the recognition of a new union).

The procedural role: policies need procedures to ensure they can be put into effect. The industrial relations officer has to design systems and procedures for the settlement of disputes, to deal with disciplinary appeals, to document shop steward appointments.

The training role: inconsistently applied procedures are possibly worse than none at all. He must assist in training managers and supervisors in their parts in the organization's industrial relations procedures.

The 'barometric' role: he should be acutely aware of the delicate shifts in employee, union and management attitudes; able to assess the motives and rationale for apparently negative or irrational behaviour; to sense the pressure points, to know and advise on the direction the next wind will come from, and on the temperature for discussions and negotiations.

The 'devil's advocate' role: managers whose operational objectives become hindered by industrial relations problems often convince themselves that they are entirely in the right. There is a strong tendency towards self-justification wherever a trade union challenges a manager's decision. The industrial relations officer, in his discussions with management, must probe for the weaknesses in the management case – must play the trade union role – in preparing for negotiations. If management is being over-expedient, he must play the lawyer; if management is hiding behind the law, he must play the buccaneer. Cases are won at law, and positions established in negotiation, by the side which is as aware of its own weaknesses as of its strengths.

The negotiation role: finally, and not necessarily the most important, he may have the delegated authority to bargain with the trade unions on management's behalf. Alternatively, he may prepare the negotiating strategies for other managers to follow.

A similar analysis could be made of other personnel specialists' work, and of the jobs of the generalist personnel manager. The simplified view of the personnel manager as merely an adviser – or as a manager who does pieces of other managers' work for them – is thus shown to be misleading and inaccurate.

The good personnel manager is a good team worker. He brings additional knowledge and skill to the work of the management team as a whole and, by so doing, helps to raise the quality of the personnel management elements which exist and remain in all managerial jobs. His biggest single contribution is to stimulate an interest in, and awareness of, the critical importance of the human factor to the effectiveness of any organization's activities.

3 Management in local government

Personnel management is, by definition, part of the total management function. The role and style of an organization's personnel function is determined partly by the employment environment in which it operates, but equally by the nature of the whole management activity of which it is a part.

Before discussing the evolution of personnel management in local government, it is therefore necessary to set the general management scene. This chapter provides a brief survey of the history and development of management style and structure in local authorities: chapter 4 traces the parallel development of the personnel function.

The historian of local authority management is assisted in his task by the almost continuous concern of central government about the efficiency of local government, a concern which has resulted in a series of reports of Royal Commissions and other Committees. For the purpose of this chapter it is not necessary to go back before 1929, and the Third Report of the Royal Commission on Local Government. The bulk of this report, was of course, devoted to an examination of local government as a governmental process: to a discussion, that is, of the nature of councils and their services.

But the report also marks the first significant discussion of the internal management of local government as distinct from its political and public-service role. And, as was to be repeated in all the subsequent enquiries, three aspects of management received attention:

the separatism of Council departments (departmentalism) and the extent to which this should be modified
the role of the chief executive officer (the Clerk, in traditional terms)
the concept of a management team (corporate management, in current jargon).

Clearly, these three factors interact and they can be discussed in parallel as the various stages of development take place.

Four commissions or committees can be used to follow this development:

The 1929 Onslow Royal Commission
The 1934 Hadow Committee on the Qualifications, Recruitment, Training and Promotion of Local Government Officers
The Maud Committee on Management in Local Government, 1967
The Bains Committee on the New Local Authorities: Management and Structure, 1972.

The Onslow report

Almost all the issues which the Bains report was to discuss over 40 years later can be found in the third report of the 1925-29 Royal Commission. Their existence, then, is important. It shows how long-established are most of the concepts of internal management and control in local government, and this in turn explains the difficulties of achieving the radical changes in attitude and organization implicit in the 1974 re-organization.

Onslow commented on these concepts, not as new but as creating problems because of their persistence.

Four items of evidence to the Committee highlight the factors on which this and later reports were to concentrate:

The National and Local Government Officers' Association (NAL-GO) (the main white collar trade union) commented on the need for complete co-ordination of departmental activities. The union saw a need, in consequence, for 'a highly qualified administrator' to head up each authority's service as something of a cross between an American Town Manager and a German Burgomeister.
The Ministry of Health (then responsible for local government) thought that the Clerk should be the permanent head of the service to 'co-ordinate the whole thing'.
Academic witnesses thought the Clerk should be 'the link, the consultant, and the co-ordinator' of all the departments.
The Association of Local Government Finance Officers took particular exception to any arrangement by which the Chief Financial Officer was required to act under the direction or supervision of the Clerk and did not consider it necessary for the Clerk to have responsibility in any way for the staff or accommodation required by the Chief Financial Officer.

These summaries of evidence illustrate the inherent conflict of interests and ideas which have dogged the growth of a clear concept of local government management. On the one hand, a feeling that the work of separate departments needs co-ordination: on the other, that at least some departments are sufficiently distinct or important to be self-contained activities and to be subject to the direct control only of the Council. And the role of the Clerk sits uneasily between these two opposing views.

The Onslow committee did not resolve these problems. Concentrating on the role of the Clerk, the report recommended that he should be in a position to 'survey the various activities of the authority and to secure that they are properly focused and co-ordinated', with a reasonable degree of uniformity and continuity. But what do words like 'survey' and 'focus' really mean in terms of management authority and activity? In any event, the effect of this recommendation was weakened by a proviso. The Clerk should not, the report said, 'interfere with the technical staff on technical questions' and technical officers should not be debarred from direct access to Council. The Clerk was clearly being given responsibility for achieving some degree of co-ordination without the authority to achieve it. Little wonder, then, that in discussing the qualities required in a Clerk, the report stated that his success would 'depend largely on his personality'.

The Hadow report
The 1934 Hadow report was concerned primarily with methods of staff recruitment, with entry standards, with the general quality of local government officers rather than with methods of management and patterns of organizations. It is therefore examined in more detail in the next chapter. It made, however, another attempt to define the role of the Clerk. He should, said the report, 'co-ordinate the work of several departments, and should exercise a general supervision over all the work . . .' – a more precise description of his work than Onslow's surveying and focusing. But the report went on '. . . without interfering with heads of departments in strictly technical questions'. And this proviso again destroyed the concept of a real head of the service.

The Maud report
That Onslow identified the problems in 1929 but failed to provide the solutions is shown by the repetition in the 1967 Maud report of precisely similar comments. On this occasion, more relevant to today because more recent, detailed research work also provided factual evidence of the extent of departmentalism and of wide differences of management organization and procedures.

The number of departments in an authority varied, so research studies showed, from a minimum of five (in a London borough) to over 30 (in a County borough). Very wide variations existed, too, in the way in which services and activities were grouped into departments. Some authorities departmentalized primarily by services –

eg housing, entertainments, public health – others primarily by function or activity – eg mechanical and electrical engineering, architecture etc. And most had a mixture of these two forms.

The research team also looked at the Clerk's job and at how different Clerks 'managed'. Some saw their job as a chief executive role in all but name and said that they controlled and co-ordinated on the basis of 'unwritten law'. Others saw their jobs very differently as the head of the administrative service but not as chief executive in the general management sense.

Some chaired regular meetings with other chief officers, others did not. One said he didn't because 'he did not want to give the impression he was holding the reins'. Another had abandoned this form of co-ordination because the meetings became a 'battleground'. The most generally stated view (or cliché) was that the Clerk was 'first among equals' – a neat tag but to any student of management almost meaningless.

The main report discussed departmentalism and the role of the chief executive officer in forthright terms.

Departmental organization was, it said, rooted in professionalism. Professional heads of professional departments had a loyalty towards their professions and their professional associations which tended to over-ride their potential concern for their local authority as a whole. There was no concept of general administration (management) as such. There was 'an unwieldy array of largely independent departments'. Work was fragmented between too many departments and, in the absence of a managing body, was seldon coherently co-ordinated. No clear definition of the role of the Clerk could be found 'in any official document'.

The report pointed to an earlier postwar attempt at this definition. In 1949 the new Joint Negotiating Committee for chief officers had published recommended conditions of service for Clerks and other chief officers, and had included brief job descriptions. These described the Clerk as the chief executive and administrative officer and as responsible for co-ordination of the whole of the Council's work. But Maud pointed out that this description could not be reconciled with that of the other departmental chief officers, who were defined as being responsible directly to the Council and whose relationship to the Clerk was not explained.

So radical changes were required. Local authorities should, the report said, adopt a systematic approach to the process of management. (The term and concept of 'management' was being used in the local government context as it had been in industry for decades).

Timetables should be included in management procedure guides which would ensure that objectives were set and progress reviewed in all fields of activity.

And the Clerk? He should be 'the undisputed head of the whole paid service', and the other principal or chief officers should form a team under him and report to the Council through him. The concept of the Chief Executive had formally arrived, though it was to be some years before the principle was generally put into practice.

The Bains report

Restructuring of local government management was linked in the Maud and earlier reports to the much broader issue of local government re-organization. Changes in government policy, and the lengthy and highly political process or re-shaping local government structure and boundaries, resulted in a seven year delay from 1967 to 1974, before a complete package of re-organization plus restructured management was eventually introduced.

In 1971, however, the government set up a Study Group on Local Authority Management Structures. Its task was to provide advice for the new local authorities which were to come into existence in the 1974 re-organization, on their management structures and management principles. Re-organization was being used as an opportunity to conduct a fundamental review of all the conflicting concepts of internal management which previous studies had identified but failed to resolve.

The Working Group which produced the resultant report in 1972 was an unusual one. Previously, local government had been considered more from an external and political viewpoint by committees whose local government members were, in the main, councillors. The Bains Working Group, however, consisted of five local authority Clerks, one County Treasurer and only one 'outsider' – the Company Secretary of ICI Ltd. Adverse comments were made in some quarters about the absence of elected members and of 'officer bias'.

Few reports have given rise to as much discussion in local government as the Bains report and, to a large extent, this has been its major success. All the old, controversial issues were highlighted and a bold attempt made to produce solutions. Many local government officers are likely to have learned more about mangement from the ensuing arguments than they would have done from a more generally accepted report, however authoritative. The report as a whole is outside the scope of this book, but its stand on three particular issues is highly relevant to the development of the personnel function:

The interlocking relationship between elected member and officers. (This is dealt with in chapter 16)
The promotion of personnel management, the subject of the next chapter
The co-ordination of departmental activities and the role of the chief executive officer, discussed in this chapter.

The report stated that 'the ingrained departmental approach to man-

34

agement' was no longer appropriate – the Group felt that there was still an absence of unity in the internal organization of most local authorities.

Changes were needed, and these should start at the top. So a job specification was put forward for the new Chief Executive (the job title most favoured by the Group). The specification stated:

> The Chief Executive is the head of the Council's paid service and shall have authority over all other officers so far as this is necessary for the efficient management and execution of the Council's functions. He is the leader of the officers' management team . . . He is responsible for the efficient and effective implementation of the Council's programmes and policies and for securing that the resources of the authority are most effectively deployed towards those ends.

This was a specification which went nearly all the way to defining the chief executive's job in industrial chief executive terms. Where it differed, the differences were justified, at least by implication, in two ways:

> Because ultimate responsibility rested with the Council and not with officers.
>
> Because a Council's activities were not commercial in nature, were concerned with public services and with the quality of community life, were in some cases defined by statute, and could not therefore be regarded as alternatives in the way in which a multi-product company could view its various activities.

Two other concepts completed this new view of local authority management: one, the overall responsibility of the chief executive for resource management – land, finance, manpower; the other, the concept of the management team, of chief officers forming a corporate management body in which each officer has a responsibility to consider and promote the interests of the authority as a whole, and not merely his own departmental objectives.

The Bains report *in toto* proposed the most radical changes in management structure and style ever experienced in local government. The formation of the new authorities on 1 April 1974 was seen as providing a unique opportunity to introduce such changes. It would be easier for a new authority to begin life with a new type of structure than it would have been for an existing authority suddenly to change its whole style.

Management structures after Bains

The report generated intense discussion in the local government world. Week after week local government journals were filled with articles setting out the pros and cons of various of the Bains proposals, with letters fiercely defending different viewpoints and with reports of numerous conferences and seminars with Bains as their main theme.

In relation to the issues with which this chapter is concerned, the subject of most discussion was that of the role of the chief executive – and in particular the question as to whether he should retain responsibility for the management of a department or conversely, as Bains proposed, be free from all departmental responsibility.

By the end of March 1974, poised on the edge of reorganization, all but one of the new authorities had adopted a Bains-type specification for a chief executive. Not all were to be free of departmental duties, though many were. Some might be changes more of intent than of eventual achievement. But the intent was clear – the old doctrine of first among equals was dead. From 1 April 1974 the principal officer of a local authority was to be a chief executive in the accepted business sense: the most senior manager, to whom all other managers were subordinate and over whose work he had the authority of direction and co-ordination.

Two other major issues – breaking down departmentalism and achieving a corporate approach through the operation of a top management team – clearly had to be linked in practice. Most of the debate centred on the formation and composition of the management team. Bains' statements that 'the team will probably number about six', and that 'a team of six may well be large enough for all chief officers in the smaller districts to serve on the team but in the larger authorities some traditional chief officers will not be permanent members' may now be a matter for regret. To keep numbers down to this figure, many authorities had either to group hitherto separate departments under a director – and thereby create a new level in the management hierarchy – or, as Bains suggested, exclude some chief officers from the team.

Not surprisingly, these proposals and alternatives gave rise to fairly heated, and often defensive debate. In the event it is perhaps as well that a wide variety of solutions have been adopted – and with a trend towards more, rather than fewer, chief officers being brought into the management team.

And despite variations, most authorities saw a value in formalizing the concept of a corporate, top management body. By providing for this in their management structures they provided a setting in which a more positive and creative concept of personnel management could be developed. A management team which becomes concerned about the quality of an authority's manpower, about management-employee relationships, about staff motivation and morale, and about future manpower requirements, is one which will see the need for consistent service-wide policies and procedures to promote employee effectiveness. A group of independent chief officers will tend merely to compete for manpower; a corporate team of chief officers should promote manpower development.

Even after six years it is still too soon after the 1974 reorganization to be at all definitive about the long-term effects of authorities' general acceptance of the Bains corporate management proposals. In any large organization the traditions of the past continue to exercise a strong influence over management attitudes for years after any restructuring – however major that restructuring may have been. In local government, the probability of really rapid changes in managerial attitudes and methods was limited by the almost total restriction of appointments to the new authorities to existing local government staff. With fears of possible redundancies when the original 1,500 authorities were reduced to their present 450, a Staff Commission was set up to oversee the staffing implications of the 1974 re-organization, and applications for the new chief executive and chief officer posts were, in the main, restricted to existing local government officers. Moreover, in the event, the majority of such appointments went to senior and chief officers who were already working within the general boundaries of the authorities in which they gained their new appointments.

In trying to reach a provisional assessment of the degree of success of the 1974 managerial revolution, some concern may be expressed as to whether too much emphasis and discussion has centred on structure – on the organization chart – and too little on the nature of management processes – on what managers actually have to do, on how decisions are made, on what information is needed at which management point. Labelling a manager a director and making him responsible for, say, engineering design, refuse collection and public transport (to take an actual example), does nothing of itself to define to what extent these often disparate activities would benefit from sharing resources, from common management or from unified control. Labelling a group of chief officers a management team does nothing of itself to define what unique contribution this team needs to make to the total process of managing the authority's activities.

If chief officers in such a team use their presence there primarily to defend their own departmental interests, to ensure that they get their desired share of scarce resources, then the team is merely a forum in which the chief executive acts as a conciliator or arbitrator in inter-departmental competition.

It would by expecting too superhuman an effort for chief officers not to use the management team for this purpose to some extent: executive directors on boards of companies are often notorious for behaving in just this way. But the board, the management team, fully justifies its existence only if its corporate consideration and decisions are of higher quality than those of its individual members. Companies try to obtain this broader, more imaginative approach by appointing non-executive directors – men with no internal axes to grind and with a wider range of external experience and contacts than the executive directors who are naturally biased towards their specialist departmental interests. The constructive mixing of narrow but in-depth views with wider outside concepts can generate ideas and decisions of higher quality than those of either set of views.

In 1976 Birmingham District Council passed a resolution to the effect that the corporate management system 'had not been conducive to the best administration of the Council's affairs' and should be replaced by a different system.

It is significant that serious reaction of this kind against the concept of corporate management began to emerge among the elected members of a number of local authorities within a few years of reorganization. Significant because elected members may, in some sense, be considered as bringing to the management of a local authority the same type of broader external interest and 'nous' that the non-executive director can bring to a company board. Lying behind elected members' criticisms of the corporate approach and of Chief Officers' Groups, there seemed to be a feeling that Chief Officers acting collectively could create a barrier between the policy-making committees of councillors and the departments which had to put these policies into effect. A Chief Officers' Group could, some councillors thought, act as a very powerful defence mechanism by which the professional managers could keep the elected members at arm's length and prevent what officers might consider as unwelcome 'interference' by councillors in departmental matters.

Alternatively, some councils saw the Chief Executive and his corporate management apparatus as an unnecessary, expensive, bureaucratic addition to an already complicated management system. The traditional system in which each major service was headed by a Chief Officer responsible to a Committee; in which each Committee Chairman thus acted, in a sense, as Company Chairman to the Chief Officer as Managing Director; and in which co-ordination between committees and the allocation of priorities (and resources) was a function of the Council itself – this system seemed simpler for the elected member to understand and gave him more direct control. In 1977 the former Chairman of the Nottinghamshire County Council, stating that there was no need for a Chief Executive inserted between 'the real policy-makers' (ie elected members) and 'the real deliverers of goods' (ie Chief Officers), forecast that within ten years there would be no Chief Executives left.

A parallel and similar reaction by Chief Education Officers within the ranks of local government management is also worth noting because it was triggered, at least in part, by the decision of some authorities in the 1974 to 1975 period to extend the ambit of their personnel departments to include teaching staff. (Traditionally, teachers have always been administered by professional educational administrators). Chief Education Officers saw such moves as the interposition of a bureaucratic screen between themselves, as professional heads of the education service, and the Education Committees to which they reported. Between the Chief Education Officers and their Committee Chairman they saw neither need nor advantage in the introduction of personnel officers who would, they felt, act as centralizing agents of an unnecessary and undesirable corporate management team, headed by a Chief Executive Officer whose organizational role as head of a Council's services was incompatible with the statutorily backed independence of the head of the education service – responsible only and directly to his committee.

This continuing controversy has certainly brought into open debate some of the serious inconsistencies between the patterns of authority and decision-making within the council committee system, and those within a Bains-type management hierarchy. If these inconsistencies are not resolved it seems probable that the role of the Council Chief Executive will continue to be a potential source of friction, both between Chief Officers and between officers and elected members. Almost any formal organizational structure can be made to work by men of goodwill. But unavoidable competition for scarce resources between disparate departments and underlying issues of personal power and status make the present management structure less stable than Bains hoped.

4 The growth of the personnel function

In the previous chapter, the evolution of corporate management structures was traced from the traditional patterns of separate departments under uncoordinated management to the introduction of the chief executive and his management team. In this chapter we go back over the same period to follow the attention given to personnel management in the various government reports, and to examine the accelerating expansion of the establishment and personnel function over the past 50 years. In succeeding chapters, we discuss a variety of pressures and influences which have affected this expansion – many of them, such as the growth in employment legislation, external to the local government scene though impinging on it. This chapter concentrates on the role of the personnel function resulting from the comments and recommendations of the various committees which have, from 1929, examined the organizational health of local authorities.

In following this development it is immediately noticeable that it has been concern for the white-collar sector of local government employment, and not problems in the manual worker field, which have provided the primary motivator for change. The formation of the National Joint Council for local authority manual workers in 1919 was not followed by any expansion in local authorities' personnel management activities. Indeed, in the 1929 Onslow report there is no evidence of the existence of any recognizable establishment or personnel function whatsoever. A number of criticisms were made of activities which are essential parts of any organized form of staff management, and from the evidence presented to the Commission and from the comments of the Commission itself it is clear that at that date there was little that would now be recognized as personnel work. The Clerk and Chief Officers recruited their own staff. Each Council committee controlled its own staff numbers, subject to overall financial limits set by the Council itself. NALGO, the primary staff trade union, commented adversely on an almost complete lack of uniformity and consistency of either entry standards, methods of selection or conditions of service. Even salary increases for individual officers were often discussed publicly by the full Council and were consequently subject to politically influenced decisions. Transferability of staff between authorities was seriously inhibited by widely varying salary levels and conditions of service and particularly by the absence of a standard superannuation scheme.

The Commission concluded that the whole topic of staff recruitment, training and promotion required further study in depth. Onslow was worried that the growing demands placed on local government would exceed the abilities of local government staff to cope with them. The ad hoc, unplanned, uncoordinated methods of staff management both locally and nationally were wholly inadequate for 1929 needs. The Commission therefore recommended that a Committee should be set up to review the whole question. It was clear that local government was not considered capable of doing this job itself.

The Hadow report

The Government accepted this proposal of the Onslow Commission and a Committee was established by the Ministry responsible for local government (Health) to review the qualifications, recruitment, training and promotion of local government officers.

The Committee examined at great length such matters as the age of entry for junior staff, the need for graduate entrants and the relevance of various technical qualifications. They paid far less attention to the staff management policies and procedures which would be necessary to secure the improvements in the quality of local government officers which they considered desirable. They were concerned, in other words, more with the quality of the manpower resource than with the methods of obtaining and managing this resource. The report does, however, provide a useful picture of the standard of staff management at that time, and marks at least the beginning of a formal establishment function at both member and officer levels.

Summarizing the staff situation, the report said that the main instruments for raising staff standards had been the various professional associations of officers themselves. Councils as such had done little: recruitment standards were uneven and recruitment methods haphazard. Little had been done to match recruitment systems to the educational system. Training was unsystematic and there was a comparative indifference to the value of training in administration. Responsibility for staffing matters was, in most authorities, divided between individual committees. Only the various professional associations and institutions (for Treasurers, Municipal Engineers and so

41

on) showed any real interest in raising standards, and each was of course concerned only for its own profession.

The Committee was particularly concerned at the almost complete absence of graduate recruitment. True, the London County Council had recently arranged to recruit one graduate annually, but in general little interest was shown by authorities in this type of intake. The Committee was, it said, in a dilemma. 'Either the entire educational system of the country is mistaken, or local authorities ought to be drawing more systematically on the universities'.

There was an air of complacency about much of the evidence presented to the Committee which does much to explain the very slow growth (or absence) of any organized staff management at this time.

Local Authority Associations were quoted as being generally well satisfied with staff standards and with recruitment and training procedures and facilities. They saw no great need for a graduate entry. 'Young officers', said one witness, 'should be willing to train themselves'.

The representatives of local government officers, too, were thought to be generally content with the situation, though both they and the local authority associations conceded that some changes were desirable. Some standardization of entry requirements, more uniformity in salary scales, and above all one national superannuation scheme were agreed suggestions for improvements.

What were Hadow's solutions? Apart from a number of detailed proposals about age of entry, minimum educational standards and the like, Hadow concentrated on the role of elected members, of Councils themselves, in determining staffing policies and on applying these in practice.

Every authority, said the report, should entrust to one committee all questions affecting the recruitment and training of staff. Only by making one committee responsible would adequate consideration of these matters be assured. In large authorities, this committee would be solely concerned with establishment work: in small authorities the finance or general purposes committee might absorb this work. The establishment committee should be made responsible for an impressive list of activities:

recruitment and job advertising
all appointments
training
all promotions
grading and salary scales
conditions of employment
transfers of staff between departments
periodic reviews of staff performance
probation and disciplinary procedures.

The report was quite unambiguous about the implication that the establishment committee itself – not officers – should be concerned with the mass of detail involved in these activities. In appointments, for example, it stated that 'members should take an active interest in all appointments', and chief officers' autonomy in making junior appointments should be reduced. The main new element of work for senior officers was to be the writing of annual progress reports on each member of the staff, and reporting to the establishment committee on staff who were rated as either exceptionally promising or not up to standard. But the report made no proposals towards the introduction of establishment departments. 'Ordinarily', it suggested, 'the Clerk should be the officer responsible for advising the establishment committee. But authorities employing very large staffs should consider the appointment of an officer to assist the Clerk'.

This modest proposal may, perhaps, be taken as representing the first formal recognition of the personnel function in local government: the first acceptance that at least one officer in an authority might be needed for staff management work on a full-time basis.

Over the next 30 years two separate lines of development can be traced: the growth of national bodies concerned with particular aspects of employment; the growth at authority level of the establishment control function.

To some extent, it may well have been the absence of well-developed personnel departments in authorities which led to the establishment of such bodies as the Local Authorities Conditions of Service Advisory Board (LACSAB) though the pressures of national trade unions played a more obvious role in this. Industrial relations, however, has certainly been something of a Cinderella function at local authority level until quite recently, and its growth locally has been influenced by the centralized system of National Joint Councils and national collective bargaining. The whole subject is dealt with in detail in a later chapter. Here it is sufficient to note that since the mid 1940s when the white-collar National Joint Council was established, the full-time secretariats of LACSAB and of provincial joint councils have supplied advisory personnel management services to authorities, in addition to their more official role as negotiators and administrators for the employers' sides of the joint negotiating bodies.

No national or central body can, however, take the place of a personnel function within an individual organization's management structure, and the expansion of national collective bargaining and its related advisory services was not matched by a parallel expansion of authorities' personnel departments.

In the training field, too, national bodies made a greater impact, and showed a greater degree of initiative and professionalism than most authorities (though there were some very creditable exceptions).

The Local Government Examination Board (LGEB), a body concerned with promoting common standards for qualified staff, proposed in 1966 the establishment of a voluntary training board to promote training on a much wider basis throughout local government. The Local Government Training Board (LGTB) was consequently formed in 1967 and was soon developing and promoting an extensive range of training activities, including such modern concepts as management development and training for training officers. By about 1970, there may well have been almost as many personnel management experts employed in LACSAB and the LGTB than in the rest of local government put together.

At authority level during the 1930-1970 period the main development was along the lines of establishment control and related management services. This is looked at in more detail in later chapters. In the context of this historical review, however, it can be noted that the widespread formation of Establishment Commitees after the Hadow Report led in turn to the appointment of establishment officers and establishment branches, usually under the general direction of the Clerk. The Committees tended to be more concerned with the control function – vetting departments' bids for extra staff – than with promoting the quality of the manpower resource; and establishment work at officer level reflected this bias. Establishment officers therefore tended to be general administrative staff and were not often trained and qualified in personnel management. Indeed, the idea of specializing in personnel work on a career basis was, in many authorities, positively discouraged.

Not that among establishment officers themselves there was no interest in a wider view of their work. A conference organized by the Royal Institute of Public Administration in 1949, attended by several hundred establishment staff, discussed many ideas which were to emerge later in the Mallaby and Bains reports and to receive official recognition and promotion in the 1970s. Semi-professional and semi-official groupings of officers concerned with various aspects of personnel management were also developing in the 1960-70 period. The Local Government Personnel and Management Services Group was formed in 1963, at that time with an almost wholly management services bias: personnel management was formally added in 1970. On a more professional basis, the Institute of Personnel Management formed a local government group for those of its members employed by local authorities. Other groups developed in the work study and operational research fields.

However, the more conventional patterns of establishment work, and the view of the establishment officer as basically a generalist administrator, received solid support from the 1967 reports of the Maud and Mallaby Committees.

The Committees were both formed in 1964 as part of the most detailed and exhaustive study of local government ever undertaken. The Maud Committee, as we have seen in chapter 3, concentrated on general management. The Mallaby Committee on Staffing in Local Government had the following terms of reference:

> To consider the existing methods of recruiting local government officers and of using them: and what changes might help local authorities to get the best possible service and help their officers to give it.

The Maud report made very little reference to the establishment function. Indeed, its only positive recommendation was that 'an effective establishment organization be set up to secure economy in the use of manpower'. This was a powerful reinforcement of the quantitative staffing control bias in existing establishment departments. It was certainly no encouragement to the development of more creative personnel work concerned with improving the quality of manpower.

The Mallaby report

Did Mallaby, whose terms of reference were related directly to the qualitative aspects of local government manpower, reach different conclusions?

The report confirmed the Hadow formula of the Clerk's responsibility for establishment matters, 'or alternatively, an officer to whom he has delegated this function'.

It stressed the control function, as had the Maud report, and recommended central establishment control to ensure the economic use of manpower, to keep a check on staff numbers and gradings, to take an overall view of the authority's staffing needs and to plan ahead for staff requirements.

Turning to what it termed the executive aspect of establishment work it saw advantages in four particular tasks being carried out centrally within each authority:

> Recruitment: authorities were recommended 'to entrust the greater part of the executive work connected with recruitment to the establishment section'
> Training: there should be one point of contact between the authority and the schools and colleges outside. There should be adequate training schemes, including management training
> Welfare: the provision of good working conditions and canteen and recreational facilities
> Record keeping: there was a need for adequate staffing information.

To carry out this work, the report envisaged that, except in smaller authorities, there would be an establishment officer. In larger authorities there was also a need for a training officer. The establishment officer should have 'the status and capacity' to undertake work at senior management level.

It would have been a short step from this view of the job of the establishment officer to suggesting that he should be a professional personnel manager. But at this point caution appeared. 'At present', said the report, 'there is no recognized training or qualification for personnel or training officers in local government and we believe this may have led to the work being undervalued'. To the 1967 personnel manager in industry – or indeed elsewhere in the public sector – where the existence and value of the one year full-time courses in personnel management, available at a number of universities, had been recognized and supported for years, this seemed a somewhat parochial view. It overlooked, too, the existence of the Institute of Personnel Management and its associated examination and training programmes. But Mallaby was clearly looking inwards (and backwards) to local government and civil service traditions, for the report went on: 'On the other hand, we are certain that establishment work should not become a new specialism in which officers make a career divorced from other duties: it should be open to the lay administrative officer'.

Whatever else the report had to say about the need for instruction in personnel management as part of the establishment officer's basic training, it failed in two primary ways to put personnel management on the local government map. First, it was unspecific about the place of the function in the management structure. It left the establishment officer as a senior officer responsible to the Clerk but without departmental authority and clearly not of chief officer status. Secondly, it turned against professionalism in personnel management and so gave it the status of a minor administrative function.

Between Mallaby and Bains, some authorities continued independently to raise standards in their establishment branches and, indeed, to begin to use the term 'personnel management'. The Greater London Council had appointed a Director of Establishments with a growing range of personnel and management services responsibilities – a chief officer post – as early as 1965. Stockport County Borough Council created a post of Chief Personnel Adviser in 1971 and other authorities were reported by Bains to be 'contemplating such appointments'. The basic staffing control function was also being strengthened and professionalized with the growth in the use of work study, O and M and other management services. Some authorities raised the standard of their staff advertising and recruitment in response to growing labour shortages. The pace and importance of industrial relations quickened – a development highlighted by the 'dirty jobs' strikes of 1969/70. The scene was being set not only for the production of the Bains report but also for its general acceptance.

The Bains report

The Bains Working Group's forthright comments on the need for a major effort to raise standards of personnel management in local government were all the more impressive for being produced by a group of experienced chief officers – and not by a group of external 'experts'. Statements such as 'the human problems of management in local government are in no way different from those in industry' might well have been rejected if made by academics or management consultants. They were less easy to ignore coming from the Clerk of the Kent County Council, the County Treasurer of Gloucestershire and the Town Clerks of Bradford and Brighton.

The report gave a useful summary of the state of the establishment and personnel art in 1971. It described 'Establishment Man' as essentially having two functions: first the day to day administration of rules about pay and conditions of service; secondly, to act as the Council's watchdog in respect of departments' and committees' demands for staff. Many establishment officers were also in charge of management services and even where these were separately organized, there were close links with 'Estab' in connection with the staffing control function. The report described this type of establishment officer as 'a prisoner of the role'. The narrow nature of the role deterred men qualified in personnel management from applying for posts in local government establishment sections; and prevented the development of the personnel management function internally. 'In the professionally orientated world of local government, the non-professional establishment function has offered little to the young man with the Chief Officer's ballpoint in his briefcase'.

Bains looked at the wider role which the personnel manager filled in industry and elsewhere in the public sector, and noted that a broad view of his positive function included the promotion of the effectiveness of human resources and the creation of a climate in which advantageous change could be achieved.

What needed to be done? In a general sense there should be 'a much greater awareness of the importance of personnel management' and this was to be encouraged by dropping the traditional 'establishment' label. In more detail, the report commented particularly on a number of work areas in which a substantial development was considered necessary:

> Manpower planning, recruitment, selection, placement and termination: Bains considered improvements in selection to be par-

47

ticularly important with more attention being paid to man and job specifications and to the development of interviewing skills.
Education, training and career development: here, too, Bains suggested that much more needed to be done. There should be a well-developed system of staff appraisal. Training needs required analysis, and to be met by effectively designed training activities. A career development system was also needed, with proper merit-based promotion procedures.
Working conditions and employee services.
Formal and informal communications and consultation through employee aand employer representatives and at all levels.
Negotiation and application of agreements on wages and conditions, and procedures for the avoidance and settlement of disputes. Bains recommended that the personnel officer should be the expert in the design of procedures and systems in consultation and negotiation. He should be the industrial relations adviser to managers throughout the authority and help to develop an atmosphere of mutual trust between the authority and its employees.
The human and social implications of change in organization and methods of working, and of economic and social changes in the community.

Bains then turned to the staffing control function and discussed the practicability of placing this within departments. The report pointed to a difference, however, in the constraints on industry and local government. In the private sector, the profit element provided a measure against which staff numbers could by assessed. In local government some other form of control was necessary and Bains felt that the exercise of central control through the establishment function was so well-founded in local government as to justify its perpetuation.

One further recommendation proved eventually to be the most controversial. Having described the role of the personnel officer in terms which embraced most modern aspects of personnel management, the report noted that in some authorities establishments work had become linked with management services (particularly work study and O and M.) Should this integration be encouraged? Bains thought not. Despite arguments that both personnel work and management services were concerned with the effective use of manpower and should therefore be integrated, the report took the opposing view that personnel management 'is a corpus of important work in its own right, whereas management services comprise a number of heterogeneous activities'. The report concluded that 'the two functions should be separate wherever the size of the authority permits, with co-ordination exercised at a high level'.

The report made one important provision: personnel management should not be seen as the exclusive preserve of the personnel department. All departments, all chief officers, must recognize their primary responsibility for the personnel management aspects of their general day to day managerial activities. The personnel officer's role was to advise, to co-ordinate, to provide specialist services, to assist in the application of the authority's personnel policies – but not to dictate or usurp other managers' staff responsibilities.

Finally, Bains discussed the status and authority necessary if the new personnel function was to succeed. The function was seen as 'central to the local authority's work and activities as a whole'. It has 'fundamental importance'. The status of the head of the department needed to be improved from that occupied in the majority of authorities. Chief officers in other departments would normally be expected to accept and act on his advice in 'exactly the same way' as they did on the Treasurer's. Given this general view of the key role, not only of the function but of the manager heading it, the organizational position of the latter might seem obvious. Any industrial manager reading Bains thus far would have assumed that the report would recommend full chief officer (or director) status for the Head of Personnel. But at this last hurdle, Bains faltered.

Yes, the Personnel Officer should have 'access' to the Chief Executive and not be subordinated to the Director of Administration or any other chief officer. But the organization location Bains proposed for him was unique and ambiguous. 'We do not suggest', the report stated, 'that at this stage the Personnel Officer should necessarily be a permanent member of the management team . . . he should, however, frequently be called in to advise the management team of proposals under discussion'. For a manager reporting directly to the Chief Executive this was clearly a position of less status than that of other heads of departments – a point emphasized by his odd position in the report's organization charts. The chart for non-metropolitan counties on the facing page illustrates this.

The five directors in this chart, with the chief executive, form the management team. And the function of the management team was to act as a corporate body in discussing policy and in reviewing progress and performance. 'There are few, if any, major decisions', the report commented, 'which can be made in isolation without some impact upon others' areas of responsibility'. Moreover, the report recognized that the contribution each member of the management team could make to its corporate deliberations was not limited to an exposition of defence of his own departmental position.

Each professional officer has a fund of knowledge and experience which is not only relevant to problems within his own field, but to the solving of problems in other fields as well and it is in the exchange of views and opinions within the management team that a true corporate spirit is likely to develop.

The chief personnel officer is not by this chart a chief officer in his own right nor, apparently, has he a fund of the kind of knowledge and experience necessary and useful within a corporate management team.

The contradiction between this organizational position and the critical importance given by Bains to a professional personnel management function is impossible to explain without reference to local government traditions and conventions. It has to be assumed that, at the end of the day, the members of the Bains Working Group were inhibited by their own local government experience from taking the final step of bringing personnel management into the organization structure at director level – and consequently produced the compromise of an officer with access to the chief executive but otherwise lacking in the organizational authority which would enable him to contribute directly to the promotion of a corporate view which takes fully into account, in its policy deliberations, the vital element of employee availability, attitudes and abilities.

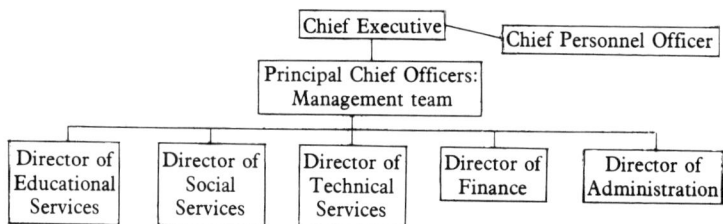

Somehow, Bains had missed the key concept of manpower as the resource common to all authority activities; and a resource markedly more complex to obtain and use effectively than its traditionally recognized twin – finance. Rightly, the Treasurer (or now, the Director of Finance) has been and continued under Bains to be a full member of any corporate management body. Without finance, the authority is dead. With finance, the traditional argument went, everything can be obtained, including manpower. So finance is the primary resource. But today most organizations recognize that finance alone will not obtain manpower of the right quality: staff look for job interest, for recognition, for career possibilities, for certain standards of facilities and employee services. Moreover, even if money will buy staff onto the books, it will not buy interest, enthusiasm, co-operation, initiative and intelligence. The manpower resource has to be planned for, competed for, developed, harnessed, involved, moti-

50

vated. And it is here that an organization should expect assistance and advice from its chief personnel officer. Provided he has the knowledge, experience and personality to contribute to manpower effectiveness in this way, it is vital that he takes part in the corporate management process at director level and so helps to shape policies and plans which can be put into effect by capable and committed staff. 'Access' to the chief executive, and reliance on his authority through a unique reporting relationship, is not enough. The personnel director must be in the team on level terms with his chief officer colleagues, and then stand or fall on his own abilities. The position allotted to him by Bains would not assist the recruitment of the best external personnel professionals into local government – as Bains suggested was necessary – nor enable the function to operate as Bains wished.

This one major disappointment excepted, the Bains report has clearly been of the very greatest importance in changing local authorities' concepts of the nature and value of the personnel function. It placed professional personnel management firmly on the local government map. It generated tremendous interest and a quite extraordinary volume of debate. And in name at least it killed the old establishment function in a period so short, in local government terms, as to be revolutionary.

Personnel management since Bains

On day 1 of the 1974 re-organization the local government Establishment Man almost vanished – at least by name. In place of one or two standard job titles – Establishment Officer, Director of Establishments – a whole forest of plain and exotic new plants sprouted. Personnel Officers, Personnel Managers, Chief Personnel Officers, Personnel and Management Services Directors, Directors of Administration and Personnel, some 30 variants of the general theme appeared.

There were two main, immediate issues which the Bains report sparked into controversy: first, the relationship between personnel management and management services; second, the place of the personnel officer in the management structure. Both issues are significant to the nature and role of the personnel function – though it is a matter for regret that far more discussion seems to have been devoted to these two topics than to the more basic issue of what personnel management really consists of, and how it can contribute to the effectiveness of the total management activity. Just as with the debate about the composition of the management team, too much attention appears to have been given to the structural elements of the personnel function and insufficient to the nature of personnel management processes.

51

Personnel and management services

Formal opposition to Bains' proposal to keep personnel management and management services separate was led by the Personnel and Management Services Group (PMSG), the most influential of numerous special interest groups active in this field.

In a report issued early in 1973 entitled *The Bains Report–another view*, the Group set out its objections to the separation of the two functions. The report was widely circulated to local authorities and received considerable backing both from individual management services groups (such as the local government group of the Institute of Work Study Practitioners) and, more influentially, from LAMSAC. (LAMSAC, the Local Authorities Management Services and Computer Committee, was set up in 1967 by the national local authority associations, with government support, to promote the use of computer and management services.)

The PMSG welcomed the Bains proposals for a wider interpretation and application of personnel management. But it considered that unless personnel and at least some other major management services were linked, the personnel function would be hampered and restricted. It considered separation to be a rejection of the corporate management approach. Personnel management and management services were both inextricably concerned with both people at work and the work itself: how could separation do other than damage this necessary integration?

There are several points to bear in mind in considering what weight to give to these views. It is fair to comment that the Group was very heavily biased towards management services in its history and membership. Until 1970 it had not formally included personnel management as an area of basic concern. Even in 1973, when it listed 11 areas of work with which it considered itself to be concerned, personnel management hardly figured prominently. These work areas were:

Work study
Organization and methods (O and M)
Operational research (OR)
Project co-ordination
Computer applications
Corporate planning
Management accounting
Management audit
Management information systems
Training
Personnel services.

Moreover, its severe reaction to Bains was triggered more by Bains' proposals to split up management services and allocate some of them to the major users, than to the personnel proposals. Bains' statements, in particular, that 'as far as work study is concerned, we do not believe that a large central unit is necessary' and that work study practitioners should operate under the day to day control of the line manager were bitterly resented by most management services officers. After all, work study was by far the largest and longest-established of local authority management services, and this proposal to distribute work study officers to the various departments which made most use of the technique amounted to an attack on a professional interest group.

Small wonder that the local government groups of the Institute of Work Study Practitioners and the O and M Society strongly supported the PMSG line and added additional arguments of their own. The O and M group commented that management services would operate effectively only if the human factors were taken into account and that, in turn, the personnel function must be concerned with such matters as work loads on staff and organization structures and systems.

One Chief Executive totally disagreed with Bains. 'Manpower', he commented, 'is the most expensive of the three primary resources (land, finance, labour) and its full development would not be achieved by regarding personnel management as 'an optional extra', hidden away in a little box attached to the chief executive and separated from related management services'. A number of authorities agreed with this view, and designed their new organization structures to achieve integration.

By no means all authorities agreed. Surrey was perhaps the leader in the opposite view. It was quoted by Bains as having decided to separate the two functions about two years before the Bains report, and as considering that this separation 'enabled both personnel work and management services to receive higher priority within the organization than before'. And other authorities, too, followed this line in planning their new structures.

A balanced, middle view, came from The Local Authorities Conditions of Service Advisory Board (LACSAB). At a *Local Government Chronicle* conference in 1973, its Secretary emphasized the value of an evolutionary approach to this type of organizational problem. Each authority should develop the pattern of relationships between personnel and management services which best suited its own needs, and made the best sense to the managers concerned in the light of their experience and of their views about priorities. There obviously had to be effective links between the two sets of activities – but the precise pattern and the level at which they were brought together were not matters to be decided in abstract argument. He sounded one warning. Management services specialists could, he thought, sometimes find objectivity difficult to establish when they became involved in aspects of human relations which were not susceptible to measurement by quantitative techniques.

The place of the personnel officer in the management structure
As important to the future of personnel management as the somewhat unproductive debate about management services were the decisions made by authorities about the position within the new management structures of the chief personnel officer. Was he to be placed, as Bains had suggested, in a special reporting relationship to the Chief Executive but excluded from full membership of the management team? Was he to be a full chief officer with equal status to other heads of departments? Or was he to be relegated to the third tier of management, below full chief officer level, by being one of a number of grouped functions along the lines of the Institute of Work Study Practitioners' proposals?

Bains' ambiguity and imprecision about the personnel officer's place seems now to have resulted in a whole variety of answers: certainly examples exist of all three of the positions just postulated. Some authorities followed 'pure' Bains, with the personnel officer in his special box, outside the main chief officer group. One district, adopting a similar approach, explained that the personnel officer was not a member of the management team 'because although he has across-the-board responsibilities these are mainly of a service nature and are not thought to involve him in the decision-making process with a view to formulating advice to the Council'.

In other authorities, the personnel officer was set at third tier level, reporting to County or District Secretaries or Directors of Administration: while elsewhere, he headed a division with the management services department. In several non-metropolitan counties, a director of personnel (or of 'manpower services') headed up two parallel specialists – a personnel officer and a management services officer.

Generalizing, however, full top management status for a personnel department separate from management services seemed still to be the exception, a situation which engendered a fairly strong response from a number of informed and experienced commentators. The Secretary of LACSAB had made his position on this issue clear on a number of occasions. As early as December 1972 he was reported as saying that Bains had been too faint-hearted on this issue. He considered it essential that the personnel officer was fully included in policy formulation in order to ensure that full consideration was given to the human relations and staffing implications of the management proposal of plans at the formative stage. In 1973, he was setting out these views even more forcibly. In a speech at a joint LACSAB/LGTB conference he said:

The top line chief personnel officer needs to be right inside the
54

thinking process of the upper echelons of management. In this respect I go much further than Bains. It is not enough for the chief personnel officer to be 'called in' to the inner circle of management thinking 'when there is a need'. It is not sufficient because more often than not the need will not be recognized soon enough and at the worst not recognized at all. The chief personnel officer must be at the centre of management thinking when it is in its embryo state – before ideas have crystallized. He will then be converting the ideas into manpower terms with all their implications. There will be many occasions when he will suggest that policies should be modified – perhaps because manpower with the right skills and experience will not be available or because progress must be geared to training or because sufficient time must be allowed to carry out effective communication.

In an editorial, the *Local Government Chronicle* supported him:

> The personnel planner must be in on the general planning from the outset: he must therefore be one of the management team, continuously observing trends and probabilities, advising and if necessary warning his colleagues about the practicability of projects in relation to manpower.

The present position
As with the whole new pattern of management, it is still too close to recent reorganization to be able to give a definitive assessment of the current state of personnel management in local government. Much has been done to bring the personnel function into a more positive and constructive posture. There are personnel departments which are operating effectively and with high standards of professionalism across a wide range of integrated personnel activities. There are still authorities in which the personnel function, placed at a low level and restricted to minor administrative activities, is not contributing as it could to the effective development of manpower resources.

Two trends may tentatively be identified, one with, one against, Bains. First, there does seem to be a development towards setting the top personnel job at top management level, and not at third or fourth tier. Secondly, and contrary to Bains, personnel and management services have remained closely linked – or have been positively so placed – in many authorities' organization structures. A 1976 LAMSAC survey showed that some 60 per cent of responding authorities combined the personnel, training, job evaluation, O and M and work study functions.*

Perhaps the main weakness is that many authorities have concentrated on the structural element – on placing a personnel officer and a

* Management Services Resources in Local Government, LAMSAC, 1976

personnel department into the organization structure – without first analysing and deciding on the tasks and processes which the personnel function should undertake.

It is a sound principle of organization planning that the sequence to follow is:

First, decide what results are required

Secondly, decide what work activities or processes are needed to produce these results

Thirdly, decide how these activities are best grouped into organizational roles

Fourthly, decide how to relate these roles horizontally and vertically within a management structure.

Did many authorities (and to some extent Bains) approach the formation of their personnel departments by deciding the structure first?

At the end of the day, the real questions for the new personnel departments will be not so much where they are placed in the organization structure but what are they doing and what have they achieved. How many of them have so far introduced career development schemes, annual staff appraisals, professional selection techniques, effective consultative and negotiating systems, grievance and disputes procedures, job-evaluated grading methods? How many chief personnel officers have gained acceptance and respect at top management level for their contribution to organization planning, to general policy formulation, to the creation of an informed and committed work force?

Two things are clear. First, progress depends on the willingness and ability of top management teams to identify aspects of their employment activities which merit change – that is, to set objectives for improvements and to ensure that manpower planning occurs and is integrally linked with corporate planning.

Secondly, the achievement of these objectives will depend more on the personal skills and abilities of personnel officers and their staff than on any merely mechanistic decisions about links with management services or the place of the personnel officer in the organization structure. A personnel officer who knows his subject, has the personal ability to gain top management interest in his ideas and who is prepared to take the initiative in proposing change will, in most management situations, gain the recognition he deserves. From now on, the future of personnel management lies as much in the hands of the staff of the new personnel departments as it does with the chief executives or the authorities generally.

5 Personnel management in industry and local government

The previous chapters have discussed how changes in general concepts of management have influenced the place and role of the personnel function within an authority's management structure. The trend towards a commercial or industrial concept of management has also been remarked. To what extent can industrial patterns of personnel management be imported into a local government setting? Why did personnel management develop so much earlier in industry; and how have the various specialisms within personnel management been evolved? This chapter describes the influences which have shaped the personnel function in industry, and compares and contrasts these with influences in the local government employment environment. Some understanding of the reasons for the differences between the industrial and local government sectors will safeguard against too ready an acceptance of industrial precedents, as well as indicating some areas of personnel work to which local government may need to pay more attention in future.

Influences in the industrial sector
Seven main influences can be identified which have had a greater or earlier impact on the development of the personnel function in the industrial, than in local government, sectors:

Welfare, and the labour pressures of world wars 1 and 2
Productivity planning and bargaining
Industrial relations
Industrial training
Management development
Employment legislation in the 1960s
Manual worker priorities.

Welfare

Industrial personnel management originated in the welfare function in the 1914-18 War. The need for maximum output of war materials led to an influx of new labour, and particularly women, into the factories. Labour shortages caused by the massive manpower drain of the Western Front stimulated interest in productivity. Longer working hours failed to bring proportionate increases in output, and the effects on productivity of different patterns of working hours, and of physical working conditions, became subjects of considerable study. Under government pressure, war factories appointed welfare officers (many of them women) whose duties gradually extended beyond employee welfare to more administrative tasks such as recruitment. Embryo personnel departments began to emerge and their value was such as to ensure their permanence and growth when the war ended and government intervention diminished.

No similar pressures arose in local government at this time. During the war, authorities were often desparately short of labour but in the war economy there was no scope for recruitment specialists. And of course, the production pressures and consequent personnel problems of large-scale factory work did not apply to the thousands of generally small-scale local authorities.

In neither the public nor private sectors was the inter-war period one of significant growth for personnel management. Labour was plentiful: in a depressed, low cost economy there were no strong commercial pressures for high productivity. But in the factories, modest welfare and employment departments survived to form a base for the next major expansion in the second world war. In the United States, the growth of mass production techniques had resulted in increasing study into two opposite ends of the employment spectrum: one, work study and the production advantages of breaking down work tasks into minute, highly specified and repetitive work units; two, the psychological effects of large-scale, repetitive work processes on the attitudes and motivation of individuals and work groups.

The second world war once again made survival depend as much on the fight for production in the factories as on achievements of the fighting services. This time, too, the developing science of applied psychology and the mathematical techniques of the emerging management services were all harnessed to the same end. Welfare expanded to include the study and promotion of high morale. Production techniques became more scientific in linking man with machine. Politically, the growth of the Labour Party, and its part in the wartime coalition, ensured that trade unions were brought into partnership in the general war effort. Joint production committees became an integral part of the factory management process. An influx of new, green labour resulted in a massive expansion of new forms of training, inc'uding the training of supervisors in the human relations aspects of their work. The government brought in far wider controls of manpower and employment than in the '14-18 war. Direction and allocation of labour, a system of resource priorities, the imposition of an arbitration procedure for dealing with disputes – measures of these kinds all generated new managerial and administrative tasks. In the Services, too, the occupational psychologists were at work. Their development of selection techniques in particular was to be picked up by industry and developed in the immediate post-war period.

This explosion of activity across the whole employment function put personnel management firmly on the managerial map. Personnel departments were needed to handle the problems of labour direction, to administer the new training programmes, to assist in the growth of joint consultation, to expand the welfare effort, to apply the new ideas about morale and motivation, to build up effective systems of industrial relations.

And, again, much of this passed local authorities by. Some impetus was given to the growth of establishment sections by the increasing administrative chores resulting from governmental labour controls. But local government was seriously drained of manpower, at management levels as well as operationally, and the war period was one more of survival than expansion.

Productivity
A combination of a growth economy and the growing bargaining power of trade unions led, almost immediately after the war, to a new situation for British industrial management. Labour had become scarce and, relative to the pre-war period, expensive. Two broad developments resulted. First, the growth of work study and other management services such as O and M and operational research which could assist in achieving a more efficient use of resources – particularly manpower. Secondly, the development of productivity payment systems and, in due course, productivity bargaining. One school, on the management services wing, promoted a massive expansion in a whole range of performance-related payments (at management as well as operative level). Another, influenced by the occupational psychologists, followed up by buying out the abuses of many bonus systems by plant-wide high day-rate, productivity deals and went on to relate job satisfaction and 'job enrichment' to higher productivity. There has been a tendency for personnel management to be identified more closely with the psychological than the management services wing and, indeed, for the personnel manager to see part of his role as being to humanize, if not to resist, the mechanistic tendencies of his management services colleagues. It is certainly far less usual to find management services as part of the personnel function in industry

than it is in local government, though this has also been due in part to the close relationship in industry between the work of the production engineer and that of the operational research scientist and other production-orientated management services.

It is largely the absence of the same degree of production pressures in local government which explains why local government did not experience the expansion of personnel work which followed these productivity developments in industry.

Industrial relations
It is an over-simplification to consider the post-war period as being marked by an escalation of industrial disputes, even though a primary reason for the expansion of personnel management has been its growing involvement and specialization in industrial relations. The intensity of strike action in the 19th century was considerable and many of the milestones of trade union history lie on pre-war industrial battlefields. Yet until the second world war, industrial relations were not considered a personnel management specialism. The situation then changed, and for two reasons. First, the effect of industrial unrest on industrial efficiency has become greater as industry has become more technologically and economically interdependent (100 maintenance electricians can practically close a national industry). Secondly, management now recognizes that industrial disputes are not merely battles about money: they involve attitudes towards work, concepts of authority, social aspirations, group psychology. So they are seen as the symptoms of complex ills in industrial society as well as having serious economic consequences. There has been a consequent demand for mangers who can blend human relations expertise and negotiating skills, and it is the personnel manager who has most frequently stepped forward into this role.

The much more recent expansion of industrial relations activity in local government, discussed in detail in chapter 6, has only just begun to stimulate the growth of this major sector of personnel management.

Training
The impetus to industrial training during the second world war died away as the skilled men returned from the forces to the factories. The cyclical economic difficulties since the war and the general effect of 'stop, go' seem to have resulted in many British managements taking a relatively short-term view of their investment in skilled manpower. The longer-term benefits of a well-trained and flexible labour force had been deferred as a result of short-term economies and by the early 1960s the government was sufficiently alarmed about the growing scarcity of skilled men, and of redundancies in obsolete trades, to intervene in the industrial training field. The resulting Industrial

Training Act 1964 provided a necessary stimulus and resulted in something of a training boom. This is not the place to debate the virtues of levy/grant, or the problems of forecasting demand for particular types of trained manpower. What *is* relevant here is that the initial efforts of many employers to maximize training grant income led to a sudden demand for training specialists and yet another boost for personnel management. Admittedly, in the early stages of the training boom, the production men moved into the training function and in some cases power struggles resulted. Should training be within the personnel function? This question was for a time as lively a debating point as the more recent local government debate about the place of management services. But as time has passed, it is generally the personnel function which has absorbed the management, if not always the execution, of training activities. The ability of many personnel departments to maintain control of a rapidly expanding training effort depended, in many cases, on the foundation established during the second world war. Of particular relevance were the three key training programmes for supervisors, produced at that time by the Ministry of Labour and used or adopted by industrial personnel officers throughout industry. The initials TWI (JR, JI, JM) should bring back memories to middle-aged readers, just as they were brought back into use in the '60s training boom. Training Within Industry (Job Relations, Job Instruction and Job Methods) – the name of the scheme and its three main training programmes – nicely sum up the biases towards industry rather than the public sector and towards the human relations and work methods wings of personnel management theory, already discussed in this chapter.

The impact of the Industrial Training Act on local government was not so dramatic. Profit-making out of the levy-grant formula could not be so immediate an influence as it was on companies for whom profit was the natural indicator of success. And in any event, local government had not got the same personnel management base from which to launch any major new effort in the employment field.

Management development
The mid 1960s also saw the rise of the management development industry, coincident, but not directly linked with, the training boom. British management, uneasy about the poor comparative showing of home industry against its expansionist overseas rivals (particularly Germany and Japan), began to look critically at its own managerial performance. Purveyors of systems and solutions – consultants and academics – fed the fires of this introspection with the fuel of an apparently endless series of remedies. Managerial grids, action–centred leadership, T groups, inter-personnel skills analysis and, above all, management by objectives were promoted, tried, dis-

61

carded, adopted or adapted in a heady round of keeping up with the managerial Jones's. A key element in many of these systems was the assessment of an individual manager's performance, and the design and re-design of performance review forms became a minor industry within many personnel departments. It was, indeed, generally the personnel function which bore the major brunt of the whole complex growth of management development. Some personnel departments led the way in pioneering the trial of new systems. Others had the task of coping with too rapid changes of direction resulting from the too frequent attendance of their chief executives at seminars run by rival consultants. The majority accepted their responsibility to sort the wheat from the chaff of all these new ideas, and achieved (and are still developing) considerable improvements in managerial standards by adapting relevant ideas and techniques to their own particular organization's management needs. Perhaps one of the most valuable lessons of this period has, in fact, been the need to view each organization as a separate social (as well as economic) unit, and to tailor its management systems to its own particular style and requirements.

Certainly, the personnel function has in many companies become even more firmly established at a high level in the management hierarchy because of its involvement in the whole process of re-shaping and developing the nature and skills of the managerial body politic.

In local government, the concept of corporate management (or even of management itself in the functional sense in which the term is understood in industry) had not been developed at the time of the management development boom. Baffled management consultants retired hurt by encounters with the traditional small-firm councillor who had sufficient self-confidence to tell them that he did not understand what they were talking about. Very few establishment officers knew enough of the background theory to act as 'change agents' (to use the jargon) by selling new management techniques within their authorities. Personnel management in local government continued to await the arrival of a more relevant stimulus.

Employment legislation and control
Since the second world war and until the early 1960s the trend had been towards a decreasing degree of state intervention or influence in employment matters, and particularly in industrial relations. Most legislation had been concerned with the disbandment of wartime controls, rather than with the imposition of new forms of legal requirement and the 1950s saw the full flower of 'free collective bargaining'. There seemed little more for the trade unions to gain from legislation, and while employers were worried about a growth in trade union power they were not directly looking to the government

for remedies. Both sides of industry preferred the Government to 'keep out'. By the early 1960s, however, the legislators were beginning to think that all was not as well as it should be in the employment world.

Safety legislation for factories was in a confused state. The trade unions' pressure for higher wages as very much the first priority left some aspects of job security at a rather lower standard than seemed socially desirable. Working conditions in offices and shops often lagged behind developments in large-scale industry. Race relations problems, including discrimination in employment, were becoming the subject of public debate and concern. Parliament turned its attention to the employment scene and the first wave of legislation began. A list of Acts introduced in the period 1958-65 illustrates this new development of legislative intervention:

1958 Disabled Persons (Employment) Act
1961 Factories Act
1963 Contracts of Employment Act
Offices, Shops and Railway Premises Act
1964 Industrial Training Act
1965 Race Relations Act
Redundancy Payments Act

The Acts required employers to provide better safety provisions and better working conditions, more job security, better training, and equal opportunities. Their impact was felt to a greater extent by the private than public sectors because it was commerce and industry which were primarily subject to increasingly rapid changes in economic pressures. These were in turn resulting in redundancies, the need for training and re-training, and the need for more protection for the weaker members of the working community: the disabled, the redundant, the immigrant. Industrial personnel management took on the task of interpreting and applying this influx of new legislation and had to develop additional expertise, particularly in safety and welfare, in personnel administration (engagement and redundancy regulations and documentation) and above all, in training.

Up to the 1960s the impact of new legislation was less severe in local government. Local authorities' administrative procedures were often in advance of those in the parts of the private sector which had led to the need for the Contracts of Employment Act. Most local government employees did receive schedules of their employment conditions, and were employed on reasonable notice periods. Redundancy was very much a private sector phenomenon: security of tenure was, and generally remains, an important aspect of central and local government employment. This first wave of legislation therefore called for relatively little action by local authorities; their establishment departments remained, in consequence, largely undisturbed.

Manual worker priorities
One other important historical difference merits comment. In following the growth of the personnel function in industry, it is noticeable that the employee group with which personnel departments have historically been most concerned has been manual workers. Factory welfare, productivity bargaining, industrial training, safety and a good deal of earlier employment legislation was concerned wholly or mainly with the manual worker and his employment environment and conditions. In industrial relations, too, it was the existence and activities of powerful manual worker trade unions which stimulated the growth of the industrial labour officer and of industrial relations specialists. The growth of white-collar trade unions has been a relatively recent development in the private sector.

Traditionally, local government has tended to pay far less attention to its manual workers than to its clerical, administrative and professional staff. The pre-war distinction between white-collar 'officers' and blue-collar 'servants' speaks for itself. In all the official studies of local government, pre- *and* post-war, there is a remarkable, almost total absence of comment about the employment position of manual workers. Not even Bains gives them a mention. In the absence of militancy (until the much more recent past) local authorities have not had to respond to the type of situations in industry which have for years called for the expertise of full-time industrial relations specialists; and the growth of personnel management has been delayed thereby. The current situation, in which traditionally staid white-collar unions have rapidly adopted the more thrusting and 'un-officer-like' tactics of their blue-collar cousins, has in consequence been a severe shock to the local government system. We shall examine the consequences of this for personnel management in a later chapter.

Other differences between local government and industrial sectors

The difference in the nature and effect of financial pressures in the two sectors is sometimes quoted as a significant factor in explaining differences in managerial approach. It clearly has some influence and is worth a closer examination.

A private company exists to make profits, though this over simplifies the motivations of the firm's managers. Their primary instincts are survival and expansion. Profits ensure the former and pay for the latter. A firm has to be competitive, expansionary and aggressive in a market sense, to be successful. Its success is measured in financial terms – profit ratios give its score in the competitive game. The availability and quality of its manpower have a very direct effect on the firm's financial results. To be successful it must obtain the manpower it needs, and it must raise output per pound of manpower costs above that of its rivals. The pressure to do something about manpower problems – and to do it fast – is intense.

So if labour is scarce, the efficient firm responds by improving the quality of its recruitment, by increasing the attractiveness of its employment conditions, by raising productivity. It will spend considerable sums in so doing, because the penalty for failure for the management team is extinction collectively and redundancy or dismissal for the individual. In any event, the rewards of commercial success will normally be far greater than the costs of, for example, trebling the job advertising budget. The volume of expenditure is almost irrelevant provided it is topped by marketing income. In a financial environment of this kind personnel management flourishes.

The financial pressures on a local authority are almost the reverse of those on a company. Survival remains as a motivator, though mainly for the elected members: for them it depends on political rather than financial success. The political danger is over-expenditure. With the traditional rating system, almost any increase in expenditure is electorally unpopular and the main financial pressure is to keep expenditure down. The relationship between higher rates and improvements in public services is not, unfortunately, perceived very clearly by local electorates. In this type of environment, a shortage of labour can thus result in 'savings' which might, at least in the short term, appear to outweigh the disadvantages of a slow deterioration in the quality of services. Certainly the incentive for an authority to embark on a massive and expensive recruitment drive, or to increase earning levels, is very much less than it is for the private company in the same labour situation. There is more scope for personnel management in an organization which places a high premium on recruitment skills, and on rapid and imaginative changes in its package of employment conditions, than in an organization with an understandably ambivalent view of expenditure of this kind.

For the elected member, expansion, too, is a singularly frustrating motivator. It brings to the fore a major divison of interest and intent between members: those who enter local government to promote the extension and improvement of public services, and those who see their role primarily as one of rates reduction and expenditure limitation. Even when the expansion of a service is agreed, it is not surprising that priority for expenditure should tend to be for the immediately tangible elements – the houses or the sports centre *per se* – rather than on the more intangible and longer term matters such as career development schemes for the staff who manage the housing and sports centre schemes. Economy – in a direct, annual budgeting sense – has taken precedence over long-term and less readily costed concepts of efficiency and effectiveness. It is one of the personnel manager's problems in local government that much of his stock-in-trade pays off in the long, rather that short, term: and pays off indirectly through changes in attitudes, skills and morale, rather than directly by cutting immediate expenditure.

At officer level too, survival and expansion are not the influences they are in the private sector. Survival of the authority is not subject to financial results but to the periodic upheavals of local government reorganization. Expansion may have its attractions, but for reasons of personal or departmental ambition rather than as a legitimate and declared objective of the authority as a whole. So departmental growth is a risky enterprise, a matter for guile and organizational politics. The scope for positive, productive personnel management has been somewhat restricted by the negative features of this traditional role.

Apart from these major financial and motivational differences, five broad influences can be distinguished in local government:

The close involvement of elected members in the management of employment matters
The growth of centralized, national collective bargaining
The need for, and existence of, a manpower control function
The 1974 re-organization
The wide range of occupations.

Each of these factors is discussed in more detail elsewhere in this book. In this chapter, the discussion centres on their effect historically on the nature and growth of the personnel function.

Member involvement
Member involvement in employment matters is a unique feature of local government. In no other large-scale employment sector do elected representatives of the public at large, working voluntarily, part-time and unpaid, and with no formal training or experience for this specific role, act as 'managing employers' to the considerable extent which has become normal in most local authorities.

In terms of principle, civil servants are also employed by the public and managed by elected representatives – government ministers. But the distance between the individual member of Parliament and any individual civil servant is enormous compared to that between the average councillor and any one of his council's employees.

True, the Minister is full-time whereas most council committee chairman are part-time; but the sheer size of a national civil service limits contact between the elected amateur in command, and the employed professional officer to a minute proportion of the whole service. And that proportion, too, is at a level (apart from chauffeurs and doormen) which to the average civil servant is lost in the mist at the top of the Whitehall pyramids.

The main and traditional area for member decision-making in employment is that of staff selection and no review of the influence of members on personnel work would be complete without reference to the very considerable extent to which members have maintained control of the appointment of new staff, and of promotions.

Historically, two strands of development can be identified. First, the long-standing practice of member patronage; second, the parallel freedom of some chief officers to appoint their own staff. These strands were brought together in 1934 by the Hadow Committee which placed all staff appointments firmly in the hands of members.

The earlier Royal Commission report (1929) quoted some fascinating evidence on member patronage. NALGO commented critically in its evidence about undesirable influences in recruitment, and particularly of personal and political influence. One witness alleged that he knew of five or six authorities in which a large proportion of the staff were relatives or friends of councillors.

The Hadow report came down strongly against member patronage which it described as 'altogether objectionable'. It was also severely critical of the practice in some authorities of chief officers selecting their own staff without reference to committees or the council. It felt this opened the door to 'undesirable pressures' being brought to bear on behalf of individual candidates and recommended that, in future, a committee or sub-committee of members should be responsible for all appointments. Canvassing should be strictly barred: all vacancies should be advertised: impartiality was to be the order of the day.

It may further surprise those without lengthy local government experience, therefore, to find that as late as 1967, in the research reports annexed to the Maud Committee's report, reference was still being made to canvassing. It was described as still relatively common, particularly in areas of high unemployment, and one county was quoted as being in favour of the practice. The County Clerk, talking more freely than might have been expected, said 'if you don't canvass, you've had it'. He went on to say that members boasted of the extent to which they were kept up all night preceding an appointments board by candidates seeking support; that they seemed to enjoy this; and that it was easier for councillors to assess candidates if they could see them in this way at their homes. To correct the balance, in another county, members were quoted as 'falling over backwards' not to appoint friends or relatives.

Patronage in public appointments was not, of course, restricted to local government. In the Civil Service, before the great reforms of the late 19th century, it was an accepted method of obtaining appointments. It did not intrinsically involve corruption – though even efficient administrators succumbed to the obvious temptations. Samuel Pepys' purse would have been somewhat slimmer had appointments to the Navy Office been in the control of a personnel manager.

Local government does seem, however, to have reacted to changes in public attitudes much more slowly than the Civil Service. Two reasons may predominate. First, the absence of strong, professional administrative controls on a service-wide basis. Departmentalism within authorities, and the lack of uniformity or co-ordination in employment matters between them, left recruitment and selection very much in the control of local councillor groups and interests. Secondly, the environments in which patronage and nepotism continued into the post 1945 period were, in the main, areas of high unemployment in which councillors were customarily local 'strong men', dominant in small, intense communities.

In most authorities, and particularly in the large ones, member control of appointments followed the Hadow principles of scrupulous impartiality through open advertising and committee interviewing.

The Mallaby Committee published figures which showed that in over 20 per cent of the 684 authorities then researched, members still selected all new entrants. And in over 30 per cent of the authorities officers were excluded from selection of middle and senior grades. The higher labour turnover rates of the late 60s and early 70s will have made it increasingly difficult for members to continue this degree of involvement and, in any event, there has been a move towards smaller selection panels as part of a process of improving selection methods. But members, both individually and collectively, remain understandably and keenly interested in the appointment, welfare and promotion of at least their staff.

The phrase 'their staff' illustrates the proprietorial feelings that many members have towards their council, its services and its staff. With common community interests, and a strong sense of local identity and pride, members (particularly of the smaller authorities) develop a paternalistic attitude towards the authority's employees which has strong parallels in the employment attitudes of owner-managers of small businesses.

It is interesting, therefore, to note that owners and managers of small firms, farmers and professional men (who are also usually small employers) have traditionally held a disproportionate number of councillor positions. Research for the Maud Committee showed that some 40 per cent of councillors in rural and county authorities, and over 20 per cent of councillors in metropolitan authorities, fell into these categories. In the whole population the proportion for these groups was then about 10 per cent. It is not surprising to find a reluctance among councillors, used in their own businesses to considering selection as a most critical aspect of business success, to delegate authority very readily to professional selectors.

Councillors with a trade union background have also exerted a considerable influence in this field. Not all may be willing to consider the professional personnel manager as being in any better position than they to assess the suitability of candidates. Some may well be concerned about the possibility of professional selectors perpetuating a conventional management view of the boss-worker relationship, and in senior appointments promoting the growth of that most distrusted feature of modern management by trade unions; the smooth, faceless, organization man.

Finally, many members are involved in local government because they wish to promote social welfare and social justice. They have a strong, personal commitment to, and sense of responsibility for, the well-being of their fellow citizens. They know that the test of collective policies to this end lies in the effect of these policies on individuals. It is not surprising that they feel a similar sense of responsibility towards their authority's employees and that here, too, they assess the effectiveness of its employment policies by the extent to which individual employees express a sense of satisfaction or grievance in their work.

In summary, taking into account the traditions of member patronage, the influence of small-business and trade union experience, the paternalism that derives from local pride, and the responsibility felt towards employees by members with a strong sense of social justice, it follows that local authorities have not been eager to delegate to personnel officers many of the employment functions which profit- and production-orientated businessmen have readily functionalized.

National collective bargaining
In a later chapter, the industrial relations system in local government is described and discussed. Here, we consider only the effect on the growth of the personnel function of highly centralized collective bargaining. It has already been noted that local government did not, until recent years, experience any really serious industrial action by manual or white collar unions. The pressure for some form of employer-based industrial relations function came mainly from the view, propounded by NALGO and generally supported by the employers, that salaries and conditions of service should be as uniform as possible throughout local government. On the white-collar side this was seen by the employers as having advantages quite unconnected with industrial relations. Consistency and uniformity would improve the image of local government as a recognized career area. It would aid recruitment, particularly of qualified professionals, and the transferability of staff between authorities.

On the manual worker side, uniformity of pay and conditions was seen as an important means of preventing industrial relations trouble. The growing power of the trade unions in the 1939-45 war and in the immediate post-war period, and the inroads of the big general unions into the public sector, was seen as a potential danger for the individual local authority. Centralization of the employers' activities was as normal a reaction to this view in local government as it was in industry. To this extent, the setting up of the various National Joint Councils and of the Local Authorities Conditions of Service Advisory Board (LACSAB) in the late 1940s, no more than paralleled the growth of national employers federations in industry.

But there was one major difference. Industry had, for many decades, lived with an active and powerful shop steward movement at local level. In engineering, for example, this movement existed in an organized capacity as early as the '14-18 war. In consequence, industry was equipped with personnel and industrial relations departments to provide the necessary support at factory level to national collective bargaining systems. National agreements laid down a broad framework of conditions and minimum rates of pay. At company and factory level, firms expanded on the conditions and built up their own domestic pay structures on the national minima foundations. Companies may well have preferred to have relied entirely on the national bargaining system and on national agreements. But the shop stewards would not accept this.

In local government, until recent years, shop steward activity (at blue or white collar levels) has been, in comparison, very limited. With most authorities treating industrial relations as a fairly negative science – the avoidance of strife –and without strong shop- or office-floor activity, there has been no incentive for an authority to become self-sufficient in its industrial relations activities.

Bargaining has been thankfully left to LACSAB, to the provincial councils and to the handful of members who form the employers' sides of the National Joint Councils.

Shop stewards may be the professional 'enemies' of the industrial personnel manager, but they have helped to bring him into existence and, by their increasing power and authority within the trade union system, to promote the importance of his industrial relations role.

It is a feature of the late 1970s that personnel officers in local government now 'enjoy' the same promotional pressures.

Manpower control

Almost all the influences on the growth of the local government personnel function so far discussed have been negative or neutral in their effect. With the exception of the 1974 reorganization itself, a natural, organic reason for the existence and development of the function seems almost wholly absent until the dramatic changes in industrial relations and in employment legislation of more recent years. What is the genesis of the personnel function? Fairly obviously, establishment control; and the history of this element of local gov-

70

ernment personnel management has been traced in an earlier chapter.

It is worth emphasizing here, however, that the control of staff numbers and grading, which for years was the dominant personnel activity in local government, occupies a very small part indeed of the industrial personnel manager's job. In direct terms it is scarcely mentioned in any mainstream personnel management literature. From a productivity viewpoint it is true that industrial work study and O and M include the determination of manning levels. But there are two key differences of approach between local government and industry to these particular management techniques.

First, the emphasis in the use of work measurement techniques in industry is on productivity – on output. It is a dynamic, positive, approach concerned with speeding-up production times, increasing unit production, raising profit levels. And with a slowly growing reaction against conventional work study based incentive schemes, the bias in the use of work study has turned towards broad-based method study. In local government, work measurement techniques have been used primarily for incentive payment schemes, and also to achieve manpower savings – to obtain the same amount of work with fewer employees. Both are necessary functions: but their character is less dynamic than in industrial applications.

Secondly, the direct link between work study and production in industry has generally resulted in this, and other similar management services being developed within the production management rather than the personnel management function. In consequence, the personnel function has been able to concentrate on the impact of management services on human and industrial relations, on coping with the changes in morale and in individual and group attitudes which result from the application of productivity techniques, rather than on the promotion of the techniques themselves. This has given personnel management the opportunity to develop its own particular specialism – the human aspects of management. In local government, the link between work measurement techniques and the conventional establishment control function has been a major reason for the development of the joint personnel/management services department. But an argument can certainly be made that this results in priority being given to the mechanistic aspects of personnel control rather than to the less easily defined but more dymanic human and behavioural aspects. There is a degree of incompatibility between the restrictive, traditional 'head-cutting' role of the establishment activity, and those aspects of personnel management which are concerned with personal and organizational development, with releasing the latent interest, imagination and abilities of individuals and groups.

Personnel management in local government thus has a well-established base in the assessment and control of numbers and grades.

71

But it is a base from which the function may well have to move if it is to develop its full potential.

The 1974 reorganization

In the more recent past, the one major factor influencing the development of personnel management specifically in local government has been the 1974 reorganization. Any major structural change in a major institution involves difficult human, social and organizational problems. Reorganization required a very considerable amount of personnel expertise, from the evolution of new organization structures for merged authorities, through the tasks of persuading staff to accept new roles in new locations, to the detailed work of marrying different local conditions of service. Overseeing the work at authority level was a statutorily appointed Staff Commission which laid down various guidelines and directions governing forms of job advertising, systems of 'slotting-in' staff to new structures, and compensation procedures for those displaced. The Commission's job, acting in a way as a national personnel management unit, was to ensure fair and consistent treatment for staff while meeting the new authorities' manpower needs and preventing unnecessary competition or 'poaching' of staff between authorities. Their even-handed and sensible approach to the massive staffing problems involved acted as a stimulus for good standards of personnel management in the new authorities, and has left a legacy of principles (of slotting-in and compensation, for example) which individual authorities have taken over for their own use when handling internal reorganizations. Some statistics of staff movements during reorganization, quoted by the Commission in their final report, illustrate the scale of the whole operation – and its generally smooth passage.

At the peak period of April, 1974, national advertisements for new posts in new authorities were running at 800 per week. These advertisements were permitted only for posts not filled within narrower geographical boundaries by slotting in, and eventually totalled 18,359. 2,878 officers opted for early retirement on the special (and very favourable) terms made available to Chief and Deputy Chief Officers in order to ease the problem caused at top management level by the reduction in the number of authorities – and hence of chief officers. Appeals tribunals were set up to handle grievances about appointments but only 47 cases were actually processed by tribunals – all other cases being resolved within local disputes machinery below tribunal level. The Staff Commission attributed the success of the staff management aspects of reorganization to extensive consultation with and between local authorities and the trade unions; but there is no doubt that the existence of the Commission was a most important feature in allaying staff fears and in setting a high standard of personnel management, particularly in terms of fair and effective selection, grievance and appeals procedures.

The wide range of occupations
Some details have been given in chapter 1 about the variety of occupations involved in local government employment. This deserves emphasis, for few industries, let alone individual companies, have to provide for so wide a range of jobs as local government as a whole or, indeed, an individual local authority.

Almost 300 different manual worker occupations are listed in the handbook of the Greater London Joint Council (covering London boroughs and the GLC) and similar lists occur in the provinces. The number of different white collar occupations is less easy to estimate but at least 60 different groups of jobs are covered by the national agreements for these staff, and each of these groups includes a variety of individual occupations. Even at the level of the individual local authority, a workforce of 5,000 may well include 300 to 500 different jobs.

Problems of pay comparisons and differentials can be formidable with this degree of variety, while the disparate nature of much of the work does not make it easy to foster cohesive and cooperative attitudes between different groups of employees. Inevitably, given the history of the trade union movement as a whole, employers have to negotiate with a large number of unions, many of which are not limited in scope to local government and therefore import industrial attitudes into a non-industrial setting. The tendency for individual professions to establish local government organizations has already been commented on, and personnel management is itself not immune from these influences, which derive very much from the occupational complexity of the employment scene and the absence of any one, strong unifying influence. Against these difficulties, however, many personnel officers would set the interest inherent in this variety of work types and occupations, and the advantages of dealing with relatively small work groups. Moreover, almost all local government work is readily understood by the layman (and the new employee) so that local government has none of industry's problems of trying to make apparently meaningless tasks purposeful. Road sweeping, preparing school meals, emptying dustbins, interviewing housing applicants, examining house-owners' plans for new garages – work of this kind may lack glamour, but it does not lack day to day meaning, and much of it involves the interest (as well as the frustrations) of close contact with the public.

Employment legislation and pay control
Particularly in the past five years, one other important influence on

personnel work has been shared by all employers. The massive escalation of government intervention, through legislation, regulation and general policy, in employment standards and practices and in pay, has imposed a considerable burden on employers and managers already preoccupied with growing economic and social problems.

Personnel departments have suddenly become necessary to help busy line managers comply with a mass of new legislative requirements, and to design and introduce a whole new range of employment procedures necessitated by statute, by various codes of practice and by an ever-growing tide of legal precedents set by the Employment Appeals Tribunal and the courts.

A summary here of the legal developments of recent years explains much of the growth in demand for personnel officers in this period, and may indicate that the need for continuous attention to, and revision of, employment policies and procedures has not yet been fully recognized in some authorities.

Four particular types of legislative intervention can be distinguished, concerned with:

dismissals
trade union membership and activities
discrimination against race and sex
pay control

The unfair dismissals provisions of the 1971 Industrial Relations Act hit many employers like a shock wave. The idea of having to pay £4,000 to compensate a dismissed worker and of needing to show at a public tribunal that a sacking was fair seemed a major erosion of the concept of 'management prerogative'. The Act, and its use of the associated Code of Practice in determining the fairness of disciplinary and dismissal methods, certainly resulted in a major overhaul of personnel policies and practices by many employers. Personnel officers througout the land got down to the job of writing new disciplinary procedures, producing standard warning letters, introducing new record systems and training supervisors and managers in a new, systematic approach to what had often been highly subjective and *ad hoc* processes.

Before long, local authorities were to discover that the mere existence of formal procedures was not enough to give them protection at law. Some illustrious Councils began to appear before tribunals and the courts, and lose on points of basic employment practice.

In general, the 1971 unfair dismissal provisions, modified and extended by 1974 and 1975 legislation have emphasized the need for proper employment procedures, operated consistently and fairly and with regard to the individual circumstances of each case.

This blend of administrative system and humanity is an important feature of professional personnel management, and personnel officers can thank legislators and the tribunals for this particular promotion of their skills.

The industrial relations facet of personnel work has also received a boost from continuous changes in relevant legislation. In particular, the 1971 ban and the 1975 lifting of restrictions on closed shops have necessitated reviews of patterns of trade union membership. Although the centralized Whitley systems in local government define the main blocks of union representation, local problems have been caused by unions not recognized nationally, by demands for closed shop agreements and by covert competition for membership between trade unions. In London, for example, the London Fire Fighters' Federation (an unrecognized breakaway union) attempted to use the Industrial Relations Act to establish its position. On the repeal of the Act, the local officials of the Fire Brigades Union (the recognized union) claimed a closed shop, partly in reaction to the activities of the Fire Fighters' Federation. More recently, other unions unrecognized at national level, such as the Retained Firefighters' Union and the Association of Polytechnic Teachers, have also used the provisions of the Employment Protection Act to seek formal local and national recognition, against strong opposition by the existing local government trade unions.

In recent years, therefore, the industrial relations function has become a live one for local government, and a personnel function with little previous related experience has had to cope with this new situation. The existence of legislation in this field has helped to ensure that coping effectively is recognized by authorities as a necessity and not merely as a choice; and it is the personnel function which is being called on to supply the necessary specialist expertise.

Equal opportunity legislation in the fields of race and sex has had less direct impact on the personnel function. The effect of the Race Relations Act has been felt by local authorities more directly in their public service functions – particularly housing – than in employment. But the Equal Pay Act and the much wider implications of equal opportunity legislation to bar sex discrimination have forced employers generally to begin, at least, to examine critically their recruitment, promotion and pay policies, and this influence will clearly grow. Again, therefore, it is the personnel function to which employers have turned to conduct these reviews of conventional and traditional employment attitudes and systems, and to suggest new policies which are in tune with current egalitarian trends.

Finally, the frequent changes of governmental attempts to control incomes since the mid '60s have imposed severe strains on all employers' pay systems and on employee relations. The unpredictable and inconsistent sequence of freeze, norms, freeze, Stage 2 and Stage 3 and Phases I to IV changed wage levels and relativities in an arbitrary and uncoordinated fashion in which minor differences in wage settlement dates were sometimes more important determinants of wage levels than any national assessment of the merits of particular claims. More recently, cash limits have imposed new constraints on pay.

In local government, particularly, the strains at local level were often intense. National wage settlements exhausted the whole Stage 2 or 3 pay pool, leaving no cash available for local bargaining. Relations between individual authorities and their employees and local union officials deteriorated. Neither was dissatisfaction limited to the main groups of manual and clerical employees. Chief and senior officers became increasingly concerned at the compression of salaries resulting from flat-rate payments and the limits to the size of percentage increases.

The personnel officer's work-load in both public and private sectors was noticeably increased by both the direct and indirect effects of pay incomes policy and control. Directly, he had to become an overnight expert in the small print of increasingly complex pay codes. Indirectly, he had to deal with the backwash of employee worries and resentment at many of the odd results of the application of these codes.

The subsequent social contract period and its related acceleration in inflation generated new pressures. Should local and immediate pressures be used to justify departures from strict cost of living-related pay changes? Was it the employer's responsibility to hold the social contract line? Was being within the contract the only justification needed for any increase in pay costs? To what extent would massive increases in pay have to be paid for by reductions in manning levels? Problems of these kinds proliferated and could not be dealt with as simply matters of finance and financial or legal formulae.

The Government's eventual response to inflation – the £6 pay limit – again changed the scene and the pressures. Local government trade unions, while negotiating agreements within this limit, either opposed the policy at the Trades Union Congress or gave at best lukewarm support. One effect of the settlements nationally at the maximum permitted level was to prevent additional local deals which might otherwise have oiled the industrial relations wheels. The later 5 per cent and 10 per cent phases continued the pattern of equal pay treatment for all, with exceptions permitted only in individual cases in which significant increases of responsibility could be demonstrated. Pressure from small groups of staff for grading changes which might, on the basis of comparisons with other groups have been justified, had to be resisted if pay policy criteria were to be met. And central government used the threat of cuts in its rate support grant to ensure that local government employers toed the pay policy line. Something, somewhere, was likely to crack; and in 1978 a national Fire Brigade strike provided a major challenge to the government's 10 per cent pay 'guidelines'. While the eventual settlement did not, within 1978, exceed this figure, a forward commitment to link firemen's pay with a point 75 per cent up the national male manual earnings league table guaranteed very major wage increases in the following two years. Similar pressures and solutions occurred in the police forces, while these moves to index fire and police pay to pay levels external to local government soon began to produce agitation from other local government trade unions. Personnel officers continued to act as guardians and interpreters of central government incomes policy; and to deal with the multiplicity of problems generated thereby. Strict central pay policy was replaced in 1979 by the new wave of comparability studies, with the manual workers and then teachers agreeing interim settlements at about nine per cent plus references of their pay levels to the newly established Standing Commission on Pay Comparability. This Commission had the task of assessing local government pay levels against external earnings, work which opened up a whole new debate about the market concept of salaries and involved many personnel officers in collecting data about pay levels among local firms in order to assist LACSAB in its task of producing evidence either for the Commission or for its own market studies for such groups as engineering craftsmen and APT and C staff.

Taken overall, the frequent shifts and distortions in relative pay levels resulting from varying national pay policies have had a social significance of at least the same magnitude as their economic effects.

The extent to which the personnel function can contribute to a solution of these social problems remains an open question: though by training and experience, the professional personnel manager is clearly equipped to take a leading role in assisting in the task of ensuring that his particular organization develops the necessary adaptability to change.

6 Industrial relations: the national system

Until fairly recent years local government would not have been considered as an important industrial relations arena. The press and public tend to think of industrial relations primarily in terms of disruptive industrial action, and local government was for many years a sector of employment in which such action was rare.

That situation has changed. Perhaps the first major jolt to complacency about the passivity of local government employees came in the 'dirty jobs' strikes of 1969/70. The annual round of national pay negotiations in 1969 included not only the usual bargaining about a general pay award but also a re-evaluation of all manual worker occupations to produce a new pay structure. Not surprisingly, negotiations were somewhat protracted though, by September of that year, employers and trade unions felt that good progress was being made and a date 29 September was agreed as the starting point for any increases resulting from the re-grading of jobs. On 22 September, however, one union branch in one London borough ignored the whole basis of both the official negotiations and the official disputes procedures, and voted for immediate strike action in support of a claim for a £20 per week basic wage. The dustmen in that borough stopped work the following day. Within two weeks this unofficial strike action had extended across a whole range of manual workers. The following autumn the situation was even more serious. A breakdown in national wage talks was followed by the manual worker unions supporting an official strike of refuse workers, sewage workers, drivers, park keepers and the like throughout London and the provinces. Before these strikes were settled, the Cabinet had had to meet to consider the hazards to public health, the TUC had been asked to intervene, and both employers and national trade union officials in local government had begun to re-think their industrial relations strategies.

At least five features of this strike illustrate the changes which had been occurring and with which a hitherto satisfactory system of collective bargaining had on this occasion failed to cope.

One of the root causes of the strike was growing resentment, at shop floor level, of the fact that local government manual workers were, to quote from the 1967 report of the National Board for Prices and Incomes, 'a large concentration of workers whose earnings are among the lowest in the country'. The strike thus highlighted the position of the low-paid – a feature that was to dominate many wage negotiations in later years and particularly in 1974 and 1978/79.

Despite the inconvenience to the public, the men received a significant level of support from the press and public for their claim for higher pay. Public opinion had to be recognized as a factor which could influence pay settlements.

The strike constituted a reaction at local level against the remoteness, complexity and duration of national level negotiations. Conflicts between local autonomy and national collective bargaining have continued to cause problems to both trade unions and employers.

The 1969 stoppage was unofficial and to some extent was as much a revolt by the rank and file against their own trade union hierarchy as it was an attack on the employers. All trade unions have found it necessary to give greater recognition to shop stewards and to the shop floor, the prompt official strike of 1970 being one expression of such support.

The whole pay situation was exacerbated (or at least complicated) by government incomes policy. In September 1969, the government-backed norm was for 3½ per cent increases and this followed the earlier 1966 freeze and later period of 'cautious moderation'. Certainly the employers were under no obligation to be other than extremely modest in their pay offers, though the lengthy re-structuring exercise was, in fact, one way of providing a little more cash than was otherwise possible within government policy. But in general, the disturbing effect of government pay policies on hitherto 'free collective bargaining' had not, perhaps been fully recognized. It has continued to be a major influencing factor on both the nature of pay settlements and on employee/ employer relations. In local government, too, central government influence may well be a factor outside periods of formal pay restraint, through the imposition of cash limits.

Since 1969, despite the efforts of the employers and the trade unions to adjust more effectively to these changes in the industrial relations environment, industrial action by local government employees has not been uncommon. A number of disputes may be selected as having attracted public attention and as illustrating other factors which currently influence the industrial relations scene.

Serious action occurred in 1973/4 in both the fire and ambulance services (in the latter, in the period immediately preceding their transfer to the new Health Authorities). Never before had the emergency services gone so far in putting life at risk by, in at least one instance, a total stoppage, and on a more general basis by a restriction of work to self-designated 'genuine' emergencies. Had the employers relied for too long on the moral pressures of this type of work to restrain industrial action, with the result that the financial rewards were, comparatively, inadequate? Was the basic issue as much one of status, caused only partly by the comparative salary position but also by a lack of occupational identity? The latter certainly seemed to apply to the ambulancemen, whose trade union membership was divided between three general unions and one unrecognized and breakaway specialist union; and whose pay was largely determined within the general local government manual worker group.

Later in 1974 many London boroughs experienced severe difficulties, particularly in maintaining their cash flows in rate income and other receipts, by strike action and overtime bans operated by white-collar staff in support of the trade unions' (primarily NALGO) official campaign for higher London allowances. Some of the employers were clearly shocked by the degree of militancy displayed by clerical and administrative staff who, by tradition, would not have been expected to behave in other than an orderly and cooperative manner. The emergence of unofficial 'action groups' within the white-collar trade unions, often with alleged extreme left political connections, has also caused reaction and concern in both employer and trade union circles. The important general point, is that employers can no longer expect their white-collar staff to exercise more restraint in action taken in support of pay claims than their blue-collar colleagues.

In the early part of 1975 there was a highly publicized, and again unofficial, strike of dustcart drivers in Glasgow and Liverpool. Two aspects of this dispute are important to an understanding of the changing industrial relations scene. First, the dispute developed from private sector settlements for heavy goods vehicle drivers – an occupation common to local government and private industry. There have been increasing difficulties for local government in pay comparisons of this type particularly where other employers have been less punctilious in observing national incomes policy. Secondly, this was another example of extremely heavy pressure being put on individual authorities by local, unofficial action, to break national agreements or to ignore formal disputes and negotiating procedures. It is unlikely that the steady increase in worker participation and industrial democracy will do other than increase the pressures on both trade unions and employers to modify their national procedures to take account of this growing shop floor and local level activity.

The new industrial relations scene in local government was unhappily illustrated in 1978/79 by a wave of industrial action which involved almost all groups of employees. Campaigns for higher pay awards than the Government's then policy permitted were spearheaded by an official 11 week strike by the Fire Brigades' Union – the most extreme strike action ever experienced in the emergency services and one of the most bitter in British industrial relations history as a whole. Government assistance in coping with the strike involved the Army in providing replacement fire cover, and in the short term the government's 10 per cent pay policy was upheld – the firemen returning to work for the same 10 per cent award they had initially rejected. However, the settlement included a future link with national pay indices to guarantee the firemen a place 75 per cent up the national earnings league table for manual workers – an index which involved very considerable additional payments in 1979 and 1980.

This strike was followed by a variety of forms of industrial action by manual workers, campaigning against the 5 per cent pay policy which followed the 10 per cent stage; and by teachers seeking the reestablishment of the pay levels implicit in their 1974 and 1975 pay awards which followed the Houghton report on teachers' pay. The disruption in some schools was particularly severe when teachers refused to cross manual worker picket lines, or when teachers refused all duties other than classroom teaching and in some cases worked only a five hour day. This round of industrial action ceased only when pay agreements were concluded at just over nine per cent together with references to the new Standing Commission on Pay Comparability from which a complicated series of additional staged pay awards were to result.

Strikes of social workers in some authorities lasted even longer than the firemen's strike and brought into dramatic focus the conflict between the ideals of social work and the drive for greater professional and economic status. The strike was unusual in that officially it was not for higher pay but for the abolition of national pay prescriptions and for freedom to bargain for pay at local authority level. The eventual settlement was a compromise in which scope for local bargaining was provided within a flexible nationally prescribed grading framework.

It would be misleading, however, to discuss local government industrial relations mainly in terms of disputes and industrial action. The long history of industrial peace in the pre- and post-war periods and the fact that, even in the highly-charged atmosphere of the 1970s, there have been so few breakdowns in employer/trade union relationships, are not the results of chance. Local government has, over many years, developed an extensive, complex and very professional system of national collective bargaining, based firmly on Whitley principles. This reference to Whitley may require a brief explanation.

J H Whitley, whose name has become synonymous with national joint councils, was the Deputy Speaker of the House of Commons in 1916. He chaired a government committee which was given the task of making recommendations to secure an improvement in 'relations between employers and workmen' throughout the economy. Labour unrest, in many cases involving the new Shop Stewards Movement, was causing much concern in the war factories.

Whitley proposed a whole new and integrated system of joint industrial councils at national level, district councils regionally, works committees at local level, a permanent arbitration court, and an extension of the enquiry and conciliation role of the Ministry of Labour. Two points of principle were stressed. First, that industries should, as far as possible, 'make their own agreements and settle their differences themselves'. Secondly, that there should be 'adequate organization' on the part of both employers and employed.

The Government accepted these recommendations and little time was lost in implementing them, at least so far as the joint industrial councils were concerned. Seventy-three such councils were established by the end of 1921 covering large sectors of industry and the public sector. Included in this first group of Whitley councils was the National Joint Council for Local Authorities' Non-Trading Services (Manual Workers), formed in 1919 to cover local government non-craft manual workers. This was the forerunner of today's National Joint Council for Local Authorities' Services (Manual Workers) commonly referred to as the Manual NJC.

On the non-manual side, today's National Joint Council for Local Authorities' Administrative, Professional, Technical and Clerical Services (the APT and C NJC) originated in the same immediate post first world war period, though its present constitution dates from 1944.

It is, in fact, a striking feature of the history of the NJCs that their two main periods of development were the two post-war periods of 1919-21, and 1944 to the 1950s. The intense manpower problems of war-time and the labour ferments in post-war societies are, of course, the reasons for this.

After the second world war, local government saw the establishment of Joint Negotiating Committees (JNCs) for Chief Officers, Fire Brigades, Building and Civil Engineering workers and many others, so that by the end of the 1950s all groups of local government employees were covered by some 40 or more joint councils or committees.

Before describing the current institutions in more detail it may be useful to summarize the key Whitley principles which have served local government so well for so many years; and to comment on those aspects of Whitleyism which have not, perhaps, been developed as fully as Whitley himself would have hoped.

Whitleyism – as a comprehensive and integrated system of employer/employee relationships – has six main features.

1 It requires all the employers in an industry (or other employment sector) to form a joint employer block. Local government has adopted this principle *in toto:* there are no authorities completely outside the NJC system, though the Greater London Council does negotiate independently and domestically with its white-collar staff. (The GLC joins with the national employers for all its other employees. The City of London is not in direct membership of the various NJCs.)

2 It requires all the trade unions in an employment sector (assuming a multi-union situation) to form a joint trade union bloc. Again, local government conforms almost totally with this principle though there are some trade unions which have some local government membership but are not members of the various NJCs' trade union sides. (For example, the Association of Scientific, Technical and Managerial Staffs (ASTMS) claims some white collar membership in Polytechnics but has no seat on the APT and C NJC.)

3 It implies a high level of trade union membership among employees: the trade unions need to be as fully representative as possible of all employees for a joint committee system to operate effectively. Here, the local government picture is varied. No reliable statistics are available about the extent of union membership, though one large metropolitan authority recently found that only some 50 per cent of its manual workers and 60 per cent of its white-collar employees were union members. One hundred per cent union membership certainly exists in some authorities in some occupations, electricians and engineering craftsmen, for example; 70 per cent-100 per cent levels exist in fire brigades. An active and highly competent trade union district organizer may achieve very high levels of membership among a group such as school meals staff which other organizers may find extremely difficult to get into membership at all. Levels as low as 10 per cent certainly exist in some locations among some employee groups. But in general, the whole local government system is operated as though *all* employees were union members and to this extent reflects the Whitley principle. Of particular note for personnel officers new to local government is the generally high level of white-collar membership, and the fact that unionism and its related collective bargaining extends up to and includes senior managers, chief officers and chief executives.

4 It does not rely solely on a national-level system, but includes joint committees at works (or local) level and regionally. These joint committees, too, should be bodies with authority to negotiate and make decisions, not merely forums for discussion. Local government's record on this point is more open to question than its national record. At regional level, it is true that there is a network of Provincial Councils for manual and APT and C staffs, and several of these Councils have histories going back well before the establishment of the NJCs themselves. But two comments might be made. First, there are quite large occupational groups for whom no regional organizations exists. Secondly, the balance of responsibility between national and provincial councils leans heavily towards the national bodies. The various national joint councils (with a degree of co-ordination through LACSAB) clearly have a much greater degree of control over pay and conditions than the provincial councils, and negotiate over a much wider spectrum. Is the whole system too top-weighted? Is the growing importance of local level employee participation creating a need for a higher degree of regional, rather than national, regulation of employer/trade union relations?

It is at local level that positive Whitleyism has perhaps been less consistently developed. Whitley (and the industrial relations practitioners who have followed him) placed a high degree of importance on works committees: joint bodies of managers and shop stewards charged with the job of jointly hammering out local industrial relations systems and agreements and for settling local disputes. Whitley himself was so far ahead of his time here that this element of his proposals was the least applied. Many works committees were formed, but too many were so restricted in their terms of reference that they became little more than talking shops where the highest level of decision-making related to the quality of the canteen tea and the standard of cleanliness in the works lavatories. Too many managers locally were only too glad to abdicate their industrial relations responsibilities to regional or national collective bargaining systems. In local government, some authorities have developed highly effective and authoritative joint committees. Others have at least a number of conventional joint consultative bodies which, while having no authority to negotiate, do provide channels of communication between management and managed. But some have done little to develop such local systems and rely heavily on regional or national assistance with any industrial relations problems which might occur.

5 It depends on pay and conditions being determined by agreement; and on permanent and voluntarily supported joint systems for bargaining and for the settlement of disputes.

At national (and generally regional) level, the local government system fully meets these criteria. Its national agreements covering pay and conditions are some of the most comprehensive and detailed in existence. For the two main groups of employees – manual workers and APT and C staffs – there is a two tier, provincial and national, disputes procedure. At local level, the position in a number of authorities is not so systematic. A lack of attention to the importance of industrial relations, commented on by Bains, has meant that local negotiations have not always been supported by an orderly system of local agreements; and by no means all authorities have a jointly agreed local disputes procedure which provides for a sensible stage-by-stage approach to the settlement of local differences.

6 It implies a readiness on the part of employers and trade unions to resort to arbitration if the standing domestic procedures fail to settle a dispute. (The Industrial Courts Act 1919 which set up independent arbitration machinery, followed Whitley's proposals).

Local government is not alone in having failed to incorporate arbitration as a standing, routine, final stage in its dispute procedures (except perhaps in the case of teachers). Provision is made for its use, but the trade unions have always reserved the right to make their own decisions about the action to take when negotiations break down. Arbitration has perhaps suffered from being used, or being considered, as a quasi-political matter by different governments. Trade union and, to some extent, employer reaction to legally compulsory arbitration during the second world war, and more recently to the implied power of the Government to this end in the 1971 Industrial Relations Act, helps to explain the relatively limited use of arbitration. Nevertheless, at both local and national level in local government, there have been numerous individual references to the various arbitration bodies which have been in existence since 1919; and from early 1975 there has been a very significant growth in the use of the Advisory Conciliation and Arbitration Service (ACAS).

The present institutions

Having outlined the main principles behind the local government system of industrial relations, we can now turn to a description of the institutions and machinery which are currently involved in operating this system.

Basically, the whole system depends on the corporate involvement of employers on one side and trade unions on the other. The number and size of the employers was described in chapter 1. In this chapter, therefore, we need to consider how the employers are grouped together for collective bargaining purposes and how these groupings are serviced. On the trade union side, we also need to describe the unions which operate in local government and how they, in turn, come together in various groups for negotiation. Finally, we need to describe the constitution of the various joint councils and committees and how, in practice, they conduct their affairs. A list of the national negotiating bodies, with details of the trade unions and other staff bodies represented on them, is given in Appendix D on page 299.

LACSAB

The growing compexity and importance of industrial relations has made it quite impossible for the employers to act as a corporate body without the existence of one central organization, with a permanent and professional staff, to act as a co-ordinator of national policies and procedures, to provide a secretariat for employers' sides of the various joint councils, and to provide information and advice to employers individually and collectively.

The Local Authorities' Conditions of Service Advisory Board was established for just these purposes in 1947. At that time, there were four main NJCs – for APT and C staffs, manual workers, county council roadmen and fire brigades. Now there are over 40 such bodies and LACSAB has had its ambit extended to include not only the newer joint committees for such employees as building and engineering craftsmen, but also services, the Burnham committees for teachers, and the police committees which differ from the rest by being established by statute and which include government appointees.

The Board itself consists of representatives, generally local government councillors, appointed by the following empoyer organizations:

Association of County Councils
Association of Metropolitan Authorities
Association of District Councils
Employers' Sides of APT and C NJC,
    Manual NJC, NJC Fire Brigades, Police Council.

There are thus two types of representation: from the three local authority associations for whom industrial relations are only a part of their total activities; and from the employer sides of the main joint bodies. However, as employer representation on the joint councils is in turn partly by the appointment of the local authority associations, the majority of employers on LACSAB are, in effect, selected by these associations.

With their heavy time commitment in their own council's affairs, councillors cannot be expected to do other than set the general directions for the Board's detailed work and monitor the results.

A big responsibility is thus placed on the officers of LACSAB, and the general absence from the Board itself of industrial relations professionals has emphasized the need for industrial relations professionalism in the Board's staff.

The Board therefore employs some 80 full-time staff under a Secretary, the scale of whose job ranks him as one of the country's top industrial relations practitioners. He acts personally as Employers' Side Secretary in the major NJC negotiations, while other senior staff carry out the same function for the other 40 odd joint councils and committees. The servicing of the collective bargaining system is thus a primary LACSAB role.

The Secretary and his staff undertake two other major functions. First, they collect and disseminate information and advice about a wide range of employment matters. In particular, they advise authorities on the application and interpretation of national agreements, on precedents established by negotiation or by disputes committee rulings, and on the handling of particular disputes. They also assess the implications for local government of new employment legislation and produce advisory notes or booklets which receive wide circulation.

Secondly, they act as a contact at officer level between local government and central government on employment issues; and liaise with other public sector employers (health, water, the nationalized industries) on matters of common concern such as the 'going rate' for public sector pay settlements. LACSAB, in turn, is used by government as one of its primary contacts with local government and to which it refers for comment on proposed new employment legislation.

LACSAB staff have to collect and collate authorities' reactions to these documents and proposals, to advise authorities on employment implications and, with the approval of the Board itself, to reply to government on these enquiries. Two 1975 examples of such work are the co-ordination by LACSAB of local authority employment figures for relay to central government in its 'manpower watch' of local government employment; and the collation of local government observations on the Employment Protection Act and other labour legislation.

The trade unions

The trade unions involved in local government have no direct equivalent organization to LACSAB. Trade unions are grouped within each NJC but have no common secretariat. This is not to say that, on an informal basis, consultation and co-operation do not exist. But trade unions – not just in local government – are very sensitive about their individual autonomy and would not welcome (or need) the same degree of detailed advisory services which LACSAB provides to

87

employers. There is, however, a local government committee of the TUC consisting of representatives of NALGO, NUPE, GMWU, TGWU, COHSE, FBU, the GLC Staff Association and three teaching unions including the NUT. This committee concerns itself less with detailed matters and more with such broad issues as, for example, the effect of statutory pay control on the public sector and the implications for trade unions of local government reorganization. It has also co-ordinated the views of these local government trade unions on matters arising from the Health and Safety at Work Act; lobbied the Government on the loss of jobs in local authorities caused by financial constraints; and discussed the application of industrial democracy principles in a local government setting. Its decisions do not, however, bind its constituents – each union retaining fully independent ultimate rights to determine its own policies.

Trade unions active in local government can be placed in three categories:

Those operating exclusively in local government
Those whose primary base is in local government but who have membership outside it
Those whose primary base is outside local government but who have some local government membership.

There are three main employment sectors in which unions exclusive to local government operate, and within these sectors they are powerful and influential bodies even though in some cases (for example the National Association of Fire Officers) their membership is extremely small compared with better known and general unions. The three sectors are the police, fire brigades, and senior and chief officers. The main employee bodies in these sectors, including organizations which are not strictly speaking trade unions, are:

Police
   The Police Federation
   Superintendents Association
   Association of Chief Police Officers

Fire brigades
   Fire Brigades Union (FBU)
   National Association of Fire Officers (NAFO)

Senior and Chief Officers
   Association of Local Authority Chief Executives*
   Association of Local Government Engineers and Surveyors

* The trade union equivalent of SOLACE – the Society of Local Authority Chief Executives

88

Association of Local Government Financial Officers
Association of Planning Officers
Society of Education Officers
and other similar associations which have a wider, professional role than that of conventional trade unions. NALGO also has membership of the Chief Officers JNC.

Those trade unions operating primarily, but not exclusively, in local government are trade unions with a predominantly local government background, but which have members elsewhere in the public sector (and occasionally in the private sector, eg private schools). This outside membership is usually the result either of an expansionist membership policy or of transfers of local government functions to other authorities (eg the 1974 transfers to the new Health and Water Authorities). There is no clear-cut division between these unions and the third category, described below, and this particular categorization is suggested mainly because it explains differences in style between unions with a primarily industrial base and those whose main interest is in the public sector. It is arguable that the education unions should be placed in the first exclusive category as the vast majority of members of the National Union of Teachers are employed by local education authorities. Taken as a group, however, the teaching unions include a significant number of members in other parts of the public sector and in a limited way in private education. They are clearly more concerned with their relationships with central government (through the Department of Education and Science) than either the specialist local government unions or the big industrially based general unions. At the other end of the spectrum is a union such as the general and Municipal Workers (GMWU) which historically has many of its roots firmly in local government but which, as the result of amalgamations and extensions of membership, now has a larger membership outside local government (about 885,000 total membership, with 250,000 in local government). The main trade unions in this category, given the provisos outlined above, are:

Education
   National Union of Teachers (NUT)
   National Association of Schoolmasters/Union of Women Teachers
      (NAS/UWT)
   Association of Teachers in Colleges and Departments of Education
      (ATCDE)
   Association of Teachers in Technical Institutions (ATTI)
   National Association of Teachers in Further and Higher Education
      (NATFHE)

Manual workers
National Union of Public Employees (NUPE)
General and Municipal Workers' Union (GMWU)
APT and C Staffs
National and Local Government Officers Association (NALGO).
Two of these unions, NALGO and NUPE, merit additional comment. NALGO's origins were of such a gentlemanly and conservative nature as to be almost a caricature of traditional local government officer stereotypes. A 19th century group of senior officers, led indeed by a town clerk, formed an association whose modest purpose was to campaign for a local authority pension scheme. They specifically abjured the use of conventional trade union militancy and, in the early days of the late 19th and early 20th centuries, certainly gained a general degree of acceptance and recognition by the employers because of their middle-class attitudes to their role as a trade union. In later years, affiliation to the TUC was to be a major issue in which many members deplored the move towards this link with the general labour movement. NALGO also experienced conflict, both with the specialist associations who resented the encroachment into their even more 'professional' preserves of a trade union, and with local staff associations who resisted the national control over their domestic affairs.

By the post second world war period, most of these battles were over, with NALGO firmly in control of the whole white-collar sector except the chief officer groups, with dual NALGO and professional association membership accepted at lower senior levels (though with NALGO taking primary responsibility for collective bargaining), and with all staff associations except the GLC's vanquished.

London County Council staff had initially seen NALGO as a basically provincial association and both their staff association, formed before the first world war and the larger and current GLC Staff Association successfully maintained complete independence, including control over independent, domestic collective bargaining for GLC APT and C staff within the context of a GLC Whitley Council.

Protection for its position within the trade union movement was obtained by the GLC Staff Association by its affiliation to the TUC (incidentally, before NALGO) and its complete independence from employer influence or control.

Meanwhile NALGO was extending its ambit beyond local government. Much of this extension was caused by various stages of local government reorganization which transferred services, and NALGO members, to new authorities. The late 1940s, for example, saw the transfer of gas and electricity undertakings from local government to the new Gas and Electricity Boards, and NALGO as a result acquired an important foothold in these new industries. More recently, thousands of NALGO members have been transferred to the Water and Health Authorities. NALGO's total membership is now around 550,000, with some 330,000 in local government.

From the 1960s, and particularly since 1972, NALGO has moved even further from its gentlemanly image of the 19th century towards that of hard-hitting professional trade unionism in the manual worker or ASTMS style. And perhaps its greatest challenge in the next decade will come not from its old local government rivals – the professional and staff associations – but from its expansionist competitors in the white-collar field. This is still a growth sector for the trade union movement and both the white-collar wings of the big general unions and ambitious non-manual unions such as the Association of Professional and Executive Staffs (APEX) and ASTMS may need more than the TUC's Bridlington Agreement to prevent their extension into local government. ASTMS certainly has significant, though formally unrecognized, membership among technician staff and some white-collar groups in some Polytechnics.

NUPE, like NALGO, deserves some additional comment. It is one of the United Kingdom's major manual unions and might well be placed in the third of the three categories used here as its membership outside local government (particularly in the Health Service) gives it the nature of a general public sector union. NUPE's total membership is very similar to NALGO's – over half a million – and it claims some 300,000 local government members. Its present nature and size stem partly from a series of amalgamations over many years, and partly from a more recent and very successful membership drive in which it has brought into trade unionism tens of thousands of workers who until recently have been largely unorganized. NUPE has an almost unique membership of over 50 per cent women (the trade union movement as a whole has been heavily male-orientated). It is among part-time women workers, particularly in school meals and cleaning services, and in similar health service occupations that NUPE has advanced its membership, a notable achievement in an extremely difficult group to organize and administer. Particular reference should be made to NUPE's rivalry with the GMWU for manual worker membership. Historically, the GMWU has been the traditional local government manual trade union and, based on membership figures of a decade or so ago, holds the largest bloc of seats on the manual workers' National Joint Council. But in recent years, raw membership figures would give NUPE dominance – a fact of which both unions are well aware, and a sensitive matter on which behind the scenes manoeuvring within the trade union world now seems to be proceeding. The relative strength of these two unions varies considerably on a geographical basis; some authorities' labour forces (particularly in the cities) still having GMWU majorities, while NUPE has increased its membership considerably elsewhere. Authorities in which both unions operate tend to consider NUPE as the more aggressive in its pursuit both of members and of local claims – a possible pointer to future developments in the relationships between these two very powerful and influential trade unions.

The third group of unions are those which, while not unimportant to local government, have their origins, priorities and major interests in other sectors, particularly in industry. Broadly, these unions are of two types: general and craft unions. The former, such as the TGWU, have local government sections; the latter may have very little in the way of any organization to deal specifically with local government and their local officials may well operate on a purely geographical basis, dealing equally with local factories and local government workplaces. It is not surprising that they display far less patience with local government systems, and accept differences between local government and industry with far less readiness, than unions with a local government base. The local authority electricians wage campaign of 1975 provides a classic example. Here, the claim was for parity with the electrical contracting industry, regardless of the difficulties within local government of conceding a pattern of wages which would change domestic relativities.

It might be argued that the GMWU should be placed in the general section of this group. But although a large part of this union's current membership lies outside local government, its historical roots are in municipal services, and it has been the transfer of such services as gas and electricity to the Corporations which has reduced its original dominance in the local government sector.

The main trade unions in this category are, therefore:

General manual unions
Transport and General Workers' Union (TGWU)

Craft unions
Confederation of Shipbuilding and Engineering Unions – particularly the Amalgamated Union of Engineering Workers (AUEW)
Electrical, Electronic, Telecommunications and Plumbing Trade Union (EETPTU)
Union of Construction, Allied Trades and Technicians (UCATT).

All the unions just listed are formally recognized for bargaining purposes and have seats on the various national joint councils and committees. It has already been noted that some large and ambitious unions such as ASTMS have some local government membership but are unrecognized and do not participate. Their possible entry to local government could come in two ways. First, they might negotiate their way in on the ground of significant membership, first clearing their lines with the other union through the established TUC machinery.

Their problem would be to avoid charges of poaching in building up their membership as the TUC's Bridlington Agreement lays down firm conditions to prevent unions affiliated to the TUC from raiding each other's territories. Secondly, they might ignore the national system altogether and by concentrating recruitment on new staff in *local* workplaces both avoid poaching and be able to present themselves to an individual authority as being representative of a particular group of employees. It would be invidious to single out ASTMS or the Technical Administrative and Supervisory Section (TASS) as being unions from which this type of tactic might seem likely.

Beyond this are one or two unions, not affiliated to the TUC and therefore free to compete with the recognized unions for membership, which have so far been markedly unsuccessful in doing more than exploit local or temporary dissatisfactions. The UK Association of Professional Engineers (UKAPE) has some local government membership and has appealed to the professional instincts of engineers against the more robust and plebeian characteristics of TUC unions. From time to time breakaway unions are formed, such as the London Firefighters Federation (and prior to 1974 re-organization, the Federation of Ambulance Personnel) which may cause local problems at the time but which have rarely achieved organizational success. Later, but now repeated, employment legislation provided (by Section 11 of the Employment Protection Act) a quasi-legal mechanism for such organizations to seek the enforcement of recognition on employers otherwise unwilling to upset existing systems of collective bargaining or to exacerbate their relationships with the recognized trade unions.

The Joint Council system and structure
Having examined the employers, LACSAB and the trade unions, we can now turn to the joint council system by which both sides regulate their relationships and determine local government pay and conditions of service.

In total there are some 40 joint negotiating bodies*. Almost all are constituted, and operate, on a Whitley Council basis. The general principle is that there is a joint council or committee for each major or distinct employee group. Each council consists of two sides, one representing the employers (the 'official side') and one the employees (the trade union or 'staff side'). The official sides consist almost entirely of local authority councillors, selected by the three local authority associations and the provincial councils. The trade union

* The 25 primary bodies are listed in Appendix D on page 299.
A number of these bodies have subsidiary panels (eg for Municipal Airports) which increase the total to about 40.

sides consist mainly of full-time trade union officers. Joint councils elect their own chairmen, the normal practice being for chairmanship to alternate annually between the sides: a trade union officer one year, an employer the next.

Each side supplies its own secretariat. All the employers' sides of all the joint councils rely on LACSAB for this function. The trade union secretaries are often trade union officers who have to combine this work with their other trade union duties.

Councils meet at various intervals – occasionally as infrequently as once or twice a year, more normally about six to eight times annually. Matters are decided at council meetings by agreement between the two sides, each side acting as a corporate body. It is not therefore necessary to have an equal number of representatives on each side. Provided a quorum exists, three or four employers, as a body, carry as much weight as eight or ten trade union officers – and vice versa. The chairman does not have a casting vote; the outcome of negotiations is quite clear-cut regardless of the numerical strength of each side: there is either agreement between the sides or a 'failure to agree'.

This absence of individual voting at council meetings requires each side to meet separately in advance of the joint meetings to determine its line. Council meetings are therefore immediately preceded by 'side meetings' at which the agenda for the joint meeting is discussed and, in the light of advice from the side secretary, decisions are taken about the policy to be followed in negotiations. This system makes it practically impossible to conduct free-flowing negotiations in the joint meeting. In consequence a normal pattern for these meetings is for one side to make a fairly formal statement and explanation of its position, the other side to make an initial response and, if agreement does not rapidly emerge, for the joint meeting to be adjourned so that each side can separately determine a new, agreed position.

If this somewhat stately forming and re-forming of the large, joint assemblies was the only method of negotiation, the progress of national negotiations would be even slower than it already is. In fact, a great deal of the real argument, manoeuvring and bargaining is conducted outside the councils by joint secretaries, often joined by one or two of their respective colleagues to form an informal, small and effective negotiating team. Occasionally this system is formalized by the appointment by each side of a small negotiating sub-committee. More frequently, and often more effectively, the process is much more informal. The LACSAB secretary will meet his opposite trade union number and, within the general limits approved by his side at a side meeting, make as much progress as possible. He may be joined by the employers' side chairman, or one or two other employers from time to time, or may call in another member of LACSAB staff. Equally on the trade union side, the union secretary will act either

94

alone or with a few officers of his own or other unions. A long round of negotiations – say an annual pay claim – may well follow a sequence along the following lines:

1 The trade union secretary contacts the official side secretary informally and outlines the general approach the union is going to take. There may be an off the record sounding out of each other's position at this stage.

2 A formal claim is submitted by letter, followed by telephone conversations between the two secretaries to clarify any uncertain issues.

3 A meeting of the national joint council is arranged at which the trade union side will formally explain and press its claim. Before this meeting the LACSAB secretary will send the employers' side a detailed explanation and analysis of the claim, with comment on factors influencing the possible response (such as the level of comparable settlements in industry or the implications of government pay policy) and pose alternative responses. Preceding the joint meeting, the employers' side will meet to discuss this brief and will agree a line of response.

4 At the joint meeting, the trade union secretary will speak to the claim, possibly followed by one or two of his colleagues. The employers' side secretary will respond, describing and explaining the employers' reaction and making a previously planned counter-offer. After a brief reply, the meeting will be adjourned while the trade union side discusses its reaction to the offer.

During adjournments, there are often interludes while the joint secretaries meet to explore possible ways forward and report back to their separate sides.

The joint meeting will then be re-convened to hear the formal trade union response and modified claim. If this has been anticipated by the employers' side secretary (or notified to him privately by the trade union secretary) an immediate employers' response can be given. If not, further adjournments and quiet backroom negotiations between the joint secretaries and a few of their side's members may be necessary. Not infrequently, no conclusion can be reached within the day, and the joint council will be adjourned for, say, two to three weeks to enable further secretary level negotiations to continue.

5 Eventually, after in some cases many weeks of intermittent meetings of this kind, the joint council will meet again for a final session at which a settlement will be formally ratified. It is rare for the details of such a settlement to emerge at a joint meeting: the final joint session is normally one at which the trade union side know in advance what form the employers' final offer is to take; and the employers know that the trade union side will accept this offer.

It will be seen that the function of the employers' side as a whole is not to conduct detailed negotiations so much as to act as a sounding board for the negotiators. The secretary, and such members as may negotiate with him, need to return to their side at each major stage in negotiations to ensure that their next step will receive employer backing. The trade union secretary has to do likewise. It is an unpublicized aspect of this type of negotiation that as much, or more, time and argument may be spent within each side in hammering out an agreed policy or strategy between conflicting viewpoints as is spent in negotiation between the two sides themselves.

One other aspect of the system merits comment: the difference in industrial relations expertise between the two sides. Every member of the trade union side is a full-time industrial relations practitioner, a professional and an expert. On the employers' side, only the LACSAB secretary and such few officers of the provincial councils as may be selected for NJC membership are normally similarly experienced. Occasionally an employer member may have such experience: Labour councils often include active trade unionists and Conservative members may be employers, but experience of this kind is a bonus which the employer system itself cannot guarantee. Very occasionally, an employer representative may be a personnel professional, a council officer rather than a member. In general, however, the employers rely heavily on LACSAB staff for the industrial relations expertise needed to match that on the trade union side and LACSAB, as a result, has built up a most competent and professional national industrial relations team. It is to their credit that they recognize the need for contact with the practicalities of industrial relations at local level and make contacts with authorities' personnel officers and with the employers' secretariat of the provincial councils to this end.

For the manual workers and APT and C NJCs, there are some 20 provincial councils, constituted on similar principles to the national joint councils to which they relate. Their functions are to negotiate those elements of pay and conditions in which national agreements permit local freedom; to negotiate matters connected with the local application of national agreements; to form the first stage in the formal disputes procedure – disagreements are referred to the NJCs for resolution; and, so far as their employers' sides are concerned, to act as a sounding board for developments in national policy and to provide a forum for provincial discussion of the national response to trade union claims. On the employers' side, members are nominated by the local authorities within their areas. They employ their own full-time secretariats which are independent of LACSAB – though close liaison is maintained between LACSAB and the provincial officers. It is with and through the officers of the provincial council's employers' sides that local authority personnel officers maintain most of their contact with the national collective bargaining system. To varying degrees of formality, the employers' side secretaries of the provincial councils inform the personnel officers in their areas of developments at national level, and obtain their views on these issues. In some areas – Southern and Mid-Southern provides one example – a group of personnel officers acts, in association with the provincial secretary, as an advisory group to the employers' side. They thus contribute not only to the process of provincial level negotiations but also to the development of national industrial relations policies.

As noted above, there are altogether some 40 joint negotiating councils and committees. Apart from the major Burnham committees for teachers and the Police Council, both of which include representatives of central government, there are joint bodies for:

Fire brigades (with an autonomous officers' committee)
Chief fire officers
Building and civil engineering operatives
Engineering craftsmen
Workshops for the blind
Probation services
Justices' clerks: and Justices' clerks' assistants
Chief Officers
Chief Executives

and a number of other minor though not unimportant groups. The whole system is, however, dominated by the two major National Joint Councils for blue- and white-collar employees and these are therefore described more fully below.

The National Joint Council for Local Authorities' Services (Manual Workers)
This NJC covers the largest group of local government workers – some 1,000,000 in all, including over a quarter of a million school meals staff, together with caretakers, cleaners, drivers, roadworkers, refuse collectors, parks and gardens staff and many others.

Its employers' side consists of 41 representatives, 24 appointed by the various provincial councils, the remainder by the three local authority associations. The full list is:

Provincial Councils	20
Scottish Council	4
Association of County Councils (ACC)	6
Association of District Councils (ADC)	4
Association of Metropolitan Authorities (AMA)	7

The trade union side is smaller though, as we have seen, this does not put the unions in a weaker position. There are 26 trade union representatives, from the following unions:

General and Municipal Workers Union	11
National Union of Public Employees	7
Transport and General Workers Union	7
Scottish Commercial Motormen's Union	1

These numbers are intended to reflect the relative membership in local government of each union, though some considerable time may elapse before changes in membership are so reflected.

The NJC also has a number of subsidiary committees, all organized on the same general basis as the main council. These committees include:

Pay and productivity – a committee dealing primarily with bonus issues

Disputes – the committee which attempts to resolve disputes referred up from provincial level

Excess rates – a committee concerned with the ratification of provincial and local additions to the national wage system

School caretakers – a general joint committee for this particular group of employees who, because of the nature of their work, have a number of unique employment conditions

Residential establishments – another specialist committee for employees working and living in old people's homes, special schools etc

Municipal airports – a joint panel which deals with local authority airport employees.

These subsidiary committees report regularly to the main NJC and, formally, many of their decisions require NJC ratification. Informally, the bulk of their work is carried out with little NJC involvement. The trade union sides through their LACSAB secretariats can co-ordinate their decisions with national policies without having to refer continually to the NJC.

The NJC itself meets some eight to 12 times annually, depending on the volume of business and particularly on the progress of the annual pay negotiations. Its meetings are normally held in London, with its annual meeting at a provincial conference centre.

The National Joint Council for Administrative, Professional, Technical and Clerical Staffs

This, the second of the two main NJCs, covers the majority of local government officers – the white-collar staff normally thought of by the public as the town hall employees. The NJC is thus concerned with about 400,000 staff including over 125,000 clerical and secretarial workers and 25,000 professional and administrative staff (solicitors, architects, engineers, planners, accountants and so on). Additionally, the NJC covers a large number of technicians and social workers. The whole group includes a diverse range of occupations and spans a far wider salary range than the manual workers NJC.

The employers' side has 36 representatives, 20 from the provincial councils and 16 from the associations:

Provincial Councils	16
Scottish Council	4
ACC	6
ADC	4
AMA	6

Four of the provincial council seats are allotted to the Greater London District Council but, unlike the manual NJC, none are allocated to the GLC. For APT and C staff the GLC is independent of the NJC and operates its own domestic Whitley with its own staff side. The GLC is, however, invited to send an observer to the employers' side meetings (not to the NJC itself) and reciprocates by inviting a LACSAB officer to its employers' side meetings. The purpose of this reciprocity is to ensure a reasonable degree of consistency in the NJC's and GLC's approach to pay and conditions, although the GLC operates a completely different salary and grading structure.

The trade union side is larger than the manual workers, mainly because the trade union sides of the provincial councils select representatives additionally to those appointed directly by the national trade unions. There are 35 trade union representatives:

Provincial Councils (primarily NALGO)	16
Scottish Council	4
NALGO	8
GMWU (through MATSA, its white collar wing)	3
NUPE	2
TGWU	1
COHSE (Confederation of Health Service Employees)	1

It will be noted that GMWU, NUPE and TGWU are represented on both the manual and APT and C NJCs. NALGO, however, dominates the trade union side of the white-collar NJC, the majority of provincial council union representatives being NALGO members.

Like the manual workers' NJC, the APT and C council also has subsidiary committees to deal with special subjects and groups. These include the Standing Joint Advisory Committee for Staffs of Children's Homes, and the Residential Establishment Officers' Committee.

The national system as a whole

From time to time the principle of national collective bargaining comes under question, and earlier in this chapter comments have been made about the possible localizing effect on industrial relations of greater worker participation at authority level. Against this must be set the strong trade union concept of the equity of consistency and equality of conditions for all local government employees. The achievement of a consistent national standard of employment rewards and security was a major plank in NALGO's campaign to establish itself as a national union. It seems unlikely that local government employees, either manual or non-manual, would accept any really significant variation in pay levels or other primary conditions between authorities. The unions no doubt see this as a possibility if authorities of widely differing political complexions were to bargain on a local basis.

Given the wide differences of outlook between councils, the achievement and maintenance of agreement nationally on the employers' side about such politically contentious issues as pay differentials and incomes policy, is indeed remarkable. It seems probable that the trade union sides, conscious of the dangers of opening up political divisions in the employment field, have assisted in maintaining this consensus by – at least on some occasions – exercising some restraint in the claims and settlements in which they have been involved. So at national level, both sides accept and promote the compromises necessary to maintain the national system.

That such a system does not always satisfy local employee groups, and particularly local union activists, is as much a problem for the trade unions as for employers. Should a union permit its members to exploit a local situation which might enable the staff of one authority to break out of the uniform limits of the nationally negotiated pay system? Such questions raise the issue of the nature of trade unions' internal authority. The concept of a union 'permitting' its members to take certain action is, after all, hardly in line with the concept of union power stemming from the grass roots, and of authority residing with the membership rather than with the elected officials. NALGO's 1978 campaign to promote more local negotiation in determining the grading of social workers and to delete the national prescription for such grades, illustrates the unions' dilemma.

Yet if present trends continue, one of the problems for the future will be that of evolving processes in which one side, with power lying at the base of its hierarchical pyramid (the trade unions), negotiates with the other side in which power lies at the traditional peak (the employers). Some change in the present system seems inevitable, if the growing demands for greater grass roots involvement in the determination of pay and conditions is to be given procedural legitimacy.

At the same time, an opposite and centralizing influence has become evident in the last two years – the involvement or influence of central government in local government collective bargaining. The need to enforce national pay policies in the public sector partially explains this tendency; and to that extent it may not be a permanent phenomenon. But the matter goes deeper than this. Local government has come increasingly to rely on central government for its sources of finance, primarily through the annual rate support grant. Central government, in its role as primary paymaster, has tended increasingly to call the local government tune, and with manpower taking up some two thirds of local authorities' revenue expenditure, this involves national industrial relations as well as the setting of various required or preferred standards of services. The trade unions at national level are very well aware of the strength of the government's financial grip and influence on local government, and in some wage negotiations have appealed directly to central government when the local government employers have, in the unions' views, been unacceptably restrictive or dilatory. This occurred in both the police and fire services' wage negotiations in 1977/78, and in both cases the Home Secretary responded. His introduction of a commitment to the introduction of a 42 hour week for the fire service, made in the context of talks with the FBU and the employers outside the ambit of the constitutional bargaining machinery, almost certainly clinched the end of the national fire strike: but it created considerable embarrassment for the local government employers who had to consider the costs involved within a financial system involving centrally imposed cash limits on local authority expenditure. The FBU, meanwhile, took the view that if it was government control of the public purse which inhibited local authorities, then the union might as well deal directly with the real paymaster.

The Police Federation had reached similar conclusions and their withdrawal from the Police Council was the first major step on the road to the 1978 Edmund Davies report on police pay*. It was central government which announced its acceptance of these recommendations, and in effect decided on their phased implementation in 1978 and 1979 – not the local Police Authorities who constitutionally are the police employers, although the Employers' Sides of the Police Council were consulted by government, and announced their support of the settlement. Department of Education and Science involvement in Burnham Committee pay negotiations, unlike the Home Office's influence in fire service pay, is formally provided for within the established machinery. Pay policy considerations seem, however, to have strengthened the DES' grip on Burnham settlements. It seems unlikely that local authorities, left to themselves, would have con-

* One outcome of the Edmund Davies enquiry was the establishment of a new Police Council under independent chairmanship, and with its own secretariat instead of LACSAB.

ducted the intensely detailed study of the costing of salary increments which was such a feature of Burnham settlements in 1977 and 1978. Similar studies of 'grade drift' also became necessary in NJC APT and C wage bargaining in those years as a result of the Department of Environment's pressure on the national employers to justify every last 0.1 per cent of any pay offer.

Even within the trade union movement, shop steward pressure for more local autonomy has been counter-balanced by pressure on low-paying authorities to come up to the general level of pay of neighbouring authorities. Indeed, the unions have used Schedule 11 of the Employment Protection Act to establish more equality of payment between authorities. The social workers and residential staffs' 1979 settlements provided for a degree of local freedom on grading standards, in accord with pressure from NALGO branches for local bargaining freedom.

The settlement was followed, however, by both employer and trade union sides taking steps to monitor the level of local settlements and using settlements in one authority to pressure other authorities into a consistent approach.

A further feature of the national scene in 1979 was a growing sense of dissatisfaction within individual authorities and in the three local authority associations with the whole national collective bargaining system. The Association of Metropolitan Authorities went as far as suggesting the disbandment of LACSAB, the bringing of Provincial Councils under national control, and the responsibility for pay bargaining being placed firmly on the AMA and the ACC. The ACC, while not supporting such a drastic reorganization, nevertheless expressed concern about the extent to which membership of the employers' sides of Provincial Councils and National Joint Councils did not reflect the different proportions of the labour force employed by metropolitan, county and district authorities. The ACC supported the AMA in the view that the Associations should more effectively set the policies for the various negotiating bodies; and that some simplification of the whole collective bargaining machinery was desirable. The Society of Chief Personnel Officers (SOCPO) also initiated national discussion of ways and means of streamlining this cumbersome machinery.

Dissatisfaction with the national collective bargaining system was not ameliorated by the impact of 'comparability studies' on the size and timing of pay settlements in 1979 and 1980. With the exception of the fire and police services, all the local government pay groups with settlement dates in the period November 1978 to July 1979 concluded only interim agreements and referred final conclusions to the outcome of external pay comparisons. Some groups – particularly manual workers and teachers – referred these studies to the Standing Commission on Pay Comparability (the Clegg Commission), an independent body established in something of a rush by the then Labour Government in March 1979, as one means of resolving a wave of public sector pay disputes. Other groups, including APT and C staffs, decided to conduct their own comparability studies using the services of LACSAB on the employers' sides, and trade union research facilities by the employee sides. In other cases (eg Chief Officers and Chief Executives) the services of management consultants were obtained. The Clegg Commission itself, with neither time nor staff to undertake detailed studies for a variety of occupational groups including health service and university workers, had to turn to the Civil Service Pay Research Unit (PRU) and to consultants for its research data.

With a variety of settlement dates, differing union pressures, no time to establish common principles and many different approaches to the form comparisons should take, the result was an unholy tangle of different levels of settlement (even for similar groups) and different staged settlement dates. Some NJCs, such as the APT and C group, agreed a one-stage settlement within the particular negotiating year. Others, such as teachers and manual workers, agreed on two-stage settlements in which the final payments of comparability studies were not to be made until after the expiry of the pay year in which they were agreed. Between July 1979 and September 1980, some type of pay increase – normal annual, or staged comparability – became payable almost every month for one or other group of local government employees. The use of external comparisons thus gave rise to a whole range of new internal relativity problems, and created a variety of precedents about the use of comparative pay data which were based not on careful consideration of the pros and cons of this form of pay determination but on a series of largely unco-ordinated responses to immediate pay pressures. These results demonstrated more clearly than before the need for local government to develop collective bargaining mechanisms which would result in a more coherent and compatible set of national agreements than could be achieved by the relatively autonomous, and differently timed, negotiations of a multiplicity of different bargaining bodies.

Little time was available, either, for the various employers' sides to get together to consider the principle of pay comparability *per se*. To base local government pay on the principle of fair comparisons with the pay of workers outside the service employed on broadly comparable work (as the 1955 Priestley Report proposed for the Civil Service) would introduce the biggest single change in pay determination in the history of LACSAB and the NJCs. Yet this is precisely what the references to the Standing Commission implied.

Gone would be traditional bargaining about the 'going rate' of current pay settlements, or of arguing about movements in the Retail Price Index, or even of the employer's ability to pay. Pay levels would in effect be set by reference to external comparitors over whose pay the local government employers would have no control or influence. Comparability might have advantages in reducing industrial action about wages, and in securing a stable labour force paid at demonstrably market rates. But none of these issues of principle received any considered attention in the few hectic months in 1979 in which one NJC or JNC after another referred their wage levels to one form or another of pay comparability study. Again, then, the need for more positive co-ordination of industrial relations policies was indicated.

7 Industrial relations at local level

For personnel officers in local government, a significant feature of the whole national industrial relations system is that it provides no formal role for them apart from the advisory role to provincial council employers' sides, mentioned in the last chapter, and their role at local level in the interpretation and application of national agreements.

Policy decisions are taken by the employer representatives on LACSAB and the various NJCs. Staff work and most of the detailed negotiation is handled by the full-time staff of the provincial councils and of LACSAB. There are two primary reasons for this non-involvement of personnel staff. First, the whole system is heavily biased towards the establishment and maintenance of national agreements and procedures. Secondly, few individual authorities until the 1970s employed experienced industrial relations practitioners in their personnel departments and the national system did not therefore have a pool of local expertise available for incorporation.

There are several factors which are changing this situation. Employees themselves, through their shop stewards and other elected representatives, are undoubtedly putting increasing pressure on their immediate local employer for improvements in local (and sometimes national) pay and conditions. They expect their own authority to deal directly with their approaches on these issues and will challenge the validity of a negative response based solely on references to national agreements. Local authorities will have to explain and argue for the existence and nature of national agreements and not merely retire behind these national barricades. Employees at local level are likely, in any event, to become concerned with an increasing range of local issues. Matters which have traditionally been decided unilaterally by management will become negotiable.

For example, it may well have been normal practice for an authority alone to decide what types or makes of office equipment to purchase.

Within the past year or so, with the development of joint consultative committees, some information may have been given to staff about such decisions and some discussion may have resulted. It should not surprise such an authority now to experience a claim by staff representatives that, in future, changes of this kind should be by agreement. Such a claim is likely to emerge from a grievance or disagreement about a particular case, such as changing makes of typewriters in the typing pool followed by the typists' refusal to accept the new machines, or as the result of new office technology.

The extension of employee participation in working decisions will, of course, hasten this extension of negotiable issues. While participation as such is not negotiation (but rather a joint employer/employee approach to problem-solving) one of its effects is clearly to erode the old concepts of 'management prerogative'. With management, as with the law, the limits of effective authority are those to which people consent. There is no absolute in these matters and the border between the negotiable and non-negotiable is moving in favour of the former.

Given this trend, councils and councillors now expect a great deal more advice and activity from their personnel departments in handling the resultant issues. The growing volume of negotiable matters is being paralleled by a growth in the sophistication of local employee and trade union claims and in the complexity of the arguments used. The old crudities of 'we want more pay' could be responded to by an equally blunt 'we can't afford to give it to you', delivered in an authoritative fashion by the chairmen of the Establishment and Finance Committees. The modern parallel may be a 10 page document prepared by a group of young, highly intelligent planners and architects (in their role as trade unionists) which purports to show that for certain jobs, assuming a Gaussian distribution of posts within the salary ranges, the authority's median salaries relative to comparable local, external, professional groups have moved from the top decile to the lower quartile. Analysing and responding to claims of this kind clearly demands more time and expertise than either busy councillors or traditional establishments men can provide.

Local government is not immune to the general social and political trends which are leading to an increasing emphasis on local level industrial relations. The tendency for small groups of employees to take instant industrial action in a dispute, the unwillingness to accept old hierarchical patterns of authority, the transfer of political influence from the centre to the periphery – all these factors point to a growing need for local authorities to give more attention to their own relationships with their own employees. This pressure will lead, in turn, to a demand for more industrial relations expertise within personnel departments.

There are four main areas to which personnel officers at local level need to turn their attention:

Policies – is there a consistent set of guidelines for management attitudes and action in the whole sphere of relations with employees and trade unions, and of pay and conditions?

Systems – is there an effective system of joint communication, discussion and negotiation between employees, management and council?

Procedures – are there effective procedures, within the general system, for the settlement of disputes and grievances?

Management involvement and training – are all managers with employment or supervisory responsibilities fully aware of the policies, involved in the systems, and trained in the necessary industrial relations skills?

Each of these areas is considered in more detail below.

Policies

The value of evolving specific employment policies is not, of course, confined to the sphere of industrial relations. But this sphere is certainly one in which, without policies, individual managers are likely to differ in attitudes and approach to an undesirable degree. Most industrial relations problems arise from feelings of 'unfairness' – and fairness is largely a matter of comparisons. It is often the inconsistency of management decisions, rather than any absolute element in a decision itself, which causes a grievance or a dispute. For the same excuse for absence one manager may approve a day's special leave, and another issue a reprimand. An employee's reaction to the latter will be conditioned almost wholly by the existence of the former – 'why should I be penalized when George had the day off?' On a broader front, differences of bonus treatment will generate a similar adverse reaction from groups of employees. The office messengers will never fully accept that their bonus should be on a 20 per cent formula, while the caretakers are on a 30 per cent scheme, however rational in 'pure' work study terms these differences may be.

In the direct field of management/employee relations, too, inconsistency will be resented. Why should one stores manager be unwilling to sit down with the shop steward in his depot to discuss the re-design of bin cards, when the manager of another depot had a meeting with his shop steward the week before to discuss a new requisition note system? Why should the members of the Council be prepared to meet a delegation of Fire Brigades Union members about the state of station housing and not be prepared to listen to a group of school caretakers complaining about their gardens being vandalized by school children?

Most inconsistencies of this kind can be reduced, if not eliminated, by a definition of policy. Policies fall broadly into two categories: first, the precise definition of local practices; second, the more general statement of aims and intentions.

For matters which are likely to recur (such as the reasons for granting extra leave) a fairly precise and comprehensive set of rules can be built up and published in the form of a code of practice. Many authorities have codes of this kind, ranging from fairly short handbooks of basic 'rules and regs' to the complexities of the GLC's two volume Staff Code. But two dangers need to be avoided:

The code may become out-of-date in its approach to specific issues. If it is built up over time, largely as a list of precedents, these codify the type of decision which was consistent with the general employment standards at the time it was made. But standards change, so the code needs regular and sensitive revision.

Without some overriding concept of employment standards, the code may have inbuilt inconsistency between its parts. It may be liberal about special leave for further professional education, but restrictive about leave for craft training. Or it may be extremely detailed in defining the circumstances and procedures for authorizing lunch allowances, but leave the authorization of weekend overtime entirely to the direction of junior supervisors. Managers and employees will resent such differences in standards and style.

These two dangers emphasize the need for general statements of policy to set the tone or style for the more detailed statements. In the field of manager/employee relations, for example, it can be made clear in a definition of policy that managers should recognize shop stewards as the normal communication link with employees collectively, and that management will discuss with shop stewards all proposed changes in work methods, systems and equipment. Depending on local circumstances and, to some extent, local political philosophy, a quite different approach to this example may be considered right. The important thing is for this to be discussed, approved at council level, and stated so that individual managers are guided in their individual actions by a knowledge of the direction and style to which their actions should conform.

A similar scene-setting approach to policy definition can operate for pay and conditions. A general policy statement that 'the Council is opposed to the use of overtime as a regular means of getting its normal and routine work done' sets the scene for a whole range of individual decisions by individual managers, and may be far more effective than a three page list of detailed conditions in which overtime may be authorized.

The personnel officer's role in relation to policy formulation is to advise and co-ordinate. He is the one senior officer with a view of the whole employment picture and it is his responsibility to identify inconsistencies of style or decision. He also has a primary responsibility to be aware of changing attitudes and standards in his locality and in society at large which should be reflected in his authority's policies. He should take the initiative in proposing changes in policy: positive industrial relations means more than merely reacting to trade union pressure.

Systems

If an authority's industrial relations are to be other than a series of bargaining sessions or disputes as and when issues are raised by the trade unions, then a system of more regular, positive contacts is required.

It is a task of the personnel officer to examine his authority's patterns of collective contacts with employees and their trade unions, to assess the adequacy of these existing systems and to propose necessary improvements.

He might do well to begin by looking at his own and his staff's relationships with shop stewards and with the full-time trade union officers. The shop stewards are likely to have more frequent contact with managers in the various service departments than with the central personnel department staff, but if the personnel officer does not meet them from time to time outside the formal bargaining session he is unlikely to be in touch with the moods and shifts of attitudes of the shop or office floor.

Leaving aside his participation in joint consultative committees for the moment, he needs to create other (and often more informal) opportunities to meet employee representatives. On his visits to offices and other work-places he can make a point of meeting the shop steward, or the chairman of a departmental staff committee, for an informal discussion about any matter that seems of interest and concern. He should make a point of talking in a similar way to employee representatives as they foregather or disperse from any formal joint meetings. (A good many thorny disputes have been settled on the basis of such 'corridor chats'). He may invite a convenor of stewards, or the chairman of an employees' committee, for informal, 'without prejudice' or off-the-record discussions in his office – or at the local pub – when he feels tricky situations are developing.

Similarly, he should get to know the trade unions' district officials as individuals and as people – and not merely as formal union spokesmen. Trade union officers (and shop stewards) may be invited to various Council and staff functions such as the opening of a new depot, the presentation of suggestion scheme awards or the annual sports day. Conversations in the more relaxed atmosphere of these occasions can benefit both sides by developing a greater degree of mutual understanding and respect. Too many managers (and some old-style establishment men) still tend to think of the trade union officer as concealing horns under his cloth cap: some trade union officers still think that whenever a manager is unavailable on the telephone it means he is away playing golf. Through informal contacts, personnel officers soon come to look on the trade union official as a fellow-professional in the industrial relations business, and in negotiations can therefore concentrate on the issues, instead of being inhibited by stereotyped concepts of the personalities.

But informal contacts, though important, are rarely sufficient and many authorities have, over a number of years, developed various systems of joint meetings between managers and employee representatives. As noted in the last chapter, the idea of joint works committees was encouraged by Whitley in 1918.

There are two particular aspects of a joint committee system which merit close attention:

What are their terms of reference; and in particular, what can they discuss and decide?

What should their membership be on both sides; should they be limited on the employee's side to trade union members; and should councillors sit on these bodies?

Terms of reference
Conventionally, joint committees are for joint consultation and, for many years, managers (including personnel officers) have considered it extremely important to keep consultation and negotiation separate. Joint consultative committees are seen as concerning themselves with everything other than the negotiable items of pay and conditions. The theory has been that the quality of discussion on these other issues would be adversely affected by the intrusion of bargaining: that a free-ranging discussion on, for example, the problems of moving into a new office block, would degenerate into a haggle about overtime payments for the extra work involved.

This traditional separation of consultation and negotiation needs to be questioned. As noted earlier, the borderline between the negotiable and the non-negotiable is a diffuse and changing one. Any management decision becomes negotiable if employees challenge it with sufficient vigour. Far better that a system exists in which management and employees can jointly discuss a work problem and, if necessary, argue out different points of view and agree a line of action in advance of the formal management decision, than that the decision itself should spark off a dispute which requires negotiation under pressure to resolve. More positively, the organization as a whole will benefit from having a system which enables the views and ideas of

110

employees collectively to be built into the general decision-making process. All this argues for a joint committee system which goes beyond mere consultation. But can the same system, the same committees, also deal with directly negotiable issues such as pay? It seems realistic to say yes. Pay (and other conditions) are clearly directly related to and affected by decisions about working methods and plans. It is unrealistic to expect employees to divorce the effect of new work plans and procedures on their pay and hours, from the nature of the plans and procedures themselves. It seems pointless to have one committee system (the conventional joint consultative body) discussing changes in work methods while another (the disputes committee) stands by to put the fires out.

The answer, therefore, may be a joint committee system which has the authority to discuss and resolve disputatious issues in the context in which they arise and to use consultation or negotiation as best fits each case. Obviously, there have to be some sensible limits on such a joint committee's negotiating authority. The joint committee of a district council could not re-negotiate the terms of the national pay agreement; and the joint committee at a local stores depot cannot negotiate changes in the authority wide subsistence allowance scheme. The sensible limits for any one committee are normally the limits of authority of the most senior level of participating management. It is no use the employee representatives on a departmental joint committee pressing for a decision on the re-design of the wage slips, if these are computer-produced centrally with decisions in the hand of the Chief Finance Officer. What is needed here is a two-tier joint committee structure on which service-wide issues can be transferred from the departmental to full authority level. The constitutional, decision-making position of the Council's Committees and the Council itself also needs to be protected, and a joint union/management committee should not be put in a position in which it takes decisions which should properly lie with a Council committee. Nor should the management side of a joint committee fall into the trap of negotiating on an issue which the elected members would consider lay with them as a policy issue. Breaking down the distinction within a joint committee constitution between consultation and negotiation does not imply that every issue is automatically negotiable. It does mean that the management side needs to know its own decision-making authority, and needs to be specific to the trade union side as to which issues it is prepared and able to negotiate on, and which it is not. At the end of a very long day, any issue to which the unions take strong objection and have the power to block implementation will have to be negotiated, even if this ultimate stage can, constitutionally, involve only elected members speaking with the authority of the Council itself.

111

Membership

The effectiveness of a joint committee system depends to a large extent on its membership. Unless each side is authoritatively representative it cannot, of course, negotiate; and if it cannot negotiate it is ineffective.

The conventional joint consultative approach often includes the view that employee representation by shop stewards is too restrictive and gives too 'hard' a character to the employers' side. Very few local authorities operate closed shops, and the argument goes on to stress the need, in an only partially unionized situation, for the non-unionist to have as much representation on these joint committees as the union member. There are two main flaws in this argument if the main point of encouraging joint committees to make decisions is conceded. First, that negotiations about pay and conditions are the business of trade unions, not of non-union members. The whole national system in local government depends, as Whitley pointed out over 50 years ago, on the existence of a collective and representative employee view. Secondly, that the non-unionist represents no-one but himself. This is not to denigrate his individuality nor to deny him the right to approach management, forcefully if necessary, on his own behalf. But if an employee in local government is interested in helping his fellow employees by acting as their representative, it is surely not unreasonable to expect him (and them) to recognize the existence of a national collective bargaining system which relies on trade unionism, and so to undertake such work under a union umbrella.

On the management side, the problems are different. There are, perhaps, three main issues.

First, there is the problem of involving sufficient line managers at sufficient levels. Frequently a complete level of management (often first-line supervision) is omitted from joint committee membership altogether and consequently feels by-passed and undercut. Sometimes the most senior level – the chief officers – may feel that they cannot spend time taking part in joint meetings with such junior employees as the representatives of cooks and cleaners. In these cases, none of the big issues can be effectively dealt with because the officers with the authority to make the decisions are absent. A solution adopted by some authorities is to have a three-tier joint committee system, each tier having management involvement by the one or more levels of management (including supervision) operating at that level in the organization. The three levels are:

Local level – an office, works, depot, or local group of work locations. It is at this level that the supervisors and foremen can participate.

Departmental level – a committee bringing together representatives of all the employee groups in, for example, the Housing

Department and, as a matter of critical importance, involving the chief officer of the department in person.

Council level – the top level joint committee for the authority as a whole, with chief executive involvement. At this level, shop stewards may be joined or replaced by full-time trade union officers.

The second management issue is the nature of the personnel officer's involvement. Too often, joint committees are chaired by the personnel officer, or he acts as the main management side spokesman. If the committees are to do more than discuss and negotiate pay and conditions, and are to play a positive role in the discussion and resolution of wider operational issues, it is most important that line managers from the chief executive down to the workshops foreman take a primary position on the management side. The personnel officer's role is threefold. He has the task of designing the whole system and, in discussion with the employees' side, of servicing, maintaining and modifying it in the light of experience. He acts as the management spokesman in his own field of personnel management topics, including pay and conditions. He advises his line managers on their role in the system and on the knowledge and skills required in joint discussion and bargaining activities. But he will devalue the whole system if he tries to run it as an extension of the personnel department. Joint committees are part of the general management process, not a welfare gloss applied to the process by a personnel specialist.

The third management issue is that of the involvement of the elected member. The employees and the trade unions see the Council, quite correctly, as the real employer and will often press for opportunities to raise employment issues directly with councillors; and for a forum in which the Council's plans and policies can be discussed directly between councillors and employees. There can be a range of reactions to such pressure.

Some senior officers will resist strongly on the grounds that their authority will be seriously undermined if employees have direct access to councillors.

Some members may support this resistance, though for somewhat different reasons. They consider that members should concern themselves solely (or at least primarily) with the Council's service policies and not with its internal management.

Other members may strongly support the trade union view and favour considerable direct contact between themselves and employee representatives: sometimes because they feel that senior officers form a barrier between the councillor and the 'ordinary employee'.

Other officers and councillors take a more middle view and consider there is a value in member involvement, with officers, at departmental and council level joint committees. Councillors can round

113

out discussions at these levels to include explanations of Council policy; and the meetings can provide councillors with a feeling for the degree of employee understanding of, and support for, the Council's plans and programmes.

Examples of the effect of these different reactions to joint committee systems can be seen in different authorities. A number – perhaps the majority – have not elevated their joint consultative committees to a level at which members explain and discuss policy. Shop stewards and other employee representatives meet officers but not members.

At the other extreme, at least one authority is known to the author in which at Council level shop stewards regularly meet councillors with no officers present.

The GLC, during the mid 1970s Labour administration, provided an example of the middle course in which members of service committees sat with senior officers on some meetings of departmental level joint committees, and other members, including the Chairman of the Establishment Board, were supplemented by senior officers at a council level joint committee on which employee representation was by trade union officers.

No one pattern is right for all authorities. Size and political complexion both provide legitimate variants, as does the extent of unionism among employees and the degree of vigour of employee and trade union activity. But the complete absence of elected members from a joint committee system can be queried. Should councillors be as remote as this from their employees? Similarly, the exclusion of officers from councillor/shop steward meetings might be thought inadvisable. Managers (and shop stewards) will inevitably have a more detailed knowledge of the working implications of matters discussed than members; and councillor/management understanding and cooperation has its importance.

Procedures

Supplementary to a joint committee system (or as a second best, in its absence) local industrial relations are assisted by at least three formal procedures to cover:

    individual grievances
    collective disputes
    disciplinary decisions and appeals.

It is useful to distinguish between individual and collective issues. The quick, sympathetic, consistent, but practical, handling of the grievances of employees as individuals not only promotes good morale; it will also reduce the incidence of collective complaints,

114

while a badly handled individual case can quickly be converted into a mass dispute by a riled and organized work-force.

Most grievance procedures, including the model procedure set out in the Scheme of Conditions of Service for APT and C Staffs, provide for at least three levels of management involvement and investigation. These may be, for example:

(i) The employee raises his grievance with his unit manager, normally after failing to get satisfaction within the normal employee/supervisor situation.

(ii) Failing settlement, the grievance is reviewed by a personnel officer, possibly at departmental level if personnel staff are employed both centrally and departmentally.

(iii) Finally, unresolved grievances are referred to chief officer level, assisted by the chief personnel officer if he has not been previously involved.

Time limits, both for registering a grievance and between stages, can be laid down to prevent undue delay. The employee should be allowed to be aided by a shop steward, trade union officer or other friend at these various hearings. If his complaint is not upheld, full reasons should be given to him, preferably confirmed in writing.

Failing resolution at chief officer level, the role of the councillors may again be raised. A number of authorities allow employees to appeal from the top management level to some form of member-level grievance panel at which the employee and the managers involved present their cases. Admittedly, it is asking managers to accept a far from conventional role to argue out their reasons for an employment decision against a dissenting employee in this way. But it is the Council which is the employer and both employees and trade unions are likely to feel that a final right of appeal to members is an essential element of any formal grievance procedure.

A variant of the members' grievance panel is a joint panel with representatives nominated by each side. The GLC's grievance panel, for example, has councillors on one side and staff side nominees on the other. These nominees are not employees, or the local trade union officials, but independent persons nominated by the trade unions, such as an academic, a retired trade union official and, more surprising, a retired establishments officer.

Model grievance procedures are recommended to local authorities by the major NJCs; and these omit member level involvement at authority level, but provide for reference to the Provincial Council. Many authorities, however, dislike cases proceeding directly from internal officer level discussions to the external agency of a Provincial Council, and have introduced some form of member level grievance forum.

A collective disputes procedure will differ from an individual grievance procedure. It needs to provide for the speedy reference of a dispute from one negotiating level to another and will therefore be less concerned with the presentation of cases before a panel, than with ensuring that the right forum exists at the right time with the right participants for effective negotiation.

If a joint committee system exists of the type described earlier in this chapter, then a disputes procedure can be made an integral part of this system. The joint committee at each level may appoint a disputes sub-committee to which disputes from the lower level are referred. Thus a disagreement between a shop steward and a foreman may first be referred up to a local level disputes sub-committee, then (failing agreement) moved up to departmental level and finally referred to the disputes sub-committee at Council level. Time limits (extensible by mutual agreement) would be laid down between stages.

With this type of fairly formal system, it is essential to make provision for the more normal and informal methods of disputes settlement – that is, for direct discussion between individual shop stewards and individual managers; and between the personnel officer and shop stewards and their union officials. Indeed, reference to the more formal disputes machinery would normally be by mutual agreement between the individual negotiators on each side.

In the absence of a committee system, it is still practicable and useful to have a disputes procedure which formalizes, and puts time limits on, the normal negotiating processes. Again, a four stage process may suit many authorities:

First, direct negotiations between the shop steward(s) and the local management (office, depot or works level).

Next, reference up to the departmental level with, say, the departmental personnel officer in a large authority and a senior departmental line manager.

Then, to top management level with the chief personnel officer and the relevant departmental chief officer – and possibly the chief executive in cases with service-wide trade union involvement.

Finally, to member level with officer support. The Chairman of the Personnel Committee, or of the Policy and Resources Committee, or on really serious occasions the Leader of the Council, may be involved.

The precise pattern of this stage-by-stage approach is very much a matter for each local authority itself to determine. The size of the authority, its departmental structure, the extent to which its personnel department is centralized, the degree to which councillors wish to be involved – all these are factors which will affect negotiating and disputes procedures.

Again, the NJCs provide guidance on disputes procedures, and for the reference of disputes from the individual authority to the regional or provincial council. Despite this procedure for referring the unresolved dispute to higher levels within the local government system, neither local management nor unions may wish to rule out the possibility of referring disputes to outside conciliation or arbitration. ACAS (The Advisory Conciliation and Arbitration Service) has regional offices all over the country and can supply conciliation officers to help in resolving a dispute, or can arrange arbitration to varying degrees of formality. The GLC, for example, has used ACAS to supply a single arbitrator to resolve a grading dispute involving only one employee – as well as using the Industrial Arbitration Board (the predecessor of the current Central Arbitration Committee) for its occasional failures to agree in its white-collar Whitley Council.

It is, perhaps, a questionable classification to include disciplinary procedures under an industrial relations heading. Disciplinary action, including dismissal, is more normally discussed in a general employment setting, and considered as a subject affecting individual employees rather than the workforce collectively. There are two reasons, however, for considering it primarily from an industrial relations viewpoint.

First, in a unionized workforce it is normal for the individual employee to look to his trade union for assistance in facing, and if necessary disputing, disciplinary action. Secondly, unfair or unskilful handling of individual disciplinary cases may well lead to collective industrial action. A good many stoppages – official and unofficial – have been caused by such action as the dismissal of a shop steward. Disciplinary action is, after all, the open assertion of managerial authority and the trade unions are legitimately in business to challenge and erode whatever might currently be considered as outdated and unacceptable concepts of the limits of this authority. There are other reasons for maintaining a disciplinary procedure. In positive terms, it helps to create or sustain the respect and confidence of the employees in the fairness of their employer. And unfair dismissals legislation has also led to a need for an employer to demonstrate the fairness of his dismissal procedures, as well as the reasons for dismissal. As with grievance and disputes procedures, no single system can be suggested as suitable for all authorities, but the following principles should be met, whatever the precise nature of the procedures:

The employee must be told what he is being accused of, and the evidence which has led management to consider the matter serious enough to warrant action.

He must be given the opportunity to reply to the charges, to rebut the management evidence and produce his own evidence.

He must be allowed to be helped, or represented by, his trade union or by a friend.

The more serious the disciplinary action proposed, the higher should be the level of management to authorize it.

In all but cases of really serious misconduct, he should be given at least one chance to mend his ways, confirmed in a written warning, before dismissed.

Management must be able to justify its action (whether internally at an appeals panel, or externally at a tribunal) by reference to a thorough investigation of the facts of the case.

For all but the most minor admonitions, the employee should have the right of appeal against both blameworthiness and the 'sentence'.

The role of the personnel officer in disciplinary matters is a sensitive one. Should he be, as it were, the management prosecutor? or should he attempt the role of the impartial investigator, leaving the responsibility for disciplinary decisions with line managers? Too often he tries to do both. Perhaps the most satisfactory role is that of the investigator – the officer whose job it is to dig out all the facts and not merely those which support the line manager's initial intuitive reaction to a breach of discipline; and of the adviser. This advisory role involves an assessment of the severity of the offence, the possible lines of action, the likely employee reaction (including the trade union response) and the legal implications, and the consequent advising of the line managers concerned. He may say, for example, 'in my view, this case does not justify dismissal and because of x, y and z, if we do dismiss, and the case goes to a tribunal, we are likely to lose. Instead, I propose a final written warning'. Or he may point out the relevance of the individual case to some collective issue: for example, absenteeism of a shop steward on May Day, to a trade union claim for an extra day's holiday on that date; and advise accordingly. In some authorities, however, including those influenced by traditional establishments thinking, the personnel officer may formally be given executive authority for the final disciplinary decision. In these circumstances, his problem is to ensure complete fairness in the earlier investigatory stages.

Particularly where dismissal is concerned, the nature of the final appeals stages is an important aspect of local authority procedures. Should this be different for different ranks? Manual workers' final appeal stage might be to their chief officers; officers below senior rank might appeal to the chief executive: senior officers might have the right of appeal to elected members. Alternatively, all employees might have this latter right of appeal – and it is the author's view that there should be no rank distinctions in this matter. Dismissal, the ultimate employer sanction, is as serious for the roadman as for the senior engineer or administrator. The Council is their employer and it is to the Council that they should all be able to appeal. It follows that the final stage in a disciplinary procedure would be some form of appeals body, constituted of elected members, before which the managers have to justify their desired action, and the employee (aided, if necessary by his trade union) has to justify his opposition to this action.

The speedy, though also thorough and fair, operation of a disciplinary procedure which follows these principles should all but guarantee the avoidance of industrial relations problems arising from individual disciplinary cases: provided, that is, that the procedure itself has been discussed and agreed with the trade unions concerned.

Management involvement and training

The last of the four areas, suggested earlier in this chapter as affecting the quality of authority-level industrial relations, is that of the involvement and expertise of managers and supervisors. In reviewing this aspect locally, a number of questions arise:

> Does each supervisor and manager know what his responsibilities and limits of authority are in his relationships with shop stewards and union officials? and what his role is in any joint consultative or negotiating systems?
>
> Does he understand that the quality of industrial relations in his section or unit is primarily his responsibility?
>
> Does he understand the accepted role of shop stewards and their relationship to the full-time trade union officials?
>
> Does he know about those parts of national, regional and local agreements which affect his group of employees?
>
> Does he understand the Council's industrial relations policies and the local disputes and other procedures?
>
> Does he understand the legal constraints and requirements which affect his authority and responsibility as a manager?
>
> Has he the necessary personal skill to communicate, consult and negotiate with employee representatives?

Many similar questions can be asked; and the answers in many local authorities, particularly those with only recent experience of trade union and shop steward activism, may show four factors which need attention:

> Some managers may perceive industrial relations as a new, unwelcome and external constraint on their authority, instead of as an integral part of the total man-management task. They will react to an industrial relations problem as though it represented an unnecessary interruption to their 'normal' work, instead of

accepting it as just one of a range of situations which managers are employed to cope with.

Some managers, too, while accepting the reality of organized labour, may consider that it is not their job to cope with this: they will wish to sub-contract their responsibilities to the personnel department and will expect the personnel officer to 'solve' all their industrial relations problems.

Managers, while willing to accept a full measure of responsibility in this field, may lack the knowledge of policies, systems, procedures and legal constraints necessary for intelligent industrial relations management.

Finally, managers may lack the communicating and negotiating skills necessary for effective industrial relations work.

All these factors point to the need for industrial relations training; and for this training to have three objectives. First, to develop a positive and interested attitude towards industrial relations as an important area of modern managerial responsibility. Secondly, to impart the necessary knowledge about the subject; to make available all the necessary information about national and local policies, procedures and agreements and about labour legislation. Thirdly, to assist managers to develop the necessary personal skills.

It is very much the job of the personnel officer to identify these training needs and to plan the necessary training action to meet them. Few authorities will have the training resources to undertake all this work internally. Help can be sought from the industrial relations and personnel management departments of some universities and local colleges. It is also a field in which consultants operate. Several authorities may combine forces, usually with the assistance of their provincial council, to develop the necessary training. Managers may be sent on standard courses run by outside organizations. But however small the authority, there is still a key role for some form of internal training. As with all supervisory and management training, there is a danger that the manager sent on the external course will find difficulty in relating the principles discussed there with the practicalities (which include the procedures and precedents) of his own work situation. The personnel officer can play a valuable part here in setting up courses or discussion groups within his authority to explain and explore the local implications of the broader issues. Particularly with foremen and other first-line supervisors, the keyword in any industrial relations training is practicability. Managers want to know how they should handle their everyday contacts with shop stewards, what policies, procedures and agreements affect their particular work group. The best case studies for training of this kind are the actual problems which the course members meet in their normal work.

Shop steward training

Just as employers are becoming increasingly conscious of the need for management training in industrial relations, the trade unions, too, are expanding their efforts to improve the standards of their shop stewards. All the major unions operating in local government have shop steward training programmes, NALGO and NUPE (National Union of Public Employees) in particular having recently expanded their training efforts as part of their broader policies of moving the balance of internal power from the centre to the branches and workplaces.

Effective shop steward training requires the employer's cooperation – at least to the extent of providing paid leave for course attendances. Granting reasonable paid time off for such training is, in any event, now a legislative requirement under the terms of the Employment Protection Act (Section 57). But there are benefits to the employer (and to the trade unions) in more positive management involvement. Some managers will understandably be concerned lest the only result of training will be for their stewards to harass them more effectively. Most managers' experience points the other way. Employee representatives who have been given a thorough understanding of the whole industrial relations system will certainly bargain more effectively, but they are also far more likely to keep their claims and actions within the agreed systems. Managers should also welcome a more professional attitude to local collective bargaining by local union members. The new, untrained shop steward not infrequently adopts the style of his public stereotype. He acts aggressively, threatens instant action, refuses to compromise. As we have seen, he has his managerial equivalent in the inexperienced, and therefore reactively aggressive, manager. Both the shop steward and his manager will behave in a more relaxed, professional manner when they have acquired the self-confidence which effective training can develop.

Personnel officers are likely to be approached by stewards or union officials for assistance with shop steward training. There are good reasons for the personnel officer himself to take the initiative in proposing such training to his local trade unions if they do not suggest it. In such jointly sponsored training, unions may be understandably sensitive about too dominant a management involvement. The training is primarily for their benefit and they need to be seen as the primary organizers and contributors. Course venues are, for this reason, often best sited other than in the Town Hall conference suite: local colleges may provide not only neutral ground but also lecturers for some of the background subjects. Courses benefit from some management contributions. The chief work study officer, for example, can give the employers' viewpoint of bonus schemes and explain the mechanics of his trade. (The fact that his consequent experience of being assailed by a group of questioning shop stewards may be salut-

121

ary and enlightening is a bonus for management training!) The personnel officer may discuss negotiating from a management viewpoint. Most trade union officers will agree that this type of management contribution is as useful to the union side as to the employer. The personnel officer would do well to consider the other side of this coin – a trade union contribution to management courses. Talks by trade union officials on union policy, and discussion groups involving managers and shop stewards, have a valuable role to play in management training. One of the aims of industrial relations training is to achieve a common level of knowledge on both sides so that friction is not generated, and energy wasted, as a result of misunderstandings about the facts of agreements and procedures. The development, jointly, of higher levels of personal skill prevents either side from retreating into savagery as a reaction against sophistication.

So the personnel officer has an interest in aiding the spread of knowledge and the growth of skills among both managers and employee representatives – and not only in his own department. There is a temptation for personnel officers to enshroud industrial relations with a mystique and to claim it as specialist, personnel territory. But in many ways the most effective contribution a personnel officer can make in this field is to promote the development of expertise among the front-line practitioners: the supervisors, managers and shop stewards. The personnel officer's job is then to advise (and the more knowledgeable the managers, the more likely they are to listen to professional advice), to innovate as new attitudes, systems or legislation emerge, and to monitor the effectiveness of his authority's whole industrial relations system.

8 Pay and conditions

The highly detailed national agreements on pay and conditions produced by the various national joint councils result in local authority personnel officers being somewhat less involved in this aspect of personnel management than many of their colleagues in industry and commerce. Many large industries, of course, operate under national agreements – building and engineering are two major examples – but these agreements are usually less detailed and less mandatory than those in local government. The building industry's Working Rule Agreement, for example, is only a third of the size of the local authority manual workers' Schedule of Working Conditions. The Engineering Industry Agreement, as another example, lays down only minimum wage rates, whereas the local government agreements define actual wage and salary levels. Local government agreements, too, cover all grades of employees whereas many industrial national agreements cover only manual workers.

Nevertheless, local authority personnel officers have to be the local experts on the substance and interpretation of national agreements, and in certain areas, such as bonus payments and job grading, individual authorities have wide discretionary powers within the general national framework. This chapter, therefore, outlines the main provisions of the two primary agreements, those for manual workers, and for APT and C staffs.

The manual worker agreement

It is, perhaps, somewhat misleading to talk in terms of a single, national manual worker agreement. Each constituent element of the whole set of provisions relating to wages, hours, leave and so on is subject to individual negotiation and amendment. Additionally, a number of provincial variations are permitted within the national framework; for working purposes, the document of most use to the individual personnel officer is his provincial joint council's handbook

123

which sets out both the service-wide national conditions and the regional additions or variations. LACSAB nationally, and the provincial councils regionally, issue regular up-datings of the various sections as and when these are renegotiated, and the whole set of conditions is reprinted from time to time. The main period of change is, of course, the time of the annual pay claim. But national or regional negotiations on other individual elements are not uncommon outside this period and the whole, complex range of negotiated conditions is really under continuous review and change.

The manual worker wage system is based on a classification of jobs into seven grades, A-G, with A covering the least skilled and G the highest skilled jobs. (Building, engineering and electrical craftsmen are covered by their own separate agreements). A number of jobs are graded on a uniform, national basis; others are graded by the provincial councils. Examples of national grades illustrate the type and range of jobs.

Group A Messenger
        Porter
        Lavatory attendant
Group B General labourer
        Street sweeper
Group C Assistant gardener
        Launderette attendant
        Stoker
Group D Laundry operator
        Sewage works attendant
Group E Refuse collector
        Rodent operative
Group F Skilled sewerman
        Craftsman gardener
Group G Specialist sewerman
        Public lighting fitter

(The pay rates extant at the end of mid 1980 for these groups, and for craftsmen, are given in Appendix B on page 295, together with comparisons in earnings between the public and private sectors.)

These national gradings were revised in 1969 taking into account skill, responsibility and working conditions. Provincial gradings are made primarily on a comparative basis, while jobs unique to an individual authority can be graded by that authority along similar lines, with provincial council ratification of the results. There are some local cases of jobs being graded above Group G.

Wages are expressed in weekly terms with an hourly rate for use in overtime and other calculations. Local government is thus somewhat ahead of a number of industrial agreements which still classify manual

124

workers solely as hourly-paid. One implication of the weekly wage is that contractually, the employer is obliged to pay a full week's wages all the while the employee is available for work. Short, unpaid layoffs (say for two days per week) when for various reasons work is scarce, cannot be implemented in local government.

The actual level of wage rates in comparison with industrial wages has traditionally been low, a factor leading to the dirty jobs strike which has already been referred to and to the move to a £30 per week minimum wage in 1974. The effect of improvements to the lower paid, and of flat-rate threshold payments, was to reduce the proportionate differentials between the wage groups and this led in turn to the 1975 national dispute about the restoration of these differentials. The introduction of a minimum earnings guarantee was another feature which raised earnings for the lower Groups closer to the higher Group levels and although this was dropped for manual workers in 1974 it continues for certain craft groups. Equal pay for men and women was introduced in full on 1 January 1975, though before this the payment of the full men's rate to women employed on male-graded jobs had already been introduced. Continued dissatisfaction with skill differentials within the 1977 pay settlement led to a renewed joint consideration of the whole manual worker grading structure, and of the principles by which it is decided that some jobs receive national gradings and others are left for provincial or local determination. The unions' wish to see differentials restored has been complicated by their desire at the same time to improve the lot of the lower paid; and by the employers' problems in preventing large increases to Group G flowing upwards into craft, supervisory and management salaries.

The 1978/79 wage disputes led to the referral of manual worker wage levels to the newly established Standing Commission on Pay Comparability – the Clegg Commission. Clegg's report in August, 1979 recommended increases ranging in total from around 4 per cent at the low, Group A end to some 18 per cent at Group G. These proposals disappointed the trade unions which had been campaigning for a £60 per week minimum wage, but went a long way towards restoring a more traditional pattern of differentials.

As is normal with manual worker wage systems, there are a variety of additional forms of payment which can boost total earnings and these are summarized below:

Service supplement: a modest weekly flat-rate for workers working at least 35 hours per week who have completed 5 years service in local authority service. (This was phased out in 1980).

Bonus earnings: bonus systems are dealt with in more detail in the next chapter. Some 70 per cent of manual workers are covered by bonus schemes; almost all are based on work study, and produce bonus

125

earnings averaging around 30 per cent of basic wage rates (though the range is certainly as wide as 15 per cent – 80 per cent).

Lead-in payments: a flat rate weekly payment to workers not on a bonus scheme but for whom such a scheme has been assessed as feasible. The workers must be willing to co-operate in the introduction of a 'genuine and viable productivity payment system', and the lead-in payments are also supposed to be 'self-financing', that is, that the costs of the payments should be covered by savings achieved either 'in a discernible way' during the lead-in period, or out of the early stages of operation of the bonus scheme itself when this is introduced.

It would be somewhat naive to claim that the application of these restrictions on lead-in payments has been either easy or consistent. There is an obvious tendency for any payments of this kind to become no more than a form of payment in lieu of bonus.

Plus payments: a variety of extra payments in specified occupations for specified factors such as the holding of certain qualifications or the existence of particular features in the work.

Parks employees, for example, can be paid extra if they hold certain first-aid certificates. Crematoria employees qualify for plus payments in crematoria handling 4,000 or more cremations annually. Home helps are paid an additional hourly rate when working in houses where various infectious diseases are present.

Some of these plus rates are laid down nationally, others are established provincially and some are left for negotiation to the individual local authority.

Proficiency payments: merit payments as such are not part of the wage system; but in certain occupations, proficiency payments are made to employees who hold specified qualifications related directly to their work.

For example, crematoria employees may obtain a Certificate of Proficiency for Crematorium Technicians issued by the Institute of Burial and Cremation Administration, and thus qualify for additional hourly plus rate.

Dirty money: extra payments made on an hourly basis for working in conditions of dirt which are abnormal for the particular occupation. 'Normal' dirtiness in any job is taken into account in its general grading. Dirty money payments are matters for local negotiations.

Overtime: overtime premiums are payable at the rate of time-and-a-half for Monday – Saturday and double time on Sunday. There are a number of detailed overtime regulations relating to shift workers, part-timers and employees 'called-out' after returning home.

The incidence of overtime working varies considerably, even within individual authorities. National averages of about four hours per week conceal a range of from nil to over 30. Most authorities, and officially all unions, oppose the use of regular overtime solely as a method of raising earnings; but in periods in which local government wage levels have been well below average levels externally, there has been understandable pressure on and from employees to use overtime in this way. Since major improvements were made to overtime in the 1972-75 period, overtime costs are considerable. It is worth noting, for example, that an employee working one hour's overtime per weekday and four hours on Saturday will increase his earnings by 34 per cent.

Shift payments: Employees on night-work or on various forms of shift-work also receive specified allowances and enhancements to the basic day worker rates of pay. These include some flat-rate payments (such as the hourly plus-rate for workers on split-duty shifts, ie two working periods per day), and percentage premia on the individual's actual basic rate (such as the one-third extra paid for night work).

It will be clear from this list of payments that relatively few employees are likely to be paid only the basic grade rate. A normal week's pay is, in fact, likely to include a modest amount of overtime, some bonus pay, and for many employees one or more 'extras' such as the shift allowance. Regular earnings of from 50 per cent to 100 per cent above the basic rates are not uncommon. In mid-1978, full-time, male manual workers were averaging earnings of about £63.50 per week; including £8.85 for overtime, £8.75 for bonus and about £1.55 for other additions. The average working week was just over 44 hours.

The working day and week
Manual workers, other than those on shift or night work, work a 40 hour week. The 40 hours is working time: it excludes meal breaks. Various patterns of shift-working are negotiable locally to cover 24 hour, seven days a week services or other activities which cannot be restricted to normal day work. The national agreement lays down the conditions of payment for work on rest, or free days between shifts, and all shift patterns must average 40 working hours. This average can be struck, however, over a complete shift cycle, allowing for weekly variations to cover unusual working hour requirements. In the course of 1978, pressure began to build up for reductions in the working week – part of the general TUC policy of moving towards a basic 35 hour week as a means of reducing unemployment.

Leave
The agreement provides for leave with pay for:

all public holidays
two 'extra-statutory' days, the timing to be decided locally
annual leave on a schedule related to length of service, with the

127

maximum entitlement of three weeks, three days after 10 years service, and a minimum of three weeks, one day.

The general level of leave entitlement has in the past been somewhat higher than the average for industrial manual workers, although there has been a strong trend towards longer holidays in many industrial agreements over the past four or five years.

Holiday pay is certainly in advance of that in many major industrial agreements in which only basic rates are payable. In the local government agreement, holiday pay includes all the main enhancements and plus rates, including payments for 'regular, scheduled overtime', and lead-in payments – and 50 per cent of average bonus earnings. There is, however, steady pressure, both in the public and private sectors, for holiday pay to be at full average earnings levels and not reduced in any way by discounting all or part of bonus earnings.

Sick pay scheme
Sick pay arrangements, are in advance of those for many manual workers in the private sector. There is a schedule of entitlements to paid sick leave related to length of service, ranging from four weeks' full pay and four weeks' half pay for employees with 6-12 months' service; to six months full and six months half pay after six years' service. Sick pay is made up to holiday pay levels by paying an allowance additional to National Insurance benefit. Fifty per cent of average bonus earnings are included in sick pay calculations.

Superannuation
A fuller description of the Local Government Superannuation Scheme is given below in the section on white-collar staff conditions.

From April 1974, however, when the scheme in its present form was introduced, it has become an important feature of manual workers' conditions of service. Before 1974 a large number of manual workers were outside the scheme, by choice or by inertia. Now, all manual employees join the scheme provided they are age 18 or over with one year's service. They pay five per cent of pay for this purpose, including bonus earnings but excluding overtime.

Normal retirement age is 65, although a pension can be drawn on voluntary retirement from age 60, provided 25 years' service has been completed. The primary retirement benefits are:

A pension of one eightieth of pensionable remuneration for every year of service, and
A lump sum allowance of three eightieths of pensionable remuneration for every year of service.

There are also provisions in the scheme for widows' pensions, a death grant and special pension arrangements for cases of retirement due to permanent incapacity.

Under the Pensions (Increase) Act 1971 pensions are revised annually in line with changes in the cost of living.

A 1971 Government survey showed major differences of treatment in private sector pension schemes, between manual workers and white collar staff. At that time only 24 per cent of manual workers in pension schemes had pensions based on final salary, and 74 per cent accrued pensions at less than one eighteenth per year of service. The Local Government Scheme is one of the most favourable for manual workers, giving 'staff' benefits for one per cent less in contributions than that paid by white-collar staff, and with its inflation-proofed pensions being an increasingly important element.

Redundancy scheme
The absence of a redundancy scheme within the national agreement contrasts with the position of many large private sector employers, and with some of the nationalized industries. Its absence, however, is not so much an adverse employment condition, as a reflection of the high degree of job security traditionally provided by local government employment. Special provisions were made to protect employees affected by local government reorganization in 1974, and special provisions relating to pension and other retirement benefits in the event of redundancy have been introduced by statutory instrument as an appendage to the local government superannuation scheme. They apply to pensionable staff aged 50 and over, with five years' service.

In summary, manual worker pay and conditions generally provide for somewhat lower earnings than in the private sector, similar hours of work and shift and overtime payments, better sick pay, leave and pensions, and much more job security, at least until the financial crisis of 1979. Even then, sizeable reductions in the numbers of employees have been achieved mainly by natural wastage, and the number of enforced redundancies has been small in relation both to the size of the local government labour force, and to the redundancy experience of much of industry.

The APT and C scheme of conditions

White collar staffs' terms and conditions are set out in the 'purple book' (the NJC's scheme of conditions) and, like the manual workers' handbook, this is a collection of all the current agreements on various aspects of pay and other conditions of service. It is more detailed and more complex than the manual workers' handbook. The index for the main APT and C section shows some 300 individual items on which national rules and regulations exist. Additional to this main section are a 26 page description of the job evaluation scheme, a longer section dealing with 'miscellaneous classes', and a section covering residential staff. Only direct reference to the purple book itself will provide detailed and up-to-date information, and all that is set out below is a summary of the primary conditions and general principles which govern the whole scheme.

Salary and grading structure

The backbone of the APT and C salary system is a 'spinal column' of 61 salary points from £1449-£10,467 at January 1980. Full details are given in Appendix C on page 297. Each salary point constitutes a rung on the salary ladder. The various salary grades for different levels or groups of staff are constructed by taking a number of consecutive points on the spine for each grade: the lowest and highest point becoming the minimum and maximum for the grade, the intervening points forming the incremental steps for normal salary progression. This progression is by annual, service increments.

The primary grades are the five used for administrative, professional and technical posts. There are two sets of grades for these posts: one for administrative and professional (AP) and one for technical (T), but all except the first grade in each set is identical. The first T grade has a lower starting point than the first AP grade to cover junior technicians and certain lower classified jobs which are subject to a bar point, past which salary progression depends on the acquisition of qualifications.

The grades are generally 'butt-ended' (they do not overlap) and each grade except the lowest is therefore relatively short. Above the lowest grade, two to four years' modest incremental progression is provided. Grade maxima are, on average, about 12 per cent above grade minima. The average size of annual increment is about 3.3 per cent of annual salary.

If this type of structure is compared with typical private sector salaries, a number of significant differences emerge. Private sector salary structures not unusually provide grade maxima of 20 per cent to 40 per cent above grade minima, with salary progression within overlapping grades on the basis of annual merit assessments. Annual merit increases are often between five per cent and 15 per cent of salary. There is a difference of philosophy between the public and private sector systems. In the private sector the emphasis is on the motivation and reward of individual performance within a competitive and therefore higher risk system: the local government system places the emphasis on collective equity and on a secure (but therefore modest) degree of salary progression. Pay policy in the 1975 to 1978 period was, of course, severely restrictive about individual merit payments, and some large private sector employers have moved towards the incremental principle.

The purple book lays down general principles relating to education, qualifications and experience on which the allocation of posts should be made, both as to the appropriate division (AP or T) and as to grade.

But the grading of specific posts is a matter primarily for local judgement and decision, as is the question of starting salary for new entrants. Inevitably, variations have occurred between authorities in their approach to grading. An authority in a high cost area, needing quickly to recruit a particular professional group in order to staff a new service, will be under strong pressure to grade the new posts at a higher level than elesewhere in order to attract applicants. A neighbouring authority may then experience pressure from its staff for comparable higher grading. It was partly for this reason that a model job evaluation scheme was evolved as a method of helping all authorities adopt a common standard and system of job grading. (The scheme is described in more detail in a later chapter). The scheme is not mandatory, however, and has not been taken up by all authorities.

The purple book also defines salary structures for several other groups of posts:

There is a *clerical division* with a three grade scale. The lower grade (C1) is a long grade to cope with junior staff and with lower grade work, in which salary progression is subject to a bar.

A *trainee grade* is provided for all AP staff employed specifically in a trainee (as distinct from junior) capacity. This grade includes a minimum entry point for graduate recruits.

A two grade structure for *senior officers*, defined as posts involving advice on policy formulation, the control of large or important sections of work, the leadership of teams of professional or technical officers, or 'individual work of a high order'. These SO grades are short and have the same service increment arrangement as the AP and T grades.

A two range structure for *principal officers*, defined as posts senior to senior officers. The salary system changes for these posts. The ranges are longer than AP and T, and SO grades, each having 10 salary points. For each PO post, the local authority is free to select any five consecutive points from either of the two ranges to form a grade specific to the individual post. Authorities are required by the purple book only to 'have regard to the scope of duties and responsibilities involved' in grading PO posts. Further, 'the salary grading of posts above PO_2 is to be at the discretion of the employing authority'. Most authorities consequently bridge the gap between the top of the PO_2 scale and the salaries of deputy chief officers by a locally designed PO_3 scale.

A pay structure for *chief officers* in which salary is related to the size of the authority, as measured by population. Salary scales for chief officers are complicated by the existence of a separate JNC for Chief Officers which specifies salaries for only a few designated senior chief officer posts – Treasurer, Secretary, Chief Education Officer and the like. The purple book scales are used for other chief officers

131

and departmental heads not designated in the JNC agreements. Both sets of scales have had to be kept compatible.

A complex set of regulations about the grading of specified 'special classes' of officers. These special classes include such jobs as librarians, careers officers, education welfare officers and social workers. In some cases (such as the jobs just listed) a specific scale is laid down consisting of some six to 14 salary points. The starting salary for a new entrant is left for local decision, and incremental progression is either to the top of the scale or is subject to some form of bar related to qualifications and experience.

In other cases (such as public health inspectors) employees with defined qualifications are allocated to one or more of the AP or T grades. In special circumstances, authorities may obtain Provincial Council approval for a higher grading than that specified in the purple book. It is the difference of approach by authorities to the grading of some of these posts – particularly social workers – which has caused increasing industrial relations friction in recent years. Some authorities have abandoned the specified grades and instead, graded social workers on the general AP grades, giving higher maxima and better salary prospects by the use of more than one grade. This in turn has led to pressure (and in 1978, strikes) by those social workers left behind on the nationally prescribed scales.

As part of a separate, complete scheme of conditions, a seven grade structure for *miscellaneous classes*. These posts are defined as being 'neither wholly manual nor wholly clerical in character'. They include supervisory and non-professional inspection-type jobs. The grades are generally shorter than the AP and T grades, all but the top grade having only three salary points (two increments). Additionally, certain special classes of these miscellaneous posts are allotted their own specific and different salary grades (eg traffic wardens and registration officers).

Taking a broad view of the whole salary structure, the main feature in recent years has been the steady compression of differentials between higher and lower grades. This compression has been the result of flat-rate payments (such as the £6 per week increase in Phase 2 of the Labour Government's incomes policy), restrictions on the maximum size of annual increase (such as in Stages 2 and 3 of the Conservative Government's incomes policy) and policy decisions to favour the lower paid. The ratio between the lowest paid adult clerical employee and a large authority's Chief Officers has been reduced since 1970 from about 15:1 to around 8:1.

Other payments
As with manual workers, there are a number of provisions in the national agreements which can enhance total earnings. These include:

132

Accelerated increments. Although the normal incremental system is for each officer to move up within his grade by one increment annually, authorities are permitted to grant additional increments for 'special merit or ability'. This may include recognizing success in professional examinations, and the award of extra increments for a high standard of work on the basis of some form of performance appraisal. The maxima of grades cannot be exceeded, and with short grades this provision merely results in a larger proportion of staff being paid grade maxima than would result solely from service increments. Pay policy has severely limited the operation of merit accelerations in the period from 1974-1979.

Standby allowances. Staff required to keep themselves available at home at the end of a telephone on some form of rota, are eligible either for a specified flat-rate allowance (eg social workers) or may be paid a locally determined allowance.

Shift pay. Below a defined salary point, officers on shift work are paid a specified rate of salary enhancement.

Overtime. Below a defined salary point, officers are eligible for overtime pay at the rate of time and a half.

Night work (as part of normal hours) carries a one-third enhancement. Work on public holidays is paid at plain time but also carries an entitlement to further leave.

Car allowances. Officers whose work necessitates the use of a car (and who are not given the use of council cars) are classified as either casual or essential users. Casual users are paid a rate per mile for business mileage. Essential users receive an annual lump sum payment plus a mileage rate.

There is also a scheme for assisted car purchase, with loans available at below commercial hire purchase or finance house rates.

It will be noted that, unlike manual workers, bonus payments are not listed as a normal means of increasing earnings. There is no national agreement about productivity or payment by results schemes for white collar staff and very few authorities have introduced any form of bonus payments. There are some examples of Office Work Measurement (OWM) being used, mainly in routine clerical work, to reduce manning levels and to justify consequential bonus payments on a share-of-savings basis. But the main bonus problem for most local authorities is that of the effect on pay differentials of high levels of manual worker bonuses. Foremen on white-collar pay (miscellaneous classes) can find they are taking home less than the bonused manual workers they supervise.

The working day and week

Normal office hours are defined as 36 in London and 37 elsewhere (though the GLC, under its separate domestic agreement, works 35).

133

Authorities are free to determine their own individual pattern of working hours on either a five day basis or with a system of periodic Saturday morning leave. Except in specific offices which are open to the public, most white-collar staff work a five day week.

Within the general specification of hours per week, local government has been somewhat of a pioneer in the use of flexible working hours. Under this system, staff are required to be present only for a designated 'core time' daily of, say, 10 00 am to 4 pm. They may arrive at work between, say, 8 00 am and 10 00 am; and leave between 4 00 pm and 7 00 pm, – actual times being a matter solely for the individual daily choice of each employee. Attendance times are usually recorded, and staff must put in the required 36 or 37 hours per week, either on a weekly basis or by a fortnightly or monthly aggregate. Different schemes have different core times, vary in their methods of time recording, and have different rules about the extent to which extra hours can be worked and 'banked' to provide for extra time off. Most of the authorities who have introduced schemes of this kind report that the working difficulties are few, and that any disadvantages are outweighed by the schemes' popularity with staff and by improvements in total attendance time. Flexible working hours continue, however, to be the subject of criticism by some senior managers, who feel that too easy-going an atmosphere may develop, and that without fairly strict recording a minority of staff may seriously abuse a scheme.

Annual leave
Annual leave entitlements are related to both salary and length of service, officers with 10 years or more local government service being entitled to three to four days more leave per annum than their shorter service colleagues. The purple book specifies leave entitlements up to an annual maximum of 26 working days, but leaves it open to authorities to grant leave 'at discretion' to staff on salaries broadly above those of the senior officer grades.

Public holidays and at least two 'extra-statutory' days are granted additionally, while a number of authorities also grant one or more further days off on a local basis.

As with manual workers, the general levels of leave for white-collar staff have been somewhat in advance of those in the private sector, though there have been clear indications since 1975 that four weeks holiday is becoming a standard provision in industry and commerce.

Sick and maternity leave
Sick leave is related to length of service and rises to a maximum of six months' full pay and six months' half pay after five years' service. Authorities can extend this scale in individual cases. Sick pay – strictly speaking a special allowance – is equivalent to full

normal pay less National Insurance sickness benefit. Maternity leave is paid in accordance with the maternity provisions of the Employment Protection Act.

Superannuation

The Local Government Superannuation Scheme in its present form was introduced under regulations made under the 1972 Superannuation Act. It does not constitute part of the purple book Scheme of Conditions and is not subject to NJC negotiation. Indeed, local government is subject in this matter to decisions of the Department of the Environment. Nevertheless, local government employers and trade unions are consulted by government on changes to the scheme and it constitutes an important element in the total packgage of employment conditions. One odd feature is that, while the scheme itself is standard throughout local government, it is financed (or at least funded) by a whole number of individual authorities' pension funds. The principle of a funded scheme is that investments must always be available of sufficient value to enable all pension obligations of existing employees and pensioners to be met if the scheme was stopped (or if the employer went bankrupt). In fact, annual payments into the scheme by way of employer and employee contributions have always matched, and usually exceeded, payments out to pensioners, so that no fund is actually necessary for solely financial purposes. It represents more of an insurance policy against the possible break-up of authorities or schemes.

The scheme is contributory, unlike that in the Civil Service. Employees contribute six per cent of their salary; the employer pays significantly more. Membership of the scheme is compulsory on entry, or on reaching the age of 18, provided the individual authority's medical requirements are met. Authorities vary in their approach to medical examinations and some do not require a medical check below certain age limits. The only age bar to entry is that new employees cannot join the scheme after age 65. The scheme does not apply to firemen, police, teachers and one or two other groups for whom alternative, statutory schemes are available.

Benefits are as for manual workers – one eighteeth of pensionable remuneration per year of service plus a lump sum of three eightieths per year of service. 'Pensionable remuneration' is the highest of the last three years salary – normally the last year; 65 is the complulsory retiring age: pensions can be drawn from age 60 provided 25 years service has been completed. The maximum pension payable is 45 eightieths and this, together with the lump sum, is approximately equal in value to the one sixtieth schemes often provided in private sector schemes but which provide lump sums only against a reduction (usually 25 per cent) in pension.

135

In fact, when the inflation-proofing of local government pensions is taken into account, the scheme is certainly as attractive as many, if not most, in the private sector.

When the inflation-proofing of local government pensions is taken into account, the scheme is certainly more attractive than most in the private sector except for 'top hat' directors' schemes.

Additionally, there are several important benefits for employees who do not complete full service at full salary:

An employee who has to take a permanent reduction in salary in mid-service may have his pension calculated on his original higher salary.

An employee absent on sick leave – even for long unpaid periods – has the whole period counted as full service but pays contributions only on the pay he actually receives.

An employee who, having completed five years' service, has to give up his job because of permanent incapacity, has his service enhanced for pension entitlement purposes on the following scale:

Up to 10 years' service – reckonable service doubled
10-13½ years' service – reckonable service made up to 20 years
Over 13½ years' service – plus 10 years up to a maximum of 40.

Additionally, if the incapacity results from an injury at work, the authority may itself pay an additional injury allowance – the amount to be decided locally.

Death benefit in service is payable to the deceased employee's estate at either three eightieths of salary per year of service up to a maximum of 135 eightieths or a year's salary, whichever is greater.

This benefit is somewhat less than that frequently provided by free life insurance in private sector schemes.

Widow's benefit is payable for three months at full salary, and until her death or marriage at half the rate her husband would have received if he had retired on permanent incapacity grounds at the time of his death. When a pensioner dies (ie death after retirement) the widow receives a pension of half that which her husband was drawing.

Employees who leave one authority and join another can, of course, transfer their pension rights. Transferability also exists between the local government scheme and other public sector schemes (such as the Civil Service and National Health Service schemes). Transfers can be arranged with some private sector schemes. Authorities also have discretion to award 'added years' on entry to service in exceptional cases in which the new officer is bringing to the service special qualifications and experience which could normally not have been obtained in local government service.

Summary

As noted at the beginning of this chapter, the agreements and related provisions on pay and conditions are complex and detailed. Only the two main blocks of conditions have been summarized. Different pay structures, and different sets of conditions exist for firemen, police, teachers, craftsmen and a number of other groups.

All, however, have some similarity in general approach and principle. The incremental system is common for all white-collar staff. Leave provisions are generally above the national average. All agreements lay down detailed rules and regulations for such items as travelling and subsistence payments and allowances of various kinds. Most permit some form of minor regional variation. The scope for local variation is limited except, in the manual worker field, in bonusing and, in the white-collar field, in grading. Here, two schemes or sets of principles are laid down for the guidance of individual authorities, and it is these which form the subject of the next two chapters.

9 Incentive payment schemes

It was noted in the previous chapter that the individual local authority could influence its earnings levels, not by negotiating local rates but by the action it took about bonus schemes and job grading. There is no direct connection between these two systems or techniques; the link is that both depend for their effect on the skill with which they are applied by individual authorities. These are not areas in which national agreements can do more than lay down guidelines and standards. Both activities, too, can be used or misused to change general earnings levels and so to create differences of treatment between authorities. When national surveys reveal differences in manual worker bonus levels for similar work ranging from 20 per cent to 100 per cent there has to be a suspicion that the high-bonus authorities are using incentive schemes more to set attractive earnings levels than to reward productivity *per se*. Similarly, in the white collar field it is noticeable how a shortage of recruits in a particular authority for a particular profession is often followed by a re-grading (that is, an up-grading) of relevant posts.

If the national guidelines of the two systems were rigidly adhered to, variations and changes of this kind should not occur. On the other hand, if a market view is taken of labour supply, then both schemes permit a rationalization of consequent earnings changes. More generally, the value of both schemes is in their adoption of reasonably objective techniques for determining pay levels and relativities, the consequent reduction in 'horse-trading' methods of negotiations about pay, and in the achievement (at least within an authority) of consistent methods of rewarding productivity and establishing pay differentials.

The two techniques involved are Work Study – for incentive schemes; and Job Evaluation – for grading jobs. The former has been applied almost exclusively to the manual worker field; the latter is designed specifically for APT and C staff, the main white collar group. It is worth noting that these restrictions are not inherent to the techniques. Broadbased work study, and its clerical equivalent, Office Work Measurement, have applications in non-manual work. A job evaluation system could be evolved for grading manual worker posts – and indeed the job evaluation approach was used (though not continued) in the 1969 manual worker re-grading exercise. And there are, of course, other systems of bonusing and job evaluation than those adopted by the local government NJCs.

In the remainder of this chapter, the NJC approach to incentive schemes is first described in some detail and the broader principles underlying incentive payments systems are then discussed. In the next chapter, the NJC's job evaluation scheme is examined.

The code of guiding principles for incentive schemes

The Manual Workers NJC, in consultation with the Local Authorities' Management Services and Computer Committee (LAM-SAC), produced a 'code of guiding principles and practice for work study based incentive schemes' in 1972. This code, while not completely mandatory, nevertheless includes a fairly forthright introductory statement that 'wherever possible and practicable, incentive schemes should be based on accepted work study principles'.

It is important to stress two elements of national-level policy. First, that incentive schemes for manual workers are a good thing. Secondly, that they should be based on work study.

The Code itself does not set out what the benefits of this scheme are. In the minutes of NJC discussions, however, and in LACSAB advisory notes, the benefits to the employers are seen primarily as:

a better utilization of manpower
lower costs per unit of service or output
a higher paid and therefore more satisfied workforce
consequential improvements in recruiting.

For employees the major benefit is seen as the possibility of achieving higher earnings.

The Code tends to deal with work study and incentive payments as though the two were intrinsically synonymous. For a clearer understanding of the whole scheme, it is useful to separate work study as a technique from payment systems. The British Standards Institution booklet which defines the terms used, and to which the Code itself makes direct reference, is quite explicit on this division. 'A clear distinction should be drawn' says the BSI, 'between the measurement of work and the methods by which payment for work is made. The aim of work measurement is to find the amount of work in a job . . . and it is equally applicable where there is no question of incentive payment, or even of any payment at all'.

139

The contribution of work study to an incentive payments scheme is thus to provide an objective technique for determining how much work should normally be achieved in a certain, defined time. That is, work study provides a common base against which employee performance in a job can be assessed and on which monetary rewards can then be placed. Work study can, however, be used quite independently of any payments system, particularly to determine the best method of carrying out a particular task and the correct manning level for a task or work unit.

Work study falls into two categories: method study and work measurement. In bonus schemes, the latter is the most obvious requirement, but method study should be considered an essential prerequisite for any scheme. The work study officer has a whole armoury of analytical techniques at his disposal to study how existing work is being carried out, to identify shortcomings in the methods and systems in use, and to propose new and improved methods.

Before a bonus scheme is introduced in, say, a refuse incineration plant, the work study team should, ideally, carry out a detailed assessment of every aspect of the operations: vehicle routing, plant operating methods, maintenance schedules, general plant layout and the allocation of tasks to individual employees and to employee teams. The Code gives little emphasis to this preliminary work, though it does state that:

. . . during the investigations which precede the introduction of changes (eg method study and work measurement) representatives of the employees and their trade unions should be invited to join the investigating team, to act on behalf of the employees in discussions with management and to be available to attend, examine and carry out any checks.

This book is not the place for a detailed exposition of method study, but the importance of ensuring that an operation which is to be bonused is first organized on an efficient basis cannot be over-emphasized. It should be noted, too, that method study techniques can cover the whole spectrum of work systems, from the physical layout of a multi-million pound incineration plant to the method by which an individual employee uses a brush and a shovel to put leaves into a park wheelbarrow.

Work measurement, particularly when applied to bonus schemes, is concerned with determining the work content or 'standard time' for a job. Standard time is defined in the BSI booklet as 'the total time in which a job should be completed at standard performance'. Standard performance is defined as 'the rate of output which qualified workers will naturally achieve without over-exertion as an average over the working day provided they adhere to the specified method and provided they are motivated to apply themselves to their work'.

140

The basic principle of bonus payments laid down in the Code is that employees working at this standard performance should be paid bonus at a rate of one third of the basic rate of pay: that is, that total earnings should be 33⅓ per cent above basic rates.

Several points in these definitions of standard time and standard performance need to be emphasized:

The degree of knowledge and skill possessed by an individual worker can clearly affect his rate of working. Standard performance is based on the work rate of a 'qualified worker'. Qualified, in this context, does not relate to paper qualifications. It means a worker who:

has the necessary physical attributes of strength, dexterity, eyesight and so on, required in the job
is sufficiently intelligent and has the requisite degree of literacy
has acquired the necessary physical and mental skills
is adequately knowledgeable about the work.

The method of working can clearly influence the time taken to complete a task, as can the standards of work. Standard performance assumes that work is being done of a required quality and within safety limits. An unnecessarily high quality of work may slow down the work rate: workers are not expected to have to cut safety corners in order to earn bonus. Further, standard performance assumes that the designed methods and procedures for the job are being followed. Of course, if a worker can evolve a faster method (within required quality and safety standards) than the work study officer then he will benefit in above average bonus earnings.

Standard performance is a steady, sustainable, 'natural' pace of working, given the motivation to work in this consistent, conscientious fashion. Workers are not expected to work themselves into the ground to earn bonus and, indeed, the key to maintaining standard performance is to work steadily, without frequent 'idle time', rather than to work in fierce, concentrated bursts of unsustainably high work-rates. It is an underlying assumption of bonusing that the motivation to work in this steady, sustained manner is supplied by the carrot of bonus earnings – a point to be discussed more critically later in this chapter.

In producing a bonus scheme for an existing operation, the work study officer's task is to produce a standard time for each identifiable task involved in the work. The BSI booklet describes standard times as being times for 'jobs' – a slightly misleading definition for the layman for whom 'job' means the whole of an employee's work. In work study, however, the whole work normally has to be sub-divided into separately measurable parts. Thus a vehicle fitter's work may well be made up of literally dozens of identifiably different tasks – replacing a clutch, re-lining a brake drum, de-coking a cylinder block, fitting a new radiator and so on – and each of these can be measured separately to produce a separate standard time. If a series of tasks is normally performed in sequence, then individual times can be aggregated, but the work study officer will have to study and measure each part separately. Assuming that acceptable methods are being worked in the job under study, then two tasks have to be performed in producing a standard time. These are *timing* and *rating*.

Timing is usually done by a stop-watch. The work study officer, having analysed the job and broken it down for observational purposes into its constituent elements, then observes the work in progress and records the time taken to complete each element. Obviously one record alone would be insufficient to give accurate results, and a whole series of studies is therefore necessary.

Rating is carried out at the same time and is a more subjective process. The work study officer has to assess the rate at which the worker under study is working, relative to the concept of the rate of working involved in a standard performance. The latter is taken as index 100: that is, a qualified worker, motivated to apply himself to his work, working to the correct method, within the quality and safety standards, and working at a natural rate. The observed worker's rate of working must be assessed as he is being timed so that the observed times can be adjusted against the common standard of a standard performance.

For example, if the time actually obtained on the stopwatch for a task is 10 minutes, and the worker under observation is rated at working at only half the standard rate (50 performance), then the time needs to be halved to five minutes to give the basic, standardized time. Similarly, if he is rated as working at twice the standard rate (200 performance), then the basic time will be 20 minutes – twice the observed time.

In practice, the observed ratings will be less variable, say from 80 to 120, as the greater the variance from standard (100) the less reliable will the rating and timing be. Rating is obviously the least scientific or objectively 'provable' element in work studied bonus schemes and if consistency is to be maintained, work study officers require frequent refresher training in this art. Workers who understand the technique may well try to give an impression, when being studied, of intense concentration and activity in order to trap the work study officer into a high rating. The work study man, in turn, must avoid being misled by this or by the apparently effortless ease of the highly skilled worker. Rating must include an assessment of the extent to which the worker matches the concept of a 'qualified worker' as well as of the effort put into the work.

Having obtained a time, adjusted by rating, a whole series of

142

additions are then built on to it before the bonus target time ('allowed time') is produced. These additions are:

Relaxation allowances: additional time to allow for minor pauses and interruptions to continuous work, needed for worker to go to the lavatory, light cigarettes, stop for a short breather after work element involving heavy exertion and so on. Relaxation allowances are sub-divided into fatigue allowances (the occasional breather) and personal needs allowances (the visits to the lavatory).

Contingency allowances: may then be added to cover normal, but infrequent or irregular extra work items or delays which it may be impracticable to measure precisely. 'Work contingency' allowances cover occasional extra items of work, such as a fitter occasionally re-sharpening a screwdriver; 'delay contingency' allowances cover occasional interruptions to work such as breaking off to answer a telephone.

Basic time + relaxation allowances + contingency allowances = standard time, but standard time may not necessarily be the target time for bonus purposes. Two further additions may be made:

A *policy allowance* may be added to provide, as the BSI booklet puts it, 'a satisfactory level of earnings for a specified level of performance under exceptional circumstances'

A *bonus increment* may similarly be added 'as a basis for an incentive scheme'.

Local government schemes which keep strictly to the Code will be based on standard times and not on 'allowed times' (standard times plus policy allowances or bonus increments), though provision is made in the Code for some easing of standards when new schemes are being introduced and little bonus would otherwise be earned. Having finally produced a standard or allowed time, a decision then has to be made as to the link between actual performance and actual earnings. All schemes have one common point: that standard performance results in bonus being paid of one third the basic pay rate. Put numerically, a worker working at 100 performance will be paid at 33⅓ per cent above his basic rate of pay. But a worker working at 150 performance will not necessarily earn half as much bonus again, nor need a worker working at 75 performance necessarily earn no bonus. Those would be the results of a 'directly proportional scheme', but the Code permits 'stabilized schemes' where conventional direct-proportion schemes are inappropriate and points out that 'it may be necessary in the interests of quality, safety and general welfare of employees, and to prevent damage to plant and equipment' that there should be a limitation of bonus earnings. The picture conjured up is one of workers motivated to such a degree by the carrot of massive bonus earnings that life and limb are endangered, and machines and equipment run into the ground. More normally, however, schemes in which bonus earnings are tapered down as production rises are justified on such grounds as the increase in production being a function of factors other than direct worker performance (such as a reduction in contingency delays caused by better managerial control), or of originally loose ratings.

A stabilized scheme, not infrequent in local government, is one in which, to quote the BSI definition, 'the rate of change of bonus is constant and the bonus follows a straight line which, if extended below the bonus starting performance, would give some pay at zero performance'. Bonus starting performance is merely the point at which bonus begins – normally a 75 performance. A stabilized scheme, in other words, is one in which bonus earnings are not directly proportional to performance and in which proportionately more bonus is earned at lower than higher levels of performance. The arguments for stabilized schemes are that they provide more incentive for workers to get into the bonus area of performance from lower levels, and they prevent too massive a difference in bonus earnings between higher and lower performers.

So far, we have talked of bonus schemes as though they applied to individuals and thus provided each worker with the possibility of earning more (or less) than his mates. The Code recognizes that individual schemes are not always practicable. While it considers the most satisfactory scheme as one in which the earnings potential of each worker is directly related to his own individual efforts, it says that the number of occasions where this is practicable or economic is very limited and that most schemes therefore have to be of a group or team nature. The difference can be seen by taking, as examples, a maintenance fitter and a team of 10 refuse incinerator operatives. The fitter's work can be measured and recorded individually. Each of his jobs or tasks can be separately timed and given its own standard time. He can book on and off each job using a time-recorded job ticket and his weekly 'clock hours' (the hours he actually works) can be set against the total time value of the jobs he completes, to assess his performance for bonus purposes (eg if he does 44 standard hours-worth of work in 40 actual hours then his performance is 110). How much work he does will depend almost totally on his own individual efforts.

For the 10 men in the refuse incinerator plant, the situation is very different. Each man depends on the next and it is *team* performance which must be measured. The crane operator, for example, who is loading rubbish into a hopper cannot operate at a faster rate than the hopper-operator, who in turn is governed by the speed of operation of a conveyor belt which may be governed primarily by the speed of two sorters alongside the belt. The bonus target for this plant may thus have to be expressed as X standard man-hours to produce a throughput of Y tons per week. *Plant* standard performance will be Y tons per week which for a designated number of attendance hours will give 100 performance (and 33⅓ per cent bonus) to all operatives. For the same tonnage, operative performance may increase if, because of sickness absence for example, the plant target output is achieved by fewer men. This example highlights the important link between work study and the determination of manning levels. In many local government bonus schemes, the justification for bonus earnings stems from a reduction in manning levels rather than from an increase in gross output. The refuse incinerator plant, for example, may never be able to exceed 500 tons weekly because that is the maximum deliverable input. Bonus is earned by a re-design of methods and a setting of manning levels at which operative performance has to be at 100 in order to produce the required weekly plant output. Most work study officer can quote studies of group jobs in which performance was as low as 30 to 50, not because each man individually was choosing to be idle, but because the operation was over-manned and work was not available to keep everyone productively busy.

The bane of both work study officers' and of bonused workers' lives is 'unmeasured', or non-bonusable, work and lost time. If 100 per cent of a man's weekly work is covered by standard times, he can potentially earn bonus for every minute of his working time. But unplanned interruptions will occur such as major machine breakdowns and other accidents. Additionally, unplanned and unmeasured extra work may have to be done from time to time. The Code sets out in some detail how such time is to be treated. It says that unmeasured work and lost time should be kept to a minimum. Lost time is defined as a period when the man or team is prevented from working for a period of 10 minutes or more, and bonus is not paid for lost time. Unmeasured work is described as work for which no targets have been set. No bonus is to be paid for the first six hours of unmeasured work in a week but, beyond that limit, time spent working on un-targeted work is to be paid at the average rate of bonus achieved on measured work. There is one further complication. If the unmeasured work is considered inappropriate for measurement because of its infrequency or variability, it may all be paid at average bonus rates.

The administrative arrangements for bonus payments are also outlined in the Code. Each employee or team leader is required to complete and sign a worksheet in sufficient detail to enable bonus to be accurately calculated. The times of starting and finishing unmeasured work and lost time must be shown. Details on the worksheet must be countersigned by a supervisor. Bonus may be calculated daily or weekly, and paid weekly, normally one or two weeks in arrears.

145

The employer is free to investigate possible improvements in methods, equipment and so on, and bonus targets can be altered at the request of either side – after consultation – where there have been changes in methods, degree of specialization, materials, equipment or working conditions; or where there has been an error or miscalculation in producing the targets. Bonus is not payable for substandard or faulty work.

The Code is particularly detailed about consultation with, and the participation of, trade unions and employees in the introduction of bonus schemes. Local authorities are asked to appoint local joint pay and productivity committees to consider opportunities for effecting savings through changes in working methods and ways and means of so doing which also increase earnings and opportunities.

Beyond this formal forum, the Code states that the employees involved in any new scheme, with their trade unions, should be invited to join the initial investigating team. It urges that such employee representatives should be given work study training. From an initial feasibility survey, it should be possible to discuss with the employees and the trade unions the benefits both sides might expect and the terms of reference for a thorough investigation.

Where an incentive scheme is being introduced, its conditions should be discussed and set out in a written work specification, in two parts:

Part 1 will set out the general conditions applying to all the authority's schemes, such as:
relationship of pay to performance
methods of work recording
lost time and unmeasured work provisions
procedure for revising targets and other matters of general principle.
Part 2 will be specific to the particular scheme and will detail:
range and methods of work, materials and equipment
rate of bonus
example of bonus calculations
any special conditions about quality and other matters specific to the particular scheme.

All schemes should include in Part I a statement about possible redundancy – normally a guarantee that, if a reduction in manning levels occurs, any surplus labour will be found comparable alternative work and that no enforced redundancy will occur. (Voluntary redundancy has been a feature of some schemes).

Taken together, the Code, the use of BSI quality work study, and the emphasis on joint employer/trade union/employee consultation and participation, constitute one of the most extensive and successful uses of work-studied bonus schemes in the British economy. With some 70 per cent of manual workers now on bonus schemes, the extent of manpower savings must be considerable, while the resultant higher earnings have gone a long way to eliminating the unsatisfactory traditions of low pay in local government service. But complacency about this situation would be a mistake, and the personnel officer in particular should be ready to examine the developing position most critically. There are five particular aspects which merit this critical discussion.

First, the acceptance of changes in work methods by workers already on bonus schemes is much more difficult to obtain than it is from lower paid, non-bonused workers. For the latter, the carrot of a potential one-third increase in earnings has often been sufficient to induce acceptance of new work methods and reduced manning levels. What incentive can be provided for the workers now earning good bonuses to change their methods as new equipment and new techniques are evolved? The ratio of bonus earnings to basic rates cannot be continuously increased. Bonus schemes condition work people to expect that their acceptance of change carries a price-tag. It reduces the workplace to a work market. With bonus schemes and bonus earnings as a normal feature of work, employers will need in the future to pay more attention to other motivators than money.

Secondly, the wider bonus schemes are applied, the less acceptable will become the existence of un-bonused work. Yet there are types of work which are almost impossible to bonus effectively. Non-repetitive building construction work, with its unstandardized working conditions and the varying effects of the weather is a notoriously difficult example. There is a high degree, too, of artificiality about bonusing some highly mechanized or automated processes such as the really large-scale, modern refuse disposal plants. Here, the number of men is determined primarily by plant design factors and output is basically machine-paced rather than determined by the efforts of the operatives. If work of these kinds is left un-bonused, the workers will feel a strong sense of grievance in being left so far behind in the earnings league table for reasons totally outside their control. If lieu bonuses are paid, or any other more subtle but still artificial form of bonusing introduced, the acceptability of 'genuine' effort-related schemes will become suspect.

Thirdly, difficulties will always arise if conditions beyond the control of management or workers lead to big fluctuations in earnings. A relatively stable and predictable level of weekly take-home pay is essential to most people's personal and domestic budgeting. Without it financial insecurity and uncertainty arise with predictably adverse effects on worker morale and attitudes. Several types of local government work – particularly road surfacing and playing field maintenanace – are both seasonal, and, during the season, significantly

147

affected by the weather. Road maintenance workers who have been averaging a steady £12 per week bonus during the spring on culvert cleaning cannot be expected to take kindly to a drop to £3 or even zero during the first few weeks of the summer's road surfacing programme if this is hit by a spell of unusually wet weather. Grass-cutting gangs on high bonus during the summer will react strongly against the reduction in earnings resulting from their reversion to a higher proportion of unmeasured work in the winter.

Fourthly, convential bonus schemes are potent sources of labour disputes. In assessing the cost benefits and savings of a scheme it is rare for any calculation to be made about the off-setting costs of these disputes. Yet too often for comfort, the introduction or modification of a bonus scheme (the only justification for which is to achieve improvements in productivity) results in the opposite: a go-slow, overtime ban or a complete stoppage with all the disruption and expense that this entails. Indirect and unmeasurable costs can occur too, in terms of a deteriorating relationship between supervisors and work people. It would be misleading and idealistic to claim that most work people and most trade unions are enthusiastic about work-studied bonus schemes. Their wide acceptance is indicative more of a pragmatic approach to wage bargaining than it is of any more fundamental belief in the virtues of work measurement. Bonus schemes are seen as almost the sole method of boosting national basic wage rates on a local basis and are often accepted on this basis alone, leaving an underlying resentment about the mechanistic philosophy of labour relations which the whole system implies.

Fifthly and finally, there is this question of employment philosophy. The work study approach derives directly from the work of that pioneer of 'scientific management', the American production engineer of the early 1900s, F W Taylor. Taylor believed in work specialization – breaking jobs down into simple, repetitive tasks – and in standardization of work methods. He considered that the planning of a job was most effectively done if separated from the actual doing of the job. He saw inefficiency in terms of unnecessary physical movements, of avoidable non-productive time, of variety in working methods and in the physical environment. His solution was to reduce the degree of control a worker had over his job, by method study and job planning: and to reduce the complexity of work by increased specialization. Above all, he believed in money as the key motivator. His machine-like model of the working man leads to a philosophy of labour management which assumes that maximum productivity is achievable when the following conditions are set:

that work is pre-planned as to method and sequence
that work is sub-divided into simple repetitive elements

that men are matched to work (not the reverse) by careful physical and psychological selection

that workers are provided with a non-distractive environment which encourages them to concentrate on their work

that they are fuelled, as it were, with the motivational agent of money to work at the maximum sustainable rate.

This 'hard', mechanistic view is not, of course, what has been in the minds of the employers or trade unions when the national agreements and Code on bonus schemes were produced. Economically, the virtues of high productivity and high earnings are not ignoble objectives; psychologically, the 'soft' view of incentive payments as a carrot to induce voluntary co-operation has seemed a better alternative than the use of the authoritarian stick. Yet even this point can be questioned. It is patently not possible for any worker continually to increase his bonus earnings. There comes a point where he reaches a certain sustainable pace of work at which the inducement of higher earnings is exactly counterbalanced by the unwillingness or inability to expend more effort. This sustainable pace provides him with a regular earnings level. At this point, the bonus scheme changes from offering carrots for more work to beating him with the stick of reduced earnings if he allows his rate of working to fall. The hard fact is that financial incentives coerce as much as they emancipate, generate tensions in the workplace, and give emphasis to the social division between management and men. There are two particular aspects to this social divisiveness. First, there is the situation in which one group of people (the work study specialists and the management generally) decide on job layout, procedures and methods; and another group of people (the manual workers) have to work within these detailed prescriptions. The quite unconscious philosophy behind this situation is that the second group is unable or unwilling to decide its own best systems of work. Secondly, in local government particularly, financial incentives are applied only to manual workers, never to managers. How many local government managers would consider it an insult to be told that, given a suitable financial inducement linked to someone else's scientific assessment of their working methods they could work 33⅓ per cent more productively? Yet that, again, is the unstated philosophy behind conventional work-studied bonus schemes. Managers and manual workers are not different sorts of human beings with different motivations and responses. Some less imaginative managers, who feel that only by using bonus schemes can acceptable output levels be maintained, would learn much from being subjected to the same constraints as their bonused men.

It would be wrong to leave this discussion with the impression that management services experts are not aware of the shortcomings of conventional bonus schemes and of the need for continual adaptation. Management services officers have kept abreast of industrial bonusing developments in which there has been a growth in the use of 'measured day work'; and a number of authorities have modified their earlier schemes to provide the stability of weekly earnings which this type of system offers. Under this system, earnings are guaranteed at a fixed bonus-type level provided a *general* standard of output is maintained over a reasonable period of time. Variations of the system involve the normal weekly meaurement of output, but the calculation of bonus on some form of running average over a period of, say, 12 weeks, thus smoothing out the peaks and troughs in earnings levels which a shorter time base gives rise to. There is nothing in the Code of Practice to prevent schemes of this type being introduced, and they go a long way to eliminating many of the irritations of the directly proportional schemes with their high degree of actual or potential variability in earnings, week by week.

In industry the period from 1977 has been marked by a sudden proliferation of 'self-financing' productivity schemes of a very different type to either conventional work-studied or measured day work schemes. This development has been caused almost entirely by the shape of government pay policy which imposed the self-financing concept in order to prevent bogus schemes being used solely as a means of breaking the basic pay constraints.

Many of these new industrial schemes have had three particular features. First, they are based on the assessment of *company* performance, rather than individual performance. Bonuses accrue from such factors as improvement in profits, sales turnover or 'value-added' during the manufacturing process. Secondly, the resultant bonuses are being paid to all employees, not merely to manual workers. Thirdly, the self-financing requirements are being met either by improved profitability or by reductions in the labour force, or both. There are several reasons why such schemes have not been introduced by local authorities. Obviously, factors such as profit ratios and sales turnover have no direct relevance to local government work. A local authority is not generally marketing its services to a potentially larger public than it currently serves and cannot therefore expand its activities in the market sense. It may, of course, be able to produce savings by maintaining the same level of service with fewer staff – by cutting jobs – and many bonus schemes have involved such savings. But as a matter of economic and employment policy, the local government trade unions are very much opposed to job losses, NUPE in particular resisting such economies fiercely at both national and local level. The likelihood of obtaining union acceptance of new bonus schemes based almost solely on job-cutting has become increasingly weaker as national unemployment figures have risen.

Beyond this, local government employers have adhered more strictly to government pay criteria than the private sector – partly by choice, partly because of direct government pressure. There have been strong suspicions that many industrial schemes are less self-financing than they may appear; that despite the Government's attempt to prevent bogus bonus payments, a number of companies have been less scrupulous in designing new bonus schemes than local authorities. Schemes under which bonuses of several pounds per week are paid if the employee is not late or absent might be thought to fall into this category.

At the same time, the concept of organization-wide incentives, paid to all employees against broad indicators of organizational performance is not one which local government should ignore. It is one significant means of securing a common identity of interest among otherwise disparate groups of employees, and of generating interest and involvement in the more efficient performance of the organization as a whole. No local authority schemes of this type are known, but the possibility of at least department-wide schemes has entered some personnel officers' minds.

Beyond this, it is very much for personnel officers to keep abreast of experiments and developments elsewhere in non-financial motivation. Building more variety into jobs (instead of specialization); giving teams of workers the freedom to plan their own work and allocate tasks within the group as they will; reducing the weight of supervision and putting responsibility for public contacts, for quality and for cost savings in the hands of the 'front-line' operator – all these are examples of a current move away from the mechanistic view of man-at-work to a more dynamic, human philosophy which may (though this yet has to be proved) result in a more completely effective system of work than F W Taylor ever imagined. In such a system, the work study officer's skills and techniques would not be redundant. But he would be less of a prescriber, more of an adviser; and an adviser, too, as much to the men as to management.

10 The NJC's scheme of job evaluation

The model scheme for job evaluation, produced by the NJC for white-collar staff, has been a more recent development than the Code for bonus schemes. One of the factors leading to its production was the 1974 local government reorganization in which it was realized that the formation of completely new authorities might well lead to problems in achieving consistent and acceptable gradings for new, and larger, groups of staff.

The Scheme with its Code of Guiding Principles, defines job evaluation, following a BSI definition, as a method of determining the relative value of jobs; and the purpose of its use in local government is that of job grading. It is concerned with jobs, not with job-holders; and with a qualitative assessment of the different nature of different jobs. It is not related to productivity negotiation and, unlike work-studied bonus schemes, is not a means of providing higher earnings for higher output. Its purpose is to provide as objective a means as possible of allocating jobs to grades – a consistent system of ranking each job against the others.

The need for a rational system of job grading arises from the complexity of the salary and grading structure for APT and C and miscellaneous staffs, and the multiplicity of jobs and occupations which are involved in the white-collar field. Employees judge the equity of a salary system mainly by comparing their salaries with those for other jobs, rather than by any absolute test of salary adequacy. Job evaluation provides a systematic method for determining salary comparisons and relationships.

The Scheme suggests that the use of a job evaluation system brings five benefits:

A clarification of the content and requirements of each job
An assurance to staff that the monetary values of their jobs have
    been determined by the use of a disinterested and objective

assessment of these jobs relative to each other, rather than by
traditional, subjective means

An avoidance of the danger of posts being wrongly valued because
of subjective attention being given more to the qualities of the job
holder than to the job

A likelihood of a greater degree of consistency between different
authorities employing similar types of staff

An aid to the identification of overlapping functions and organizational defects.

Two types of benefit emerge from this analysis. First, the improvements in job definition and in job systems which can result from the
preliminary task of producing detailed and accurate job descriptions.
Secondly, the improvements in staff relations resulting from an equit-
able salary system.

The Scheme recommends that, wherever practicable, job evaluation should be preceded by a review of organization and methods, and
to this extent follows the same principles as for bonus schemes – in
which method study is an almost essential prerequisite. An O and M
study is, however, less essential to job evaluation as the evaluation
process itself involves a very thorough analysis of each job, an analysis
which can be used to identify weaknesses in the definition of responsibilities and in the organizational relationships of jobs.

The Scheme gives three further points of principle which have been
endorsed by the NJC:

That the use of private consultants to undertake job evaluation is
not recommended

That if authorities wish to use job evaluation they should follow the
Code of Guiding Principles laid down in the Scheme

That an authority without management services staff or a specific
personnel function would not normally be able to introduce job
evaluation but should ask the joint secretaries of their provincial
council for assistance. (The implication is that other authorities
might be able to provide the necessary specialist staff).

The Code of Guiding Principles

The Code of Guiding Principles sets out the recommended system in
detail. This system was produced by LAMSAC (Local Authorities'
Management Services and Computer Committee) and applies to
authorities outside London. London boroughs (but not the GLC)
operate a similar but not identical system produced before the
national scheme by the LBMSU (London Boroughs Management
Services Unit).

The Code recognizes that in introducing and maintaining any
scheme there must be the fullest consultation with staff and union

representatives. Staff representatives should be fully informed about the whole scheme and there should be safeguards, too, for individual staff who may, as a result of job evaluation, be in posts found to be over graded, that is, posts which already carry a higher grade than that resulting from the application of the evaluation system.

The system of job evaluation in the Code requires two types or groups of staff for its operation: job analysts and members of evaluation panels. Job analysts should be staff with a personnel and/or O and M background. Their task is to produce job descriptions. Members of evaluation panels should be senior officers and the Code suggests that the optimum number per panel is four; the personnel officer or chief executive, 'a chief officer selected on a consensus basis', a management services or personnel officer, and another senior officer. The Code suggests that 'a knowledgeable officer normally senior to the post-holder's immediate supervisor' might attend to answer factual questions but not to participate in the evaluation. The whole emphasis is on impartiality and an avoidance of the bias that might result from too close a contact between members of the panel and the job (or job-holder) under evaluation.

The procedure suggested in the Code assumes that an authority is introducing job evaluation and wishes to review, and if necessary regrade, all its posts. The following procedure is then to be followed:

1 A programme of work should be drawn up and agreed with the staff representatives
2 Meetings should be convened with all the staff to explain the purpose and procedures of the exercise
3 Agreement should be reached as to which posts to include; and to evaluate only single, typical jobs where numbers of staff undertake identical or essentially similar work (eg only one of a group of twenty rent collectors' posts may need to be evaluated to determine the grading for the whole group)
4 Each job-holder whose post is to be evaluated completes a job questionnaire. The job questionnaire establishes the facts about the tasks undertaken, responsibilities, supervision given and supervision received, type and degree of contacts between the job-holder and other staff
5 The completed questionnaire is checked and agreed by the post-holder's immediate supervisor
6 A job analyst then interviews the post-holder, using the completed questionnaire as a basis for the interview. This is intended to be an extremely thorough discussion of the whole nature of the job
7 The job analyst then interviews the job-holder's supervisor to clear up any points of doubt arising from the first interview
8 The job analyst then completes a detailed job description to a standard format which lists the job's purpose, its major tasks and

various working activities, and the standards of performance required. It goes on to analyse and describe the job under nine headings, or 'factors':

Supervisory and managerial responsibility
Decisions made
Supervision received
Work complexity
Special conditions
Contacts
Creative work
Education
Experience

9 Following vetting for clarity and completeness by the job analyst's supervisor, the job description is then agreed with the post-holder and his supervisor, and signed by both as an accurate and full description
10 The evaluation panel, either individually or jointly, then considers the job description and allocates a 'points score' for each of the factors listed in Stage 8 above.

The Code suggests that it is better for panels to discuss their initial ideas, and reach a consensus on each factor, than to average individual and differing scores.

The Code provides a scoring matrix giving a range of scores for each factor, with accompanying notes for the guidance of the evaluation panels in scoring each factor.

The evaluation panel's work is completed when a total points score is produced for each job.

The points scoring system
The scoring matrix, which the evaluation panel uses to allocate points to each factor is set out below:

Factors	Levels								
	1	2	3	4	5	6	7	8	9
Supervisory responsibility	16	24	32	40	48	56	64	72	80
Decisions	20	30	40	50	60	70	80	90	100
Supervision received	12	18	25	31	37	43	50	—	—
Work compexity	20	30	40	50	60	70	80	—	—
Special conditions	20	—	—	—	—	—	—	—	—
Contacts	10	20	30	40	50	60	70	80	—
Creative work	10	20	30	40	50	60	70	80	—
Education	10	20	30	45	55	85	105	115	125
Experience	20	40	60	80	100	120	140	150	160

It will be noted that each factor is subdivided into up to nine levels, and that each level carries a designated points score. The panel therefore first decides what level of each factor is appropriate: the points can then be read off the table, the total score for each job being the sum of the scores for each factor.

It will also be noted that the factors carry different points values; that is, some factors are 'weighted' higher than others, the three main factors being education, experience and decisions.

Guidance notes are provided to help panels achieve a consistent approach to the allocation of points. These notes define both the factors and the levels. The nine factors are described thus:

Supervisory and managerial responsibility

This factor deals with the number and type of staff for whose work the post-holder is responsible or accountable. Control of staff and management of their work is also relevant.

Decisions made

This factor deals with the responsibility of the post-holder for taking decisions during the course of his duties. Decisions to recommend a course of action are included. The extent of the effect of a decision becomes progressively relevant in making assessments beyond Level 4.

Supervision received

There are three aspects of supervision which should be considered. These are controls by the supervisor (who is anyone with sanctioned authority to give the post-holder instructions about his work), control built in to the system and advice and guidance.

Work complexity

This factor deals with the complexity of the work dealt with by the post-holder and includes consideration of the diversity of tasks and functions, the skills required and the pressures involved.

Special conditions

This factor is designed for minority application. It recognizes features of jobs involving specific personal hazard or permanent conditions of work of an abnormal character which on balance render it significantly less attractive than work in average non-manual conditions.

Contacts

This factor appraises the degree *and purpose* of personal contacts made by the post-holder during the course of his work. Contacts can involve simple fact finding, furnishing of information, or the collection of money etc but may, at the higher levels, include negotiations with outside bodies and the reaching of agreements on behalf of the Authority.

Creative work

This factor deals with the work content of the post from a creative point of view. Some posts have a responsibility for creating by the use of words whilst others create by plans, drawings or by casework. It is important to distinguish between the element of creativity in a decision area and the decision itself. Decision making relates to the choice of action whereas creativity is the force of imagination required to translate the objective into effective action.

Education

This factor looks at education in its broadest sense and defines the level of work allotted to a post in relation to the appropriate educational qualifications required by the post-holder.

Experience

This factor deals with the minimum period of experience which the average post-holder would require for the post in addition to the educational requirement inferred from the education element.

As an example of the definition of levels, the experience factor, which carries the highest points values, is subdivided thus:

Level 1 Under one months' experience
Level 2 One month and under three months' experience
Level 3 Three months and under six months' experience
Level 4 Six month's and under 12 months' experience
Level 5 One year and under two years' experience
Level 6 Two years and under three years' experience
Level 7 Three years and under five years' experience
Level 8 Five years and under 10 years' experience
Level 9 10 years and over.

More complex definitions are given for some factor levels: for example, Level 6 of supervision received, is defined as:

Carries out high level work within established policy. The post-holder has a particular major function delegated to him and therefore organizes his own workload, contacting his supervisor only to notify progress or to seek specialist advice on an unusual project.

Supervisory and management responsibility is scored according to the number of staff the post-holder supervises or is accountable for. This is not done simply by totalling the actual number of staff but is defined in terms of the number of 'staff units'.

One manual post is equivalent to 1½ 'staff units'
One clerical post is equivalent to three 'staff units'

One administrative or technical post is equivalent to seven 'staff units'

One professional post is equivalent to 12 'staff units'.

Supervision of one to 10 staff units rates Level 3 and over 400 scores the maximum Level 9.

Points and gradings

Using the scoring matrix and the level definitions to produce a total score for each job is not the end of the procedure. Total scores then have to be translated into grades. The Code does not provide any standard tables for relating total scores to the various national APT and C grades but does suggest a procedure for individual authorities to follow in producing such a table:

(i) A small committee of officers should identify a proportion (say 5 per cent) of all the posts evaluated and covering a broad spectrum by function and grade, which can be regarded as already correctly graded. This is necessarily mainly a subjective exercise, hence the need for a consensus view by officers well acquainted with the total work situation. It is important to select these 'benchmarks' in consultation with staff representatives to ensure local acceptability.

(ii) When these posts have been selected they are plotted against two axes, one being total points awarded and the other existing grades.

(iii) A line of best fit for the scatter of locations on the graph is then drawn. The points total awarded to each of the remaining majority of evaluated posts relative to this line will enable the appropriate grade to be read off from the other axis.

(iv) Authorities may find it necessary in exceptional circumstances to weight certain posts to take account of local market factors usually relating to shortages of particular skills.

In other words, a number of jobs considered typical of each grade are selected and evaluated. The point scores for each grade can then be chosen to fit round these typical or benchmark jobs. Other jobs can then be scored and graded in relation to the benchmark scores.

Although the Scheme describes a job-grading operation primarily in terms of a complete review of all jobs, the major benefit of having a job evaluation system is that it provides a permanent means of deciding the correct grading for new and revised jobs. No authority's job structure is static; departmental re-organizations change the nature of existing jobs; new policies and new statutory requirements introduce new jobs and these jobs all have to be allocated to grades. Without a job evaluation system this has to done on an *ad hoc*, comparative, basis

158

ssues Receipt
University of Plymouth Library
Date: Wednesday, October 04, 2006
Time: 2:12 PM

Item ID: 9002662533
Title: British Civil Service / Robert Pyp
Due date: 11/10/2006

Item ID: 9003583992
Title: Civil service / Keith Dowding.
Due date: 11/10/2006

Item ID: 7001317721
Title: Personnel management in local ç
Due date: 25/10/2006

Item ID: 9006939566
Title: Staff appraisal and development
Due date: 25/10/2006

Item ID: 9006345125
Title: Dynamics of employee relations ,
Due date: 11/10/2006

Item ID: 9006131978
Title: Strategic human resource manaç
Due date: 11/10/2006

Total items: 6
Please keep your receipt until you
have checked your Voyager Account

and often leads to disagreements and bargaining with the trade unions. There is a tendency, over time, for 'grade drift' to occur as staff side pressure leads to new and changed jobs being edged higher and higher in the grading hierarchy. Job evaluation can maintain consistency over time, as well as consistency between jobs in an initial comprehensive review.

A critical view of job evaluation

The very real advantages to be obtained from job evaluation should not be allowed to obscure its shortcomings. A job evaluation system of the type in the Scheme has at least four aspects which merit close attention:

It is almost wholly subjective
It has questionable internal logic
Its ultimate test is its ability to confirm existing relativities
It cannot adequately cope with changes in the salary market.

Each of these points is examined in more detail below.

Subjectivity
Sophisticated and complex job evaluation schemes, with their factors, levels, scoring matrices and points ratings, appear to offer an objective method of job assessment. To reduce a job to a number, or points value, creates an impression of statistical validity about what is, in fact, a highly subjective set of assumptions.

Consider first, the choice of factors. Why choose the particular nine in the NJC Scheme? Other schemes use quite different factors for very similar jobs. 'Responsibility' is sometimes assessed in financial terms – the value or cost of capital or revenue for which the job-holder is responsible. 'Pressure or stress' might be considered as important a factor as work complexity. Some schemes attempt to analyse and score for 'judgement'. And 'time span' – the time that elapses between a decision being made and its effectiveness or validity being checked or proved – has been claimed as sufficient alone. There are no absolutes about the choice of factors. Factors are chosen which, in practice, seem to provide sensible results and this choice is clearly subjective.

Look next at factor weightings – the relative importance given to factors in points values. In the NJC Scheme, 'Experience' can score twice as much as 'Work Complexity', and 'Supervision Received' scores half as much as the type of 'Decisions'. Where do these differences in weighting come from? Not from any independently objective 'correct' criteria but, just as with the choice of factors, from a trial and error system of obtaining acceptable results.

159

Internal logic

The more closely the detail of any job evaluation scheme is examined, the more questions arise as to its basic logic.

Consider, for example, the scoring table and Notes for Guidance for the most important factor, 'Experience'. This is defined as 'the minimum period of experience which the average post-holder would require'. It is then divided into nine Levels, ranging from under one month to 10 years or over. It might be asked whether it is possible to be at all accurate in distinguishing between a requirement for under two years and over two years, or between, say eight years and 12 years. There is no way of measuring this. Yet very significant differences in points scores result from such choices. Look more closely at the actual points values in the scoring matrix. Note that each Level from 1 to 7 is 20 points different from the next. But from points 7 to 9, the difference is only 10 points. A difference of, say eight years experience between Level 7 and 9 gives an extra 20 points; while a difference of three years between Level 4 and Level 7 gives an extra 60 points. There is no hard logic in this.

Look, too, at the definition of staff units quoted a page or two back, and relate this to points scores. Supervision of a manual worker rates 1½ units, of a professional employee 12 units. The logic of this would be an assumption either that it is eight times more difficult to supervise a professional than manual worker, or eight times more important. Even supervision of a routine clerical job carries twice as much weight as supervision of a skilled craftsman. The results of this in points scores are obviously significant. To score a highish level 64 points, the supervisor of professional posts need have only nine subordinates, the clerical supervisor 34, and the manual supervisor 68. These points differences do not really reflect the realities of supervision.

The more closely the details are examined, the clearer it also becomes that a great deal of 'double-counting' is involved. The factors interact and overlap and what is being evaluated is not nine distinct job attributes, but a whole series of related phenomena. The Experience factor in particular, almost wholly overlaps at least five others. Jobs which are complex, carry extensive supervisory responsibility, involve a high level of creative work and demand a high education level, all result in lengthy experience being necessary.

Indeed, it might well be that the use of the experience factor alone would suffice to place jobs in an acceptable ranking order. The suspicion arises that the complexity of the scheme is necessary, not for logical reasons or to establish the cold facts about jobs, but to ensure its acceptability as an apparently sophisticated and therefore reliable system.

160

Acceptability
Ultimately, the test of the system is its acceptance by the employees
whose jobs it evaluates and by their managers. A scheme, however
apparently logical, which resulted in wholesale changes in existing job
relativities would be considered unsatisfactory by managers and staff.
The test is thus the extent to which it produces results generally
consistent with currently established ideas about relative job values.
As the Notes for Guidance put it when describing how to relate points
to grades, it must be constructed to fit a framework of jobs 'which can
be regarded as already correctly graded'. Proponents of national
schemes of job evaluation to resolve problems of wage relationships
between different groups of workers overlook the fact that a scheme
which, for example, placed mineworkers below deep sea fishermen,
or agricultural workers above car assembly operatives, would be
inoperable. The same position exists within any one employment
sector. The NJC Scheme rates the supervision of professional posts
higher than that of administrative, and clerical higher than manual,
not because this is 'right', or can be established by any strictly logical
data, but because it has to be in order to produce acceptable results.
And acceptability means an acceptance or confirmation of the grading
standards and differences which existed before the introduction of the
scheme.

Market influences
A less philosophical objection to job evaluation derives from its inability to cope directly with changes in the job or salary market. A growth
in demand for taxation accountants in the economy at large will lead to
a rise in their salaries relative to other job groups. A job evaluation
system, having to confirm job values which existed when the scheme
was designed, will start giving the 'wrong' answers for taxation
accountants when external job values change in this way.

The Code suggests that this can be handled by a conscious weighting of such posts and says that 'an addition on these grounds to the
evaluated salary should be clearly recorded so that these factors can be
reviewed at a later stage'. In time, many jobs would acquire such
special weighting because the job market is in continual flux. The
Code's advice is sound in the short term as there is no alternative,
when job evaluation comes up with too low a salary or grade, but to
pay what the market necessitates and to record this. But on a longer
term basis either the scheme will need a thorough re-weighting and
re-scoring so that it catches up with changes in accepted job
relativities; or a greater emphasis in salary determination needs to be
given to effective pay research into market levels and changes.

Criticism of the kind discussed in the preceding paragraphs might be
taken as indicating that this author has no time for job evaluation.

This is not the case. His objections are to claims that job evaluation is an objective or scientific technique. There is only one test for any job evaluation system – does it work? If a scheme helps an employer to allocate jobs to grades in a consistent and orderly manner, with results satisfactory to management, trade unions and staff, then the mechanics and logic of the scheme are almost wholly irrelevant. Any scheme which inhibits undesirable grade drift, which significantly reduces employer/employee conflict about grading matters and which provides an agreed and orderly method of resolving such differences as do arise, is worth its salt. So the main question to be raised about the NJC Scheme is whether it is as important as the Scheme avers for all authorities to use this system and this alone. The London boroughs have used a different scheme with equal satisfaction. Other large employers of white collar staff use very different but still satisfactory schemes. A professionally trained and experienced personnel officer should be capable of designing a tailor-made scheme to meet the particular needs of his own authority and such a scheme may include neither factor levels, scoring matrices nor job analysis. But the NJC Scheme has the merit of being formally approved by the national staff side, and if it can gain local acceptance, is clearly to be recommended. It may also help to create common grading standards between authorities.

In recent years, the likelihood of the universal adoption of the NJC scheme seems to have become much weaker than was envisaged on its introduction. The number of authorities introducing it on a complete basis, agreed with their local NALGO branches, have been relatively few, while some authorities who do use the scheme have run into some of the difficulties outlined earlier in this chapter. On the other hand, the pressure at local level to review and revise individual job gradings has grown, partly as a response to the restrictions of pay policy on any systematic restructuring of salary systems. NALGO's approach to job grading has also been equivocal. On the one hand the union has supported the NJC job evaluation scheme in principle, and does expect grading decisions to be made rationally and equitably. On the other hand NALGO has progressively turned away from national grading prescriptions (and so, national consistency) and supported the freedom of local branches to bargain for the best grading they can get – a recipe for inequitable variations between authorities. The 1978 NALGO campaign to take social workers and environmental health officer gradings out of the purple book and so leave the field free for local bargaining exemplifies this approach. Perhaps the view has been that strong local branches can become wage improvement leaders by achieving high grading levels on which weaker branches, with national NALGO backing, can then base comparative argu-ments for similar improvements. NALGO has also displayed some interest in using the provisions of Schedule 11 of the Employment Protection Act to achieve pay parity between authorities for similar jobs. This Schedule provided for contractually enforceable Central Arbitration Committee awards to bring pay levels for specified jobs for a particular employer up to the general level for such work in the trade or industry – provided the levels complained of are not determined by collective agreements (see chapter 15 for a fuller discussion of this legislation).

The hankering by trade unions to base salary and therefore grading levels almost solely on a comparative basis militates against the effective use of job evaluation. It follows instead the classic trade union ploy of pushing up wage levels in areas where market pressures or employer weakness can be exploited and then using such bridgeheads to secure a more general advance – to be followed by other local campaigns and so on and so on. Against this background, it is not surprising that a common use of the NJC job evaluation scheme is for it to be used, privately as it were, by personnel or management services sections as their professional method of reaching an employers' view of a job's grade, with NALGO being aware of this method without objection or acceptance. This approach at least partially satisfies management's need to reach grading decisions on a consistent and rational basis, while leaving the union free to campaign for a particular grading decision on any grounds it feels appropriate.

Given, then, that some form of job evaluation is a useful grading tool, whether fully agreed by the unions or used as a technique within the personnel department, it remains important to keep in mind that it is the existence of a system, rather than the system's internal logic, which really counts: and that it is the psychology of job evaluation and not its pseudo-science which justifies its use. In this author's view, job evaluation is not a management services technique in the accepted scientific sense. It should be seen as part of the personnel manager's armoury of methods for influencing attitudes and for creating an employment environment in which potentially contentious issues can be resolved in an unemotional, cooperative and systematic manner.

11 Manpower planning

General background

Manpower planning is a subject which has tended to become surrounded by somewhat abstract and academic theorizing; and to be described as an activity essentially involving advanced statistical techniques.

Management textbooks not infrequently open a discussion of manpower planning with a comment on the problem of definition. Thus:

Various attempts at defining manpower planning have not met with universal approval. Given a subject which craves the involvement of statisticians, behavioural scientists, economists and organization development specialists, it is hardly surprising that there is disagreement as to its precepts[1]

When definitions are offered, they range from very general statements such as:

a strategy for the acquisition, utilization, improvement and retention of an enterprise's human resources[2]

to narrower definitions such as:

the art of balancing an organization's demand for manpower with the supply[3]

The weakness of the wider definitions is that they seem to cover every aspect of personnel management and so do not aid either understanding or organizational decisions as to where a manpower planning function best fits *within* a personnel department.

[1] Bramham J, *Practical Manpower Planning*, IPM, 1975
[2] Department of Employment, *Company Manpower Planning*, HMSO, 1974
[3] Ray K, Northamptonshire County Council, Local Authority Manpower Planning, *Local Government Studies*, April, 1976

The disadvantage of many narrower definitions is that, by their concentration on manpower supply, they may well exclude some other objective (eg improving the quality, or reducing the cost, of manpower) which, for a particular employer, is best aided by the existence of a manpower planning function.

However, despite differences in definitions, a common core of concepts can be identified among most expositions of the subject. This envisages the existence of some form of corporate plan which defines the organization's policy objectives in operational (or 'business') terms. From this corporate plan can be identified its manpower component, representing the organization's future manpower requirement.

The manpower planning activity is then concerned with analysing and forecasting:

Manpower supply – both from its own stocks and within the general manpower market

Manpower demand – both from its own corporate plan and from forecasts of levels of general economic activity and of demographic change

The surplus or shortfall between the current manpower stock and the projected future requirement.

Planning *per se* then occurs when plans are evolved to eliminate the projected manpower surplus or shortfall. Additionally, a feedback is usually shown between the manpower plan and the corporate plan by which the latter may be revised to take account of any manpower surplus or deficiency which appears otherwise ineradicable. Manpower planning of this kind is usually described as a long-term activity, linked to a three to ten year rolling corporate plan.

From an individual local authority's viewpoint, this whole concept has certain shortcomings. Because of the disparate nature of local government services, there are very few situations in which the whole authority's workforce can be treated as a homogeneous group. Long term factors of critical importance in education will not affect the fire service; and manpower supply in the engineering field will have no impact on social services. The degree of realistic manpower detail that can be produced within any long term plan is also severely limited. Changes in central government policy and in local political control are two key influences on the range and extent of an authority's services: both make three to ten year manpower planning an exercise in which speculative rather than statistical skills are paramount. Further, the forecasting of manpower supply from the external market is notoriously difficult at local level. Broad indications can be identified nationally and these will obviously affect the local situation. But more detailed local variations are usually dependent on very unpredictable short-term changes in the local job market.

Comprehensive manpower planning across an authority's whole labour force – in the sense of detailed, statistical supply and demand forecasting – is thus rarely practicable. This should not be taken, however, as indicating that manpower planning is an unnecessary or useless activity. Manpower planning in the more academic sense outlined above certainly has a role in national economic and manpower policy formulation; while locally, manpower planning in the sense of basing manpower decisions on an analytical assessment of current facts and future trends is central to the whole personnel and management services function.

Manpower planning at national level

The assessment of trends in manpower supply and demand has become an essential and integral part of national economic management and has consequently been developed within central government as an aid to the development of national economic policies. Forecasting the national demand for, say, teachers or doctors (having made the necessary assumptions about the level of services) is somewhat easier than making similar forecasts locally. A good many national projections of this kind are based primarily on demographic projections*, and national population forecasts tend to be more accurate than those for small, local areas in which migration looms large as a potential major source of inaccuracy. At the same time, knowledge of official forecasts of these national trends is a very necessary part of local planning, and local government personnel officers would be well advised to follow the wide range of national manpower planning data produced by the Department of Employment's Unit for Manpower Studies. This is by no means the only organization working in this field nationally – the Institute for Manpower Studies is another notable body – but the publication of the Unit's studies in the Department's monthly *Employment Gazette* makes much of the academic work readily available, and these studies often draw together research from wider sources into specific and practical manpowers studies which are of direct use to the local practitioner. For example, the Unit's 1978 studies included a projection of school leavers at different ages for the period to 1981 – essential information for manpower planning within Education Departments; a study of age restrictions on entry to various occupations which might well have triggered a

---

* For example, the fall in the birthrate from 876,000 in 1964 to 569,000 in 1977 can be used to project demand for teachers through into the 1990s when secondary and further education are taken into account.

re-examination in local government of age limits for entry to administrative careers and, perhaps, to library work; forecasts of the supply of 'highly qualified manpower' of various categories – useful when considering locally the extent of graduate recruitment into social work and other local government professions; and a series of studies on the effects on unemployment and labour costs of shortening working hours, reducing overtime and lowering the national pensionable age. These latter studies should clearly influence the national negotiators in local government who have to assess the effect of growing trade union claims for a 35 hour week – as well as helping personnel officers at local level to set local decisions within national trends.

The Manpower Services Commission also treats national level manpower planning as an integral part of its work in assessing national employment trends and in 1976 published a document, *Towards a Comprehensive Manpower Policy*, setting out its views of the need for, and nature of, a co-ordinated planning approach to the national tasks of reducing unemployment and ensuring the availability of the right mix of skills and abilities within the nation's labour force. The objectives of the Commission's two operational wings – the Employment Services and Training Services Divisions – have been determined by this broad-based planning approach. The Commission and its Divisions operate within the context of five year forward programmes, and local authorities need to be aware of the Commission's plans if they are to take full advantage of the development of these national manpower agencies in forecasting, and helping to meet, local manpower needs. Local authorities have, in particular, co-operated extensively with the Manpower Services Commission in the operation of a variety of schemes to assist unemployed school leavers and the long-term adult unemployed; and these schemes should be seen as originating in a national manpower planning approach.

National manpower planning in local government

In varying ways, three national local government bodies are involved in national level manpower planning – LGTB, LACSAB and LAMSAC.

In determining its training priorities the Local Government Training Board clearly needs to make assessments of the changing and future manpower needs of local authorities generally. The Board has conducted some manpower studies of its own into the training needs – qualitative and quantitative – of specific occupational groups and over the past few years has, for example, collected a considerable volume of data in this context about the developing demand for trained personnel and training officers. The Board has not, however, attempted any comprehensive manpower supply and demand forecasting, tending in recent years to select for detailed study particular manpower issues drawn to its attention by other bodies. A 1976/77 survey of employment and training for catering staff, for example, resulted from broader action in this field by the Hotel and Catering Industry Training Board which sought LGTB's co-operation in extending their survey into local government. The survey revealed that the 363 authorities which participated, together employed over a quarter of a million catering workers – a hitherto largely neglected sector of local government manpower in terms of any positive and planned approach to training to meet future needs.

LGTB has also worked with the Central Council for Education and Training in Social Work on adapting social worker training to meet the changing demands of social work; and jointly with LACSAB carried out a major manpower study in 1977/78 of environmental health staff.

LACSAB's involvement in this joint study, which was one of the most detailed manpower research projects yet undertaken at national level in local government, illustrates how manpower planning activities affect a wide range of personnel work. At district council level, concern had been growing since 1974 about the ability of the Environmental Health Service to cope with the increasing weight of legislative measures in the consumer and public protection field. Questions arose; were there sufficient Environmental Health Officers (EHOs) of the right calibre? Were their qualifications and training appropriate to their developing role? From whence could new EHOs be recruited? Were their grades and salaries adequate to attract and retain staff of the requisite calibre?

It will be seen that questions of this kind cover training, recruitment and conditions of service; and if effective plans (ie manpower plans) were to be produced to resolve staffing difficulties, a comprehensive view was needed of all these factors. LACSAB's responsibility for pay and conditions of service, as well as their ability to collect statistical data about the numbers and grades of EHOs in employment, brought them into this manpower planning arena as well as the more obvious LGTB interest in EHO's qualifications and training.

The resultant joint study, published in 1978, raised other matters, too; particularly suggestions about the more effective use of non-professional staff in environmental health departments, and the organization structures of these departments. The whole exercise, while criticized in some quarters for being excessively detailed, does provide an interesting example of a perceived manpower problem at local level being set within a national framework of trends and corrective action, as a result of a comprehensive study being made of the facts of the existing situation, and a projection of possible future directions. In a word, practical manpower planning in action.

A more controversial aspect of LACSAB's work that can also be described as a manpower planning exercise is the Board's collection and publication of the numbers employed in local government for the Joint Manpower Watch, already referred to in chapter 1. Statistically detailed quarterly returns of manpower are made by all local authorities to LACSAB, which consolidates the figures to give a detailed breakdown of the national local government labour force (in England and Wales). This analysis is used by central government as a means of monitoring – and by implication restricting – the growth of public sector employment; and is a standing item on the agenda of the meetings of the Consultative Council, a central/local government body at ministerial level which was set up to improve relationships and communications between the leaders of local government (the policy makers in the Local Authority Associations) and government ministers and top civil servants. The creation of the Joint Manpower Watch itself seems to have been a reaction to growing public criticism of an alleged escalation in the numbers of 'bureaucrats', and does not appear to have been used for any very positive purpose. No doubt it is wholly necessary and justifiable for the size of the total local government labour force to be measured and monitored. But whether the mass of detailed statistics is worth the administrative effort of collection and collation has been a question asked forcibly by local authority chief executives and their council leaders. Indeed a few councils, noting that there is no statutory requirement to complete the statistical returns, have unilaterally decided not to do so.

Aware of the criticism from local authorities that manpower information is being collected by LACSAB which gives no benefit at local level, LACSAB have experimented with the issue of feedback returns, based on Joint Manpower Watch data, in forms which it is hoped could prove useful for local manpower planning purposes. For APT and C staff, an additional (and optional) return has been included with the general Manpower Watch returns for this specific purpose. It provides a good deal of detail about the distribution of staff between and within the various APT and C salary grades and can be used by an individual authority to compare its grading distribution with those of other similar authorities. One 1977 return showed, for example, variations in the proportion of clerical staff employed in Education Departments (within the whole range of APT and C grades) of from 69 per cent to 84 per cent: and the proportion of officers at Principal Officer Grade 1 and above in non-metropolitan county authorities as a whole varying from about 2.5 per cent to over 4 per cent. Local study of figures of this kind might lead to reassessments of the ways in which clerical staff are used, or in the shape of management hierarchies. More frequent reactions, however, tend to be either that comparisons are meaningless because each local authority is unique; or that whatever position one's own authority is shown to occupy in any comparative table is the right one. High-graded authorities tend to argue that this shows that they set out to attract and retain the highest calibre of staff. Low-graded authorities argue that they are demonstrably more responsible in their attitude towards the expenditure of public monies.

Some of LACSAB's work in this field has consequently been subject to the criticism that statistics are being produced first, and the indentification of issues which the statistics might serve then follows. Effective manpower planning works the other way round: a problem or issue is identified and the figures are then produced to aid the production of the necessary action plans.

There is one major area, however, the very mainstream of LACSAB's primary role, in which statistical analysis has become increasingly necessary, to an increasingly sophisticated degree. This is the assessment of wage movements and possible alternative formulae in national wage settlements. Relatively minor changes in pay and conditions can generate extremely large expenditure for local government's massive labour force. It is essential in national wage bargaining to know the relative importance of different items in a pay settlement. How much, for example, would it cost to remove the bar point in the Clerical 1 scale? What would be the cost of an addition of one increment to the Technical 5 scale? To what extent are the earnings of skilled craftsmen on bonus overtaking unbonused supervisory salaries? A multiplicity of issues of this kind arise in every annual pay negotiation. To identify the most cost-effective solution and, more important, to develop any sort of long term incomes strategy, requires as an essential feature the availability of accurate and up to date information on current earnings levels, the distribution of employees in and between grades and data on turnover and recruitment. LACSAB's growing work in this field should not be seen by individual local authorities as the unnecessary or over-centralized collection of superfluous information, but as an extremely important element in maintaining effective control of the national wages systems.

Manpower planning at local authority level

A starting point for consideration of manpower planning within a local authority is to set aside for the time being the concept of manpower planning as some form of specialized function, and to consider instead the extent to which most ordinary, week-to-week decisons about manpower are, in effect, manpower plans. Looked at in this way all the following can be described as constituting or involving such plans:

a decision to hold the authority's total manpower at its existing levels for the next budget year a decision to reduce the number of APT and C staff by 10 per cent, without enforced redundancies, by a certain date

a decision to introduce a career grade system for social workers in order to reduce staff losses and aid recruitment

a decision to make more effective use of non-professional staff in the environmental health service

a decision to increase the number of road maintenance staff in order to achieve improvements in road standards

a decision to apply more liberally the 'interests of efficiency' early retirement provisions among teachers in order to encourage the departure of dead or dying wood

an objective of achieving 'flatter' organizational hierarchies when management structure reviews are undertaken.

The list is almost literally endless. Each department individually and the authority collectively is involved continuously in decisions which change the constitution and/or volume of manpower – either generally, or more usually in specific organizational or occupational groups. And almost all these decisions involve a view being taken of the future, and (whether formally defined or not) some forward objective as being the reason for current action.

Manpower planning, therefore, does not exist only when a specialist unit with that title is established. The real question is not whether such a unit is necessary, but whether the quality of managerial decisions about manpower objectives can be raised by the application of more systematic and analytical methods. And if so, what are the essential features of these methods? Is their application aided by the provision of a specialist manpower planning function? And where, organizationally, might this function best be placed?

In broad terms, decisions in the manpower field of the kind exemplified above may be seen to have a number of common requirements if more system and analysis is to be introduced.

There should be a direct link between the manpower plan and an originating policy or operational requirement. Thus, a policy of improving road standards leads to a decision to recruit roadmen; and a largely political policy of holding or reducing staff numbers generates a need for a variety of specific manpower decisions about freezing vacancies or introducing voluntary retirement schemes.

For the decisions to be realistic, there is a critically important need for accurate information. Can a 10 per cent run-down in APT and C staff be achieved in nine months without enforced redundancy? Accurate labour turnover information is needed to provide an answer. How many roadmen are necessary to achieve the required improvement in road standards? Information about the ratio of units of labour to units of output is needed to answer this type of question.

171

Further, it can be seen that in many cases it is information itself about some aspect of the constitution of the labour force which triggers the action. Thus, a decision to make more effective use of non-professional staff may originate from an analysis showing an unbalanced professional/non-professional situation. And unsatisfactorily high labour turnover and vacancy statistics may lie behind the decision to institute a career grade. All such decisions require a change to be effected – often by a specified date and this requirement generates two further needs:

First, for the evolution of procedures or strategies to effect the change. Thus an early retirement scheme for teachers needs a whole framework of actions and procedures – consultation, publicity, administration etc. And a change of emphasis in the design of organizational structures is likely to require a programme of management discussions, definitions of objectives and departmental reviews and reports.

Secondly, for a monitoring process to check on progress, determine whether objectives are being met and if necessary generate corrective action – by modifying either the plan or the procedures being used to fulfill it. Monitoring essentially involves a further collection and assessment of information.

In that a whole variety of manpower plans and changes will be proceeding contemporaneously, there is a need for co-ordination – both in the decision making process itself and in monitoring. Two wholly independent policies may unwittingly become incompatible. Thus, a staff reduction exercise without redundancies may conflict with a policy of reducing the proportionate number of 'Chiefs to Indians', through the effects of higher natural wastage at the lower grade levels. And the introduction of career grading for the professionals in a particular service may depress the career prospects of the non-professionals to a degree which prejudices their more effective employment because of low morale and high turnover.

Co-ordinating manpower and other policy plans

Some of these points require more detailed discussion and the link between manpower and other policy plans merits particular attention. It may seem that a statement that many operational or policy plans and objectives have manpower implications hardly needs saying. In practice, however, this link is not always identified. For example, a number of local authorities have stated as one of their broad policy objectives, the aim of encouraging the growth of local industry and commerce – ie the promotion of a healthy local economy. In one such

172

authority, the declaration of this policy coincided with two developments in the manpower field. First, an agreement was concluded with the local trade unions to the effect that no work would be placed with contractors or consultants which could be undertaken as normal routine by direct labour. Secondly, the management services section was promoting the concept of a centralized supplies warehouse in order to achieve economies by a switch from small local purchasing contracts to bulk ordering from national suppliers. Both decisions militated directly against the policy of stimulating the local economy; both resulted from a failure to consider how that policy affected the manpower field.

It can indeed be argued that such cases not infrequently arise and that manpower problems consequently occur at a later implementation stage, for which urgent or *ad hoc* solutions have to be found which might not be as effective as the plans which a more positive analysis at the early stages could have generated. For example, recent problems in staffing recreation centres seem to indicate a lack of prior consideration of issues such as staffing standards, specialist training, payment and shift systems.

In other cases, the manpower content of new policies may have been noted, but the need to adjust the policy to ensure its compatibility with these manpower implications (or with other manpower policies) may not have been provided for in the decision process. Thus the staffing implications of joint funded social services projects may well have been assessed, and the projects started, only to conflict at a later stage with an overall policy restriction on manpower numbers. If manpower factors had been taken fully into account at the initial decision stage, the joint funding project policy might have been adjusted to give a priority to, say, projects which involve increases in the staff of voluntary organizations, rather than in the authority's.

In considering how the link between manpower and other policy plans can be better developed, and co-ordination between manpower and operational decisions achieved, two particular considerations arise. The first is to ensure that some regular or routine mechanism exists whereby manpower considerations are analysed and reported on when programme area, and Council-wide, policies are being formulated. The second is to ensure that within the authority's decision-making process, the identified manpower implications are effectively considered and discussed, and plans made to achieve whatever objectives emerge.

If the authority has a corporate planning section or unit, the first of these requirements is met by establishing an active working link between that unit and the personnel department. It should become routine for the corporate planning officer to consult the personnel officer on the manpower implications of the policy plans of the various programme area committees, and of the Council's strategic plans as a whole. For example, a social services plan to change the emphasis in social work from residential to domicillary care will have major manpower implications in phasing out, or retraining, staff with experience and qualifications in running children's and old people's homes, and building up the home help service and general fieldworkers. These changes need quantification, costing and the evolution of action plans to ensure that the rate of change required in the operational policy plan is matched by the rate of change in the constitution of the social services labour force.

It is in the construction and adoption of plans to meet operational and manpower objectives that the second factor arises – the securing of a manpower component in a corporate decision-making process. At top management level this implies the involvement of the authority's personnel manager (Director of Personnel, County Personnel Officer, or whatever title is used) in the process by which policy options, and key operational plans, are formulated by the Chief Executive and his management team for presentation to the authority's committees and full Council. If the Chief Executive chairs a Chief Officers' Group or other form of corporate management team, the personnel manager should be involved. His exclusion in a number of authorities from this formal top management group is usually a matter of status: he is not one of the principal chief officers, or if located in the Chief Executive's department is not technically a departmental head. A more constructive view would be to consider the functional need for his contribution to the management decision-making process regardless of the niceties of organizational protocol. If he or she does not carry the formal status for a seat on the group, then an appointment as 'manpower adviser' to the Chief Officers' Group can get round the problem without upsetting the status-conscious inner cabinet.

But the co-ordination of manpower and operational policy and planning does not depend solely on the personnel manager's involvement in the central corporate management team. There is an equal need for a personnel contribution to management decision-making at departmental level. One of the major disadvantages of too centralized an approach to personnel department organization is that it removes personnel officers from the week-to-week 'sharp end', operations and may leave departmental management teams without the benefit of personnel expertise when important departmental policies are being evolved. Thus, the Director of Personnel may have been involved at corporate management level in evolving a broad-based plan for using the new early retirement provisions to reduce teaching staff numbers. The Education Department now needs to work out the detailed application of this plan to the various parts of its schools empire; and to ensure the skilled and sensitive handling of the detailed plans which emerge. The educational administrators would thus benefit from the close involvement of a personnel officer in the evolution and activation of these plans – and a personnel officer who understands the department from the inside and is part of their own team, not a busy officer from the central department who can do little more than attend the occasional policy-level meeting. Manpower planning needs to be worked through the whole management system, not left to deal solely with the big, broad, central policy objectives if it is to make a practical contribution to securing better decisions, better implemented, right down to the point of action at the departmental 'coal-face'.

Compatibility between manpower plans

Just as it is necessary to secure compatibility between manpower and other policy plans, so it is necessary to ensure that the various manpower plans interlink, and reinforce each other's effectiveness. When manpower planning is not considered as a co-ordinated activity, and merely happens because a variety of decisions are made which have forward objectives, it is almost certain that different plans will pull in different directions.

In a period of manpower constraint, for example, one decison (or *ad hoc* plan) may be to freeze all vacancies; another may be to guarantee the unions no enforced redundancies; and a third may be to try to reduce the proportion of senior, relative to junior, staff (ie less chiefs, more Indians). These three 'plans' are almost wholly incompatible. Staff in clerical grades have a higher turnover rate than those in higher grades, so a freeze on recruitment will result in a steadily growing proportion of senior staff. Yet without redundancies, nothing can be done about this proportionately growing army of 'chiefs'. A fourth plan may be the missing co-ordinating link – a voluntary early retirement scheme available only to the senior grades.

Incompatibility also arises quite frequently between personnel and management services plans and approaches. Influenced by the work of behavioural sciences, the personnel unit may be promoting the concept of enlarging or enriching jobs in order to build in greater employee interest and involvement. At the same time, a conventional management services unit, applying text-book O and M and work study principles, may be busy breaking jobs down into smaller, more easily measured and managed components in order to secure the economies of a flow-line approach to clerical, administrative and other work systems. Some O and M practitioners, too, find difficulty in defining, charting (and therefore accepting) the concept of varying multi-disciplinary project teams in, say, a surveyor's or engineering department, which the personnel unit may be advising is more appropriate to the management of a continuously changing mix of projects than a conventional 'line and staff' hierarchy.

The introduction of a sensitive personnel element into management services planning, and the hard disciplines of a quantified management services approach into personnel thinking, are both valuable antidotes against the dangers and inefficiencies of incompatible plans made separately by each. This view leads to a conclusion that the managerial co-ordination of personnel and management services is an important consideration, underestimated by Bains in his promotion of the separation of these activities.

The need for information

Information lies at the heart of effective manpower planning. It may be categorized into four main types:

1 *Analyses of the manpower content of operational and policy plans.* Broadly, this involves applying known or estimated utilization data to assess the type and quantity of manpower necessary to achieve a given type and level of service. The collection, assessment and regular revision of indices, ratios and yardsticks is an important element in this work (eg staff/population ratios, man hours per unit of output, etc)

2 *Analyses of the constitution of the authority's existing labour force* – normally in terms of particular occupational groups. Different operational plans may dictate the need for different analyses, but a strong case can be made for the routine collection and monitoring of certain basic data for all groups. In particular:

numbers employed, both actual (full and part-time) and full time equivalents
labour turnover and stability rates
age distribution
grade distribution
incidence of overtime.

Additionally, in many services there is a value in monitoring the ratios of qualified or professional to non-professional or unqualified staff, while some fairly simple statistical techniques can be used to assess the frequency with which promotion opportunities occur within a particular department or occupational group. A knowledge of the statistical probability of an employee at one grade obtaining promotion to another is often a useful indicator of the causes of employee disillusionment with career prospects, or of bottlenecks in career progression.

Data of these kinds are of value in at least two ways. First, when the current manpower stock – and its quality – is compared with the estimated future requirement, shortages or surpluses may be iden-

176

tified and the necessary corrective action can then be planned. Secondly, an examination of the data itself may reveal the need for corrective action.

Age distribution analyses not infrequently show undesirable 'humps' in future retirement patterns, caused by on-off recruitment policies in the past. A knowledge of these irregularities can result in changes of emphasis in recruitment – for example, a higher priority being given to mature entrants rather than young trainees.

Grade (and qualification) distribution data can indicate areas for investigation about possibly uneconomic staffing patterns, particularly if trends and not just current data are kept under review. An increasing proportion of posts at Clerical 2, for example, as against Clerical 1, might show the need for a check on either unwarranted grade drift, or an over-specification of job requirements.

Turnover rates are vital for planning any staff reduction programme; and with stability rates, may also indicate areas for attention, leading for example to the introduction of career grades to improve promotion prospects and aid with staff retention.

The regular monitoring of overtime may again lead to plans to increase staff (or to contract work out) rather than pay for it continuously at high overtime rates. Without overtime analyses only an incomplete picture can be presented of total manpower utilization.

3 *Comparative data* – both between departments and between authorities. Internal analyses may reveal significant and unwarranted differences of employment practice between departments. Interauthority comparisons may provide useful indications of other matters for correction*. Study of the LACSAB 'feedback' of APT and C manpower surveys certainly shows a fairly wide range of practice both in staffing levels and in grade distribution, though such studies are unlikely, by themselves, to be more than rough indicators of areas which might repay closer study. That study may well involve an authority in making its own more detailed enquiries of apparently comparable services elsewhere.

A study of the use made of staff in clerical grades in the library services of three major counties showed a variation of from 48 per cent to 70 per cent in the proportion of clerical staff, and in one county this triggered an O and M review of how library systems might be redesigned to make more effective use of non-professional staff. Other external comparisons will lie outside the LACSAB field. Local com-

---

* LAMSAC is undertaking a variety of comparative staffing studies in nonmanual employment. Two systems of comparison are available on a consultancy basis for examining staffing levels in Housing and Architecture. Work is in hand on similar systems for Education and Social Services staff.

parisons among the area's employers generally of the extent of shortages of skilled workshop staff, or of local levels of turnover/shortage among general clerical and secretarial staff, or of sickness and absence rates, may prove useful in showing whether the authority is in a favourable or adverse comparative position and will help prevent unnecessary action occurring, for example, in response to the too-ready assumption of many managers that recruiting difficulties result almost solely from allegedly too low salaries.

Contact also needs to be maintaned with the various bodies, internal and external to the authority, which work in the field of population forecasting. Many local government services are directly influenced by population changes. Increases in the numbers of old people, and decreases in child population both need quantification for the calculation of manpower requirements in Education and Social Services Departments.

4 *Information about broad social, economic and legislative trends.* There is a danger of concentrating on quantifiable information – often in considerable detail – and ignoring powerful over-riding, but unquantifiable trends. These trends will include national factors affecting all local government or, indeed, all employers ; and local factors particularly in the field of employment trends. For example, local authorities in the early 1960s, located in areas subject to major office development schemes, were subject to major changes in the supply (and market value) of clerical staff and needed to take this factor into account in their own forward planning about forms of clerical recruitment, the extent of clerical training, and grading policies. More generally, an extensive range of important trends can be identified which to a varying degree affect all employers and must be borne in mind when making manpower plans. These trends may currently include:

the increasing disinclination of employees to accept working systems (such as standby duties) which significantly interfere with normal social life

the slowly increasing pressure – legislative and social – for sex equality, and the potential effect of this in areas such as Surveyors' and Engineering Departments which have traditionally been male-dominated

a whole range of changes in salary relativities such as those between teachers and educational administrators; and between index-linked firemen and the non-indexed civilian staff

the steady growth of social and unionised pressure for greater employee involvement in decision making. The rejection of employee participation at Council or Committee level is likely to be balanced by pressure for more involvement in the officer-level decision-making systems below Committees

178

the continuing political importance of the numbers of staff employed in the public sector as a distinct and separate issue from manpower costs.

When plans involving manpower changes are being considered – changes in organization structures, career patterns, training programmes, job design – the identification and analysis of relevant trends will often assist to a major degree in determining the practicability of various options. In the social services field, for example, the growing disinclination of staff to have their social life disrupted by standby duties may lead to the alternative method of covering out-of-hours periods by special emergency duty teams.

The organizational role of the manpower planning function
Given that most operational and policy plans have a manpower component; that consideration of this component requires reliable and comprehensive information; and that other manpower analyses may themselves trigger managerial action, the question arises as to how the work involved in linking operational and manpower plans and in producing manpower information might best be organized. What job roles, what pattern of organizational relationships, can ensure an effective manpower planning activity?

It would not be sensible to suggest that one precise organizational structure would be appropriate to all authorities. Size, the existence (or not) of a corporate planning function, the policy towards the relationship between the personnel function and management services – variations in these and other factors will all influence how best a manpower planning function might be organized. What might be considered, however, is a systematization of the types of activity outlined in the preceeding part of this chapter.

In a very broad sense, this activity falls into three categories:

the regular production of a range of manpower information ('headcounts'; overtime analyses; turnover, age and grading analyses, etc); initiation of and participation in LACSAB, LAMSAC and other inter-authority surveys; detailed analyses of the manpower content of departmental/authority forward plans; statistical manpower projections in the supply and demand areas

injection into the top management decision-making process (corporately and departmentally) of the implications of detailed manpower data; and of broad local and national trends

evolution and implementation of specific manpower action plans to achieve specified objectives (eg recruitment, training, grading, etc). This will include the monitoring and control activities inherent in a manpower budget.

179

The first of these categories involves a good deal of detailed clerical and lower-grade administrative work. This work needs to be defined, designed and supervised in an intelligent and selective manner to ensure that the right information is produced in the right form to meet the practical needs of the particular authority. It is very much the specialist manpower planning function and in larger authorities may well be of sufficient volume to justify a reasonably senior specialist appointment with a small clerical/AP support staff. In a smaller authority, the personnel officer himself should be able to set up and supervise this work.

The second category is very much one for the authority's most senior personnel appointment – though a specialist manpower planning officer in a large authority should certainly be expected to take the initiative in pointing out trends and planning needs to his senior manager. He may also provide the necessary organizational link with a corporate planning unit, if one exists. But only the head of the personnel function can really be in the right organizational place to ensure both that that function is aware of the development of authority plans and policies, and that consideration can be given within that development process to significant facts, projections and general trends in the whole manpower and employment fields. He can also see that departmental personnel officers have the knowledge and competence to participate similarly in department policy discussions.

The third area of activity will involve both personnel and management services staff centrally and, if they exist, within departments. It represents the translation of plans into the action needed to achieve them and any detailed discussion of recruitment, training, grading and the like lies outside the ambit of this chapter. What needs emphasis, however, is that operational issues such as the design and scale of graduate or school leaver recruitment programmes, in-service management training, and grading and staffing criteria need to be consistent with authority and departmental policies and plans; and to be worked out on the basis of sound manpower information.

The specialist manpower planning function can thus be seen as central to both personnel and management services work. Organizationally, therefore, it might best be placed in neither of these two common 'wings' of the whole manpower function, but to constitute a third area of activity contributing information and advice to both – and upwards to top management.

In a large authority in which personnel and management services are managed by the Personnel Officer (under whatever job title) the organizational logic of this view leads to the organization pattern on page 181.

The working relationships between these four positions are as follows:

```
                        ┌─────────────────┐
                        │ personnel officer│
                        └─────────────────┘
          ┌──────────────────┼──────────────────┐
  ┌─────────────┐    ┌─────────────┐    ┌──────────────┐
  │ personnel   │ ─ ─│ manpower    │─ ─ │ management   │
  │ services    │    │ planning    │    │ services     │
  └─────────────┘    └─────────────┘    └──────────────┘
```

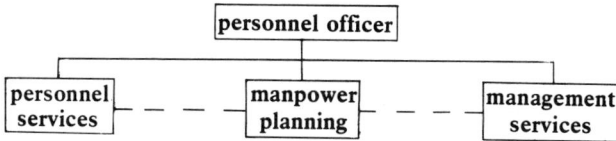

on the personnel side, manpower planning feeds in an influence
  particularly on recruitment and training programmes; and receives
  back raw information on engagements, losses, training volumes
  and the like
on the management services side, manpower planning feeds in an
  influence, particularly on staffing ratios, organization policies and
  optimum grading distributions; and receives back the raw information on employee/output ratios, and on the results of O and M
  reviews
for the personnel officer, manpower planning supplies a whole range
  of suitably processed monitoring data for use in manpower control
  and policy and procedure evolution and receives general direction
  as to internal and external trends and directions.

The extent to which these personnel department activities need to be
converted into separate posts (each with support staff) is a function
primarily of size. But even the smallest authority's solo personnel
officer can still follow the same pattern of working logic in the
organization of his own work.

The manpower planning function also needs to be the main link
between the personnel department and three main areas of activity in
other departments:

  finance: to ensure compatibility between manpower and financial
    projections and budgets
  corporate or strategic planning
  research planning: particularly in the demographic field.

This type of approach to the organizational location and operational
nature of manpower planning, views it as an activity which can
contribute to any and all policy and operational plans at authority or
departmental level which have a manpower component – rather than
as the production of one integrated, centralized and statistically
sophisticated authority master-plan.

Manpower planning can thus be seen to be a practical, not
academic, component of the whole personnel management process.

12 Training in local government

Traditionally, training in local government has had three characteristics:

It has been primarily concerned with the acquisition of professional and other qualifications by examination

Responsibility for training, and for setting standards, has been considered as much that of the professional associations and individual officers, as of the employers

Training has been considered mainly in white-collar terms, with little emphasis placed on manual worker training.

Several quotations illustrate the general position in the mid 1960s, just before the impact of the Industrial Training Act. The 1967 Mallaby report commented that:

One of the most notable features of local government is the great number of professional bodies conducting their own examinations and with each body having its own registrable qualification.

And again:

Local authorities attribute great importance to examination qualifications of many kinds apart from the professional qualifications of, for example, the medical practitioner and the solicitor: promotion, even for officers engaged on routine clerical work, has been governed to a great extent by examination success.

And later:

Many authorities have been content to leave officers to make their own arrangements for study outside normal working hours . . .

The Mallaby Committee found it necessary to make a formal recommendation that:

Employing authorities should accept responsibility for arranging training facilities and for enabling their officers to make full use of them.

By 1972, the Local Government Training Board was able to report significant progress in developing staff training. But in its report for that year, it commented:

> There is unfortunately a major disappointing feature. This is the continued failure to recognize the importance of manual worker training.

These characteristics are in marked contrast to the history of training in industry. There, traditional training consisted almost wholly of craft apprenticeships, with a major expansion in white collar and management training not occurring until the 1960s. It has also become generally accepted in industry that training means employer action to improve work performance; and, compared with local government, relatively little importance has been placed on examinations or on formal qualifications.

The role of the NJC

It would be wrong for the preceding quotations to be taken as indicating that local authorities as a body have, until recently, failed to take any real interest in training. To the contrary, training has been an established part of national employment policy for many years.

Any brief survey of the development of national policy and national training institutions in local government, has in fact to start with the role of the National Joint Council for APT and C Staffs, founded, as has been noted in an earlier chapter, in 1943. From the beginning, and with equal support from authorities and the trade unions (particularly NALGO), the NJC has seen one of its important functions to be the general encouragement and oversight of staff training. As the Scheme of Conditions (the 'purple book') has it:

> Local authorities should advise their staff on, and encourage them to undertake, approved courses of study and training, as this is in the interests of the service as a whole, of the individual local authority and of the officer concerned.

The Scheme goes on to set out the principles governing the provision of training facilities and recommends that four types of training should be available:

> Induction and other training for junior entrants to the service
> Day-release for officers studying for GCE 'O' or 'A' levels either as a continuation of general education or as preparation for further studies; and for preliminary stages of other relevant professional, technical, administrative or clerical qualifications
> Assistance for officers preparing for qualifications recognized by the NJC for promotion purposes

'Facilities which help to equip an officer for the better performance of his existing or possible future responsibilities in the service'. This includes attendance at non-examination courses.

Additionally, the Scheme states that the NJC considers that local authorities 'acting as good employers' should sponsor selected officers to attend full-time courses including university courses.

The heavy emphasis in the NJC provisions on training for promotion-linked qualifications, is emphasized by the appendices to the purple book which deal with training matters. In these appendices are listed some 140 different examinations, many of which are further subdivided into intermediate and full qualifications, making a grand total of almost 300 recognized examination qualifications. Many of these qualifications are specific to individual posts or to specialist groups of staff (eg examinations of the Advertising Association, Illuminating Engineering Society and the Institute of Municipal Entertainment). Others cover large groups of professional staff, such as the qualifications awarded by the Royal Institute of British Architects. Others are of an even more general nature such as the examinations originally set by the Local Government Examinations Board (now by the Local Government Training Board) for the Diploma in Municipal Administration.

The NJC Scheme also sets out in some detail, the particular role of Provincial Councils in providing training facilities and generally stimulating an interest in, and co-ordinating, training activities. For many years before the establishment of the Local Government Training Board (LGTB), Provincial Councils had taken a leading part in sponsoring or providing induction courses for new entrants, and in arranging other short courses, particularly to help officers preparing for local government clerical and administrative examinations. In 1970, following discussions between the LGTB and the National and Provincial Councils, Provincial Councils were asked to develop their training role in two ways. First, in the provision of more courses; secondly, in developing group training schemes whereby smaller authorities combine under Provincial Council co-ordination to form training groups.

Regarding courses, Provincial Council training officers were seen as providing a link between local authorities and colleges – though this concept was, of course, developed before the 1974 local government re-organization and at a time when the average size of authorities was significantly smaller than now, and when few authorities employed their own training officers.

The LGTB's 1970 bulletin, which set out these new tasks for the Provincial Councils, also stressed the need for course activity to go beyond the traditional examination field. The bulletin made particular reference to the need for:

A wide range of short courses: for example, training for management and supervision, specialist and appreciation courses, courses in management services techniques, updating of professional skills, revision courses for examination students, and so on.

The need for advice on the suitability of courses of this kind offered by a wide range of outside bodies was stressed, as was the value of commissioning short courses to meet identified training needs.

In recent years, Provincial Councils in many areas have taken a leading a part in providing training facilities of this kind. Their strength in this work is their ability to tailor training to meet the specific and local needs of the authorities in their areas, and to group together the training requirements of a number of authorities which individually would provide too small a group of trainees to merit tailor-made training.

By 1970, the NJC system with its important Provincial Council component, was moving into a broader-based concept of training than that outlined in the opening of this chapter. The Local Government Training Board's leading role in stimulating this change requires more explanation; to provide this we need to go back to 1946.

The Local Government Examination Board

One of the first actions of the newly formed NJC was to establish, in 1946, the Local Government Examination Board (LGEB). The Board's primary function was to develop and administer an examination and qualification system for clerical and administrative staff which would match the situation already existing for professional and technical staff.

At the same time, the LGEB was to review and advise on the suitability and relevance of all examinations used within the NJC Scheme for promotion and appointment purposes, and to advise generally on staff recruitment standards and post-entry training.

In its 22 years' life from 1946 to 1968, the LGEB became established as the national focus for training and, as well as administering the Clerical and Administrative examinations, was providing an information and advisory service about a wide range of formal training matters. Its activities had also been extended into the manual worker field where it took responsibility for the Parks and Gardens Apprenticeship Scheme and serviced the Joint Training Committee set up in 1965 by the Manual Workers' NJC and the NJC for County Roadmen.

Nevertheless, the primary role for the Board remained its examining function. The three primary examinations developed by the Board were:

The Clerical Examination; designed to provide an introduction to local government studies

The intermediate examination for the Diploma in Municipal Administration; designed at about the level of the first year of a general degree course

The final examination for the Diploma, designed at pass degree level and to provide (on the intermediate base) evidence of an intelligent understanding of UK political, governmental and administrative systems. The emphasis was on a broad-based approach within a liberal studies tradition – rather than on a highly detailed study of administrative principles or techniques.

Other examinations which the LGEB conducted included those leading to the Certificate of Education Welfare and the Diploma in Local Government.

In 1968 the functions of the LGEB were transferred to the Local Government Training Board and the LGEB then ceased to exist.

The Local Government Training Board (LGTB)

It has long been a matter of concern among employers in all sectors of the economy that, unless training is undertaken on a fairly uniform basis, the employers who spend money training staff lose them to the less responsible employers who undertake no training. One of the three primary objectives of the 1964 Industrial Training Act was to remedy this situation. Training Boards were established on a statutory basis in all the large industrial sectors, and each Board had to work towards the three objectives of:

assessing its industry's present and future manpower and training needs

taking action to ensure that its industry trains at a level to meet these needs

re-distributing the costs of training across its industry by raising a general training levy and paying grants to employers who carry out training at the required level.

The Act did not apply directly to local government but the LGEB, with the support of the local authority associations, followed the Act by setting up a working party in 1965 to examine the question of training costs. Its terms of reference were: 'To examine the ways in which a more widespread pooling of the cost of training could be achieved, and to analyse the administrative and financial issues which would be involved'.

In its 1966 report, the working party recommended that a training board should be established in local government to carry out the same

186

functions as the industrial training boards. Following discussions with the NJCs, the associations and the trade unions, it was eventually agreed, in 1967 that such a board should be established – though on a voluntary, not statutory, basis. The Local Government Training Board first met in September 1967.

Its membership consisted of employer representatives nominated in the main by local authority Associations; trade unionists from NALGO, NUPE, TGWU and GMWU; educational members and assessors from central government.

In its first bulletin, issued late in 1967, the new Board set out its aims as being:

> To increase the efficiency of local government by ensuring that sufficient training of the right type and quality is given to the staff and employees of local authorities at all levels
> To use a system of training levies and training grants so as to ensure that the cost of this training is spread fairly and evenly among all local authorities.

The Board also decided to follow the general principles adopted by the industrial training boards in putting forward a series of training recommendations for different groups of staff. The four basic principles on which each training recommendation was to be based are worth repeating here, as they set out a new and systematic philosophy of training for local government. These four principles are:

> That each training recommendation should be based on a thorough analysis of the occupation and work involved, and should specify not only a training programme but also the standards of performance which the training should achieve, and methods by which the effectiveness of the training can be evaluated
> That all the education and training necessary for an employee to carry out his job efficiently should, as a general rule, be given during working hours
> That training should not be envisaged or conducted as an isolated process but should be part of an authority's total personnel policy, related to future manpower needs and aiding any necessary technological or organizational change
> That training and any related further education should be built into an integrated training programme with close liaison between authorities and educational institutions.

Decisions also had to be taken as to the local government employees to be covered by the Board's activities. It was decided to exclude employees for whom, in the Board's view, adequate arrangements already existed and teachers, police, firemen and civil defence workers were thus omitted from the LGTB's terms of reference. Additionally, local government employees in occupations covered by any of the statutory training boards were left under those boards, the largest group being building and civil engineering workers under the Construction Training Board.

Having laid a foundation of defined aims and principles, appointed a Chief Training Officer with supporting staff by the end of 1968, and taken over the LGEB, the Board could 'go into business'. Its work, from about 1968, can be examined under seven headings:

Financial arrangements (levy and grant)
Manpower planning
The training of training officers
Personnel management training
Management development
Training recommendations
Examinations

and each of these areas is discussed in turn in succeeding paragraphs.

Financial arrangements
The possibility of spreading training costs was a primary motivator in the establishment of the LGTB and the Board had rapidly to produce its first levy/grant scheme.

In the absence of suitable manpower figures, the Board's first levy was based on the size of authorities as measured by their populations, with participating authorities paying between 2½d (old pence) and 7½d per head of population.

Financial success depended on the extent to which authorities joined the scheme – its voluntary nature has been noted earlier.

In the event over 90 per cent of the larger authorities joined (County Councils, County Boroughs, London Authorities) and about 70 per cent of the smaller Rural and Urban Districts. £1,800,000 was raised against a target of just over £2 million.

The LGTB had also to give high priority to launching a grants scheme. The difficulties of constructing and maintaining such a scheme are formidable, as other training boards had already discovered. With no accurate information about either the volume of training being undertaken or about the real costs involved, the setting of grant levels against a projection of the volume of grant claims could be no more than intelligent guesswork.

The LGTB produced a grant scheme and asked authorities to estimate their grant income within the scheme. Against a known levy income of £2 million the Board was surprised to find that the full payment of grants would cost around £7 million. Either grants would have to be scaled down to keep within the levy income or the levy had to be raised. Neither solution was thought wholly satisfactory. If levy income was kept at a level well below the total cost of training, a full re-distribution of training costs could not be achieved and most of the cost of training would continue to be borne by those authorities which undertook training. On the other hand, a major increase in levy would have resulted in a rise in costs for authorities not undertaking very much training – and this at a time when the Government was asking authorities to limit their expenditure.

As a compromise, a levy target of £3.5 million was agreed for 1969-70, and £3.2 million was collected. There was a slight fall in the number of authorities in the scheme. The Board redefined its financial objective: instead of ensuring 'that the cost of training is spread fairly and evenly', its aim was 'to redistribute *some* of the cost of training and to provide a financial incentive to local authorities to improve their training practices'.

In the next two years, the Board continued to experience difficulty in balancing levy income with grant expenditure, in obtaining a full recovery of targeted levy, and in finding an acceptable basis for levy calculations. In the two years ending March 1972, levy targets totalling around £14.3 million were under-recovered by some £1.6 million and grant commitments were in excess of levies by some £1.5 million. The number of participating authorities fell from 1,054 (74 per cent) to 942 (66 per cent) and it was becoming clear that beyond a fairly modest level higher levies merely resulted in fewer participants.

Against this background, the 1972-73 year saw a complete review of the whole levy/grant principles. In order to prevent any financial deterioration, grants in that year were limited to the availability of levy income. But the Board proposed a more fundamental change, coinciding with a change in government policy towards the levy/grant system in the industrial training boards: the abandonment of the principle of the redistribution of costs. The emphasis in the Board's role could then become more clearly that of providing focus for the promotion of effective training in local government and less that of a financial regulator of training costs.

In 1973, too, the Employment and Training Act established the Manpower Services Commission which, unlike the statutory industrial training boards, was to include local government employment within its scope. The voluntary nature of the levy/grant scheme was confirmed against a background of lengthy and complex discussions about the Board's long term policy. Levy income was reduced from £8¼ million to £4¼ million, grants cut back to about £3½ million, and arrangements made to hold the 1974/75 levy/grant at similar levels pending more fundamental decisions about the future.

For 1975-76 a complete change in financial policy was eventually agreed. Grants would be eliminated except for a modest degree of support for some manual worker training and for training staff. The

Board's income was to be raised, not by a levy on participating authorities but by a deduction from the Rates Support Grant. These financial changes carried broader policy implications. In future, the primary role of the Board would be to provide training assistance and services to local authorities rather than to control, direct and finance local government training. One other significant change resulting from this form of financing was that all local authorities could now use LGTB services, not merely those who, under previous arrangements, agreed to pay the levy.

By 1977 when these changes were in full effect, the Board's income from the Rate Support Grant (the general central government subsidy to local government finances) was around £1½ million for the year and grants were running at:

Training officers' courses:	£94,000
Training centres:	£260,000
Craft apprentices:	£415,000
Subsidies to Provincial Councils:	£193,000

In 1977-78, too, the Board became heavily involved in the application to local government of the various central government schemes to ameliorate unemployment, such as the Clerical Training Awards Scheme. LGTB acted as local government's liaison link with the Manpower Services Commission and its Training Services Division in the design and vetting of such schemes, and in advising authorities on their application.

Manpower planning

For two reasons, the LGTB had to build up statistical information about local government manpower. First, this was required for levy purposes as it was seemingly fairer to raise levy on numbers employed rather than on population. Secondly, and much more important from a training point of view, the Board had to know the size and occupational mix of the labour force for which training was to be provided, and to be able to measure and forecast changes in demand for manpower, in order to assess training priorities. Had local government all the planners, social workers, building craftsmen it needed now? Were any of these occupational groups growing or diminishing faster than changes in demand? Were the numbers of trainee entrants matching the losses of retirements and resignations? A myriad questions of these kinds needed to be asked and, in the absence of accurate manpower statistics, could not be answered.

In 1969 the Board began a series of manpower surveys to get the facts and sent questionnaries to all local authorities in England and Wales asking for details of the numbers of their employees in different categories. Unfortunately, in this and later surveys, not all authorities replied and the Board has consequently been forced to make extrapolated projections from the replies received in order to produce estimates of the total local government manpower. Nevertheless, the LGTB's surveys provided the Board with a most valuable and necessary picture. The 1969 survey, for example, immediately spotlighted the existence of a large number of part-time employees with consequent special training problems.

Subsequent surveys investigated this aspect of employment in more detail, the proportions of male and female employment in various occupational groups, the age distribution of employees and the extent to which non-manual staff held relevant qualifications – as well as increasingly detailed analyses of the size of various occupational groups. Some of this data is quoted in chapter 1.

The large number of different occupations in local government makes the Board's task of collecting manpower statistics and forecasting manpower changes difficult. Some 450 different occupations were listed by the Board in a booklet sent to authorities in mid 1975, asking for views about future training priorities.

These jobs ranged from abattoir labourer, through landscape architect and ceremonials officer, to woodman and work study officer. Forty-two 'position statements' were also given, each covering one of the listed jobs for which the Board had been involved in some form of training activity.

The problems of accurate planning in the absence of accurate statistics are illustrated by listing some of these position statements together with the Board's comments on the numbers employed.

Position	Numbers employed
Building control officer	Provisional estimate – 3,500
Crematorium attendant	600 (approx)
Education officer	5,000 (approx)
Planning officer	5,000 (approx) holding an appropriate qualification
Pool plant operative	3,000 plus
Receptionist	Not known
Recreation officer	Not known
Road safety officer	Several hundred
Shop steward	Not known
Social worker	9,000 with CCETSW certificate
Supplies officer	3,000 (approx)
Public relations officer	Employed in about half of all local authorities
Trading standards officer	1,500 (approx) qualified
Warden of sheltered houses	Minimum estimate 3,000
Waste disposal employees	Not known

There are two particular features in this list. First, the number of areas in which training has been undertaken but in which the scale of employment is not known.

Secondly, in a number of occupations only the number of qualified staff is known – through membership figures obtainable from the professional institutions. For training purposes, the number of unqualified or partly qualified staff is of at least equal importance.

The LGTB would readily admit that a great deal of work is still necessary before adequate manpower and training planning can really be established.

A significant recent development was a joint study of the staffing and training problems in environmental health departments, undertaken by the Board in conjunction with LACSAB. This has been perhaps the most comprehensive study of its kind yet undertaken in local government, and the link with LACSAB recognized the reality of an employment situation in which salary and grading levels were as important a component in manpower supply, as was the volume and nature of professional and job training. A study of catering staff, undertaken for the Hotel and Catering Industry Training Board, showed the very high total of 258,000 catering workers in local government (the largest group being in school meals work) and perhaps highlighted a somewhat neglected sector from a training viewpoint.

The training of training officers
Appropriately, the first formal training recommendation issued by the Board in its first year dealt with the appointment and training of training officers. As was pointed out in its first report, although the Board itself could help to provide a national framework for training, 'the appointment and proper use of a well-qualified corps of training officers within local government is an essential part of any future development plan. Little effective training could be developed on any co-ordinated basis unless authorities themselves employed properly trained training officers to assist in the identification of local training needs.

It has been estimated that when the LGTB was set up there were only some 50 training officers employed in the whole of local government. By 1978 there were well over 1,000 and the LGTB's work in stimulating this expansion of local training effort is one of its most significant achievements. The Board arranged training courses for new training officers at a very early stage, some lasting six weeks and providing a basic, general course; others of shorter duration on specific subjects such as training evaluation and management development. Two series of national conferences for training officers have helped to provide a forum for the interchange of ideas and experience – particularly useful for training officers who, as the sole training specialists in their own authorities, might otherwise feel rather isolated.

The early years of the grants scheme were also used to provide a strong financial incentive for otherwise cautious authorities to appoint their own training staff. In its 1975 discussion document, the LGTB listed its current activities in relation to the training of training officers as:

development of diagnostic courses

linking of courses to IPM Affiliateship regulations

preparation of a training officers' handbook

publication of a training recommendation for instructors (a necessary distinction has to be made between the generalist training officer as a training adviser and administrator, and the specialist instructor)

a further series of national conferences.

In subsequent years, another range of training courses for training officers has been introduced with an emphasis on the identification of the individual training needs of each course member. These courses include project work, individual tutoring, and course work on the identification of training needs, on designing and implementing training activities and on the evaluation of training. In 1976/77 the Board also introduced a training co-ordinator's scheme for those authorities unable to support full-time training staff, but who could identify someone – usually in the personnel department – who had responsibility for advising and assisting on training as part of the duties of a more general post.

Personnel management training

With one eye on the personnel workload implied by the Mallaby report, and the other on the forthcoming 1974 re-organization, the Board gave personnel management training a fairly early priority. A survey of the work of establishment officers was carried out in 1968-70 although it was not until 1972 that any very extensive training began to be provided, and then mainly by short single subject courses and seminars.

The Board then produced three important publications to stimulate a greater interest and sense of urgency in the need for better training in this field.

In 1971 the Board produced a training recommendation, Staff Engaged in Personnel Work, which dealt with the need for wider-ranging professional training, as well as with the shorter-term, practical training needs. This recommendation suggested that there would be a need for 'a corps of professionals in the personnel field' and concluded that the qualifications of the Institute of Personnel Management were the most suitable for local government personnel staff.

A booklet entitled *Personnel Management in the New Authorities,* produced in 1973 and looking towards the 1974 reorganization, set out a comprehensive new view of personnel work for local government. It suggested that personnel work fell into three categories:

Analytic activities;
  manpower utilization
  records and statistics
  job descriptions
  job evaluation
  manpower planning

Personnel development activities;
  recruitment and selection
  performance appraisal
  training and career development
  salary administration

Human relations activities;
  communications
  industrial relations
  organization development.

The booklet suggested that the personnel officer required two broad sets of skills:

Problem-solving skills – which were described in somewhat abstract terms (eg an ability to discern and interpret corporate objectives, strategies, tactics, constraints and opportunities)
Communication and social skills – such as effective speaking and writing, the ability to establish rapport with a wide range of individuals and groups and to 'mediate in resolving conflict'.

To assist in training towards this concept of personnel management, the Board produced a comprehensive training package, called Personnel Practice. It contained training material (tutor's notes, a case study exercise etc) for the use of colleges, provincial councils or individual authorities in running training sessions for new personnel staff. By the end of 1975 most authorities had purchased this package, and although not all had actually used it in any formal training, many newly appointed personnel officers had benefited from the information and advice it contained.

Despite all this work, the Board had to report in 1974 that the response to short courses in personnel management arranged through polytechnics had not been very encouraging. It seemed likely that the heavy pressures on establishment departments in the periods immediately preceding and following reorganization was preventing any real development in long term planning towards the kind of personnel professionalism that the Board envisaged. However, during 1975 an encouraging increase was noted in the use of courses and in particular in the development of courses for personnel staff organized by provincial councils.

In its 1975 policy discussion document, the Board listed its main current activities in personnel training:

Development of further courses and of additional training material

Linking of courses to IPM Affiliateship regulations (for other than the professionally qualified officer)

Establishment of a linked correspondence and face to face tuition system for full IPM qualifications, organized through the NALGO Correspondence Institute

Preparation of training material on health, safety and welfare

'Advice on a very limited scale'.

Training for personnel work seems to be developing in two ways. First, an expansion of training for professional qualifications with young personnel staff for IPM examinations. Secondly, the use of short courses run by a variety of organizations, within broad LGTB recommendations, to improve specific skills and to up-date personnel officers' knowledge of their work.

It remains for personnel managers to carry out practical training, among their own staff, on a formal and informal basis. In personnel work, as in much of management generally, the best case study material is the work which arrives on each officer's desk – provided his senior officer takes a positive interest in the use of this live material by on-the-job coaching.

Management development

The LGTB was founded at a time when management development was a subject of extensive and lively debate in industry, and when most large organizations were introducing or recasting formal management development schemes. With this background it was not surprising that the Board's next training recommendation after that for training officers was on the subject of management training. Rapid action was also taken on the provision of management courses. In addition to supporting the extension of the 10 week management courses offered by the Institute of Local Government Studies (INLOGOV), the Board also mounted its own series of shorter courses – particularly for officers over the age of 45 who were ineligible for attendance at INLOGOV courses. The University of Birmingham, and the Polytechnics of Bristol, Leicester, Portsmouth and Sheffield, and the Anglian Regional Management Centre have cooperated closely with the Board in this work. By 1978 over 3,000 local government officers had attended general management courses – though it must be said that this represents a very small proportion of the number of local government staff who have managerial responsibilities. More recently short, single subject courses have been introduced to supplement the general management courses. The LGTB has also promoted the use of the Diploma of Management Studies (DMS), with local government or public service options, as being an appropriate general management qualification.

The Board's second management training recommendation (1971) was entitled Management Development and was supplemented by a booklet on *Identifying Training Needs* and another on *Management by Objectives in Local Government*, accurately reflecting the interests and jargon of the times. Considerable interest was shown by authorities in the staff development aspects of management training: that is, in the regular review of individual performance and individual strengths and weaknesses, and in action on-the-job as well as on training courses to capitalize on strengths and overcome weaknesses. A number of authorities, following the Board's advice, appointed management development advisers, either on a full-time basis or as an additional role for the personnel officer or other senior manager. Special courses for management development advisers have also been introduced, involving a mixture, over several months, of course attendances, project work and other tuition, some of which also involves the line manager in whose departments the adviser is to work. In 1977/78, the Board conducted a thorough survey of authorities' experience and views of management development which generated much discussion in and between individual local authorities. It revealed considerable management (and elected member) interest in the need systematically to develop the skills and potential of staff – not only managers – but some disillusionment, too, about the difficulties of implementing effective development programmes.

It seems that full-scale management development is still relatively rare in local government. Some authorities have introduced staff assessment systems, some make a planned use of management training courses, some regularly review their management resources and forecast future needs, some have developed forms of internal training, some have encouraged their senior managers to use on-the-job 'coaching' methods to train and develop subordinate staff, some have experimented in self-assessment systems, some have applied the target-setting and review principles of management by objectives. Few have linked *all* these activities in one, integrated development programme.

There is still a great deal of scope for most personnel officers to do more in developing effective development programmes – and the LGTB can be one of the main sources of advice for those inexperienced in such work.

Other training recommendations
A brief summary of the more important of the Board's other training recommendations illustrates the range of training activity necessary in local government with its multiplicity of occupations.

Supervisory training received early attention and, in addition to a formal training recommendation, training material was provided for provincial and local courses, and pilot courses were also run by the Board to validate the course organizers' handbooks. A study programme was also evolved with the National Examinations Board in Supervisory Studies, for supervisors to obtain the Certificate in Supervisory Studies.

Clerical and administrative training was clearly important, given the high volume of office work in local government. Apart from the main clerical examinations (dealt with in a later paragraph) the Board produced training recommendations including one for on-the-job training, and worked with the Department of Employment in preparing courses for clerical staff instructors.

Much of this material was based on a study of administrative and clerical work undertaken by an LGTB working party in 1969-70, when the work of some 2,000 office staff in 57 authorities was surveyed.

Training for roadmen has been given quite a high priority since a training recommendation was produced in 1972. As with clerical training, a national working party has monitored training developments in this field, which have included the production of training manuals, the training of instructors, and the sponsorship of courses and of research into work methods. Some 21 training centres have been established across the country with full provincial council involvement and the volume of training for road workers has more than doubled since 1972. This work represents one of the relatively few large-scale developments in manual worker training, though similar work is also being expanded for parks and playing field employees. By 1977, some 21 training centres had been registered for these workers, too; and their level of training was up to that for roadworkers.

A similar programme for heavy goods vehicle drivers has not developed quite so smoothly, with a number of training centres being closed due to financial pressures. However, the remaining centres continue to provide a useful output of trained drivers for an occupation in which market pressures in industry and commerce have pushed wage rates beyond those easily payable within local government scales.

Other occupations for which both training recommendations and training material have been produced include:

school caretakers – the training material is a manual on the operation of school swimming pools
catering employees – primarily school meals service workers
heavy goods vehicle drivers
pool plant operatives
shop stewards – the training material was produced in consultation with the trade unions and LACSAB.

Training material has also been produced by the Board on subjects, as distinct from occupations, such as:

metrication
decimalization
safety in sewers
social service legislation
industrial relations.

Examinations

The LGTB's inheritance of the work of the LGEB has already been described. The Board's role as an examining body is a unique feature in the Training Board world. Other Boards have been able to leave professional examinations to the professional institutions, but the combination in local government of an absence of a general administrative professional body, the existence of a major occupational group of administrators and the tradition of professionalism made the LGEB's work necessary, and the LGTB's takeover of this role desirable. A major advantage of the Board's involvement has been its ability to integrate formal, examination-type training into the spectrum of occupational training as a whole. It has also been the Board's policy to take an open rather than introverted view of its examination work, and to broaden the various qualifications rather than restrict them too severely to local government topics.

With this view in mind, the Board undertook an early review of the two main examinations conducted by the LGEB – the Clerical Examination and the Diploma in Municipal Administration (DMA). The result of the review, following intensive discussions with both local authority and educational interests, was the termination of both the Clerical and DMA Examination and their replacement by new schemes. The last Clerical Examination was held in December 1973 and the last Intermediate Examination for the DMA in April 1974.

The peak years for the old Clerical Examination had been 1964 to 1966, when some 6,000 candidates sat the examination annually. The pass rate was just under 50 per cent. (About 1,500 candidates took the final DMA annually, with a pass rate of just over 50 per cent.) The Clerical Examination had been under criticism for some time before the LGTB abandoned it. It failed in two ways, being neither a test of clerical competency nor a widely recognized qualification in the educational sense. The Board's solution was that it should not be directly replaced. Instead, clerical staff were to be encouraged to sit for more widely recognized qualifications and to have a choice in these. The two qualifications the Board selected were the Certificate in Office Studies (COS) and the Ordinary National Certificate (ONC) in Public Administration. For the clerical officer, a significant career advantage of each of these was its recognition as a valuable qualification outside the world of local government. The ONC, for example, is widely used by the Civil Service, as are the successor BEC courses.

On the administrative side, the Board raised the standard of final qualification by introducing two levels of examination. The first, a new Certificate in Municipal Administration, was to be equivalent in standard to the final of the old DMA. The entry standard is five approved GCE subjects, two at A level. The CMA examination is in two parts:

Part A Government and Public Administration 1
Economics of Public Finance 1
Local Government Administrative Practice
Part B Government of Public Administration 2
Economics of Public Finance 2
Social Policies and Social Needs

Each part represents one year's work on a day release basis. The CMA is also an intermediate qualification, although many students are now using it as preparation for the second new qualification introduced by the Board – the new Diploma in Municipal Administration. This is designed to match the general intellectual and professional standard of other major professional qualifications. The training for this qualification is more intensive than for the CMA. It was LGTB's intention that DMA studies should be on a full-time basis. During 1975, however, it became clear that this requirement was resulting in a serious reduction in entrants to the course, and the regulations were changed, with some reluctance, to permit part-time day release studies. Students have to provide evidence of suitable practical experience, and carry out a project on which a paper had to be presented and of which an oral examination is made. The main examination consits of six papers:

Local Government Law
Local Government Finance
Social Administration
Personnel Practice
Local Government Administrative Practice (two papers).

Entry to the new DMA course is either via the CMA, or by a university degree or Higher National Certificate (HNC) in Business Studies with public administration options.

199

By 1980 it was evident that the DMA was failing to attract support, with less than 100 students enrolling annually. The Board's alternative proposal was to revise the examination in association with a professional institute – most likely the Institute of Chartered Secretaries and Administrators. Why had the DMA failed? In the private sector, the general administrator has practically disappeared and his place has been taken by the professional accountant, personnel manager, taxation specialist and the like. General business studies have never really flourished, other than on a post-graduate or post-experience management studies basis. Professional qualifications of a high standard are available in each of the four broad vocational areas in the DMA's final examination; law, finance, personnel management and social studies. Will the generalist administrator and generalist administrative qualification survive? And, if so, would courses such as the more general Diploma in Management Studies be more appropriate? A number of authorities think so, and have continued to sponsor administrative trainees for DMS rather than DMA courses. They argue that too early a concentration on purely local government studies does not take advantage of the broader approach of a more general management course, and may unwittingly encourage a narrowness of vision which the future local government manager must avoid.

The LGTB, in any event, has had to undertake a thorough review of its approach to both business and technical studies in the light of the major changes being introduced in colleges to the long-standing pattern of ONC, HNC and HND courses of all kinds. The new national courses, developed by the Business and Technical Education Councils (BEC and TEC) can respond more flexibly to the particular training needs of the main occupational sectors such as local government, and many large authorities are in direct contact with their own further and higher education colleges about the local government content of new BEC business studies courses. To complete the outline of the Board's examination activities, mention must be made of the Certificate in Education Welfare for education welfare officers (EWOs). About 150 candidates have been sitting for this qualification annually, without a 50 per cent pass rate. As a result of a review of the whole training picture for EWOs (a training recommendation was produced in the 1974-75 year) the Certificate was discontinued from April 1976. Instead, the Board has liaised with the Central Council for Education and Training in Social Work (CCETSW) on the provision of places for EWOs on courses for the Certificate of Qualification in Social Work. Additionally, the Board had encouraged the growth of in-service training for EWOs, and the provision of short modular courses by colleges.

The Board has also established its own Careers Service Training

Committee to oversee the development of training in this field, and the award of the Board's Diploma in Careers Guidance.

Finally, the Board also acts as the examining agency for the Fire Services Central Examination Board and the Police Promotion Examination Board. Some 5,000 fire service and 19,000 police candidates for promotion are examined annually.

Other training institutions

It would be misleading to give the impression that only the LGTB has been involved in promoting training. The Board has become a focus for training and its activities have spanned a wider spectrum than those of any other body. But there are at least four other sources of training effort which merit comment. The work of the primary one of these – provincial councils – has been noted earlier in this chapter. But the work of a number of educational institutions, of the Institute of Local Government Studies and of local authorities themselves, must not be overlooked. The Royal Institute of Public Administration has also consistently promoted higher and more professional standards among local government administrators. Several polytechnics, particularly Leicester, Portsmouth, Bristol and Sheffield, worked with the Board in developing management courses and their knowledge and skill in management training contributed to the growth of interest in this hitherto neglected field of local government training. The Anglian Regional Management Centre also contributed to this work. Sheffield undertook a practical research study into the identification and analysis of training needs in a county borough, as the basis for providing wider advice on this key aspect of effective training.

Local authorities work with many other institutions. For example, the Oxford Centre for Management Studies has worked closely with the GLC for several years evolving senior management training and, with other authorities, has supported the Henley Staff College's Master courses. The use of carefully planned, individual project work, with coaching by both college tutors and by senior management, is a particular feature of these courses and the projects are authority, and not college, based.

The CMA and DMA courses depend almost entirely on the work of colleges and polytechnics, Middlesex, for example, being responsible for the first of the DMA courses. On a more local basis, many colleges have worked with provincial councils and individual authorities in developing courses to meet particular local needs.

The Institute of Local Government Studies (INLOGOV) has provided a research foundation for a number of training developments. The LGTB has maintained a close relationship with INLOGOV and has commissioned research, as well as benefiting from the Institute's own studies. INLOGOV's more direct training contribution to local government has been in the provision of management courses and its 10 week advanced course has been its central training activity. But it has also provided a steady stream of short seminars, courses and conferences on a variety of management subjects, with a particular bias towards the training and information needs of senior and chief officers.

INLOGOV together with theLGTB arranged for some 400 councillors to attend seminars on the Bains report.

In the research field, the Institute has been particularly concerned with management structures and with management development. Two research projects, both commissioned by the LGTB illustrate the Institute's work in this field.

In Derbyshire, INLOGOV has been working with the County Council in studying the application of organization development (OD) theories to a local authority. This includes an analysis of the whole organizational structure and ethos from a socio-psychological viewpoint as well as operationally.

INLOGOV has also been involved in a national study of changes in management education needs, arising from changes in local government management structures and processes following reorganization.

The Institute sees, in its future work programme, the development of:

further research into management structures, into corporate planning, management accountancy, decision stimulation techniques and other aspects of managerial activity and development

graduate courses for younger local government officers and for academics

work with individual local authorities to assist in problem solving and improvement projects at local level

the flow of information about management and organizational ideas and techniques into and out of the Institute.

INLOGOV's interest in working more directly with the local authorities on the solution of identified local problems illustrates the more general need for an effective training function at local level. As the LGTB itself pointed out in 1969, 'the efficiency of the training given will always rest primarily on the shoulders of the individual local authority'. In a formal sense, a good deal of progress has been made to this end. Upwards of 100 training centres have been established at provincial and local level; some spanning the whole field from manual to management training; others (such as the regional roadworker training centres) concentrating on instruction for one occupational group. A number of local government services have, for a number of years, organized and promoted professional training at departmental

202

level. Indeed, of the 1,000 or so full time training officers registered with the LGTB, over 600 appear to be located within particular departments rather than in central training units. Departmentally, the largest group of these training officers is in Social Services, followed by the Catering and School Meals service, and the departments concerned with roadworkers and heavy goods vehicle drivers.

The training activities of the various professional institutes must also be recognized, particularly in promoting training for qualifications. It is less easy to determine the effectiveness of the growth in courses and in course attendances which has followed the expansion of national, provincial and local training facilities. Yet in the end, the real test is not the number of examination successes or the number of man-days course attendances. It is whether this growth in training is improving the quality and efficiency of local government work, organization and services. Thus in the training of a manager the real question is not 'how well did he do on the course?' but 'is he a better manager as a result of his training?'. The traditional emphasis in local government training on the acquisition of professional qualifications creates a danger that training might be seen to too great an extent as an end in itself. Perhaps the biggest challenge for the training officer (and for the personnel manager) at local authority level is to develop ways of monitoring work performance, in order to assess not only where training is needed but also to ensure that, when time, effort and money are put into training, there is an identifiable return in terms of raised standards of quality and performance. This can only be done 'at the coal-face'. The training officer who spends his time running courses in the training centre, or booking staff on to external courses and quizzing them on their return ('re-entry debriefing' to be fashionable!) is not merely doing only half his job. He runs the risk of being totally non-productive – because he is not assessing the impact of training in the work situation. Formal training can provide the conceptual framework for more effective job performance. But the most effective training, learning how to apply knowledge and skill in real-life work situations, can take place with full effectiveness only 'on the job'. The best training officers at local level are those who make their reputations, not by running eye-catching courses but by assisting managers to create the type of learning environment at the workplace, which stimulates the effective self-development of every member of staff – including the manager himself.

For authorities generally, more emphasis may need to be given to developing comprehensive training policies and strategies to meet the identified needs – future as well as current – of each authority for its own unique mix of manpower, and to ensure a better assessment of priorities. In the training budgets of many authorities it is noticeable how expenditure is concentrated on relatively small groups of staff, particularly those employed in the politically sensitive social services. Yet this may not be where the most effective improvements in manpower might, by training, be achieved. The whole manual worker area, for example, is still relatively undertrained. It is as well, too, for each authority to build up some internal training capability, and not to rely too heavily on the services of the LGTB or other training institutions. A growth in the number of authorities' internal training courses and an increase in the number of instructor appointments have been noticeable in recent years. Both are encouraging signs of the growing independence and self-confidence of individual authorities in standing on their own training feet. On this matter, the emphasis in this chapter on LGTB activities should not be taken as other than a convenient way of describing the local government training world as a whole. In real terms, authorities will achieve the maximum pay-off from training only when they are able to assess their own needs, and can bring to these needs the best blend of internal and external resources and skills.

13 Establishment control

Establishment control – control of staff numbers and gradings – became something of a Cinderella of the personnel department in the period immediately after the 1974 reorganization. At least, that is the impression from the lack of discussion of this traditional local government personnel activity in the journals, and its absence as a topic from courses and conferences at that time. In reality, it still constitutes an important feature in most personnel departments' work.

The financial pressures which began to emerge in 1976/77, and the growing public and political concern about the need to restrain the growth of public sector employment, soon placed establishment control back in its traditionally central position in local government personnel work. The emphasis, however, has changed somewhat. Pre-1974, it was seen as a primarily administrative task. In recent years, the emphasis has been at a much higher manpower policy level – the achievement of 'value for money' in local government's massive expenditure on wages and salaries. In many authorities, too, control of manpower numbers is seen as being of equal political importance to control of manpower costs. Indeed, it has not been unknown for an authority's financial budget to allow a greater expenditure on manpower than the manpower budget permits. The demonstrable control of numbers employed – or more specifically, cutting the staff – has been seen as an urgent and over-riding political priority, and to achieve such reductions elected members have insisted on some fairly Draconian measures. Edicts have been issued that there has to be a 10 per cent cut, or that so many hundred posts must be disbanded by a certain date. Freezes on recruitment, a thorough vetting of every vacancy before it is filled, a ban on any growth in numbers – measures of these kinds have become commonplace, with the result that the steady growth in local government employment in the period 1970-75 has been stopped and indeed reversed.

It cannot be said that the fairly rough and ready measures which pressure from elected members has necessitated have been met with enthusiastic support by chief officers and senior managers, let alone by the trade unions. The latter, however, have generally had their potential resistance weakened by guarantees of no enforced redundancies, by quite extensive consultation on the implementation of staff reduction schemes, and by a higher priority than normal being given to internal candidates (over external recruits) when vacancies are filled – a generally popular measure with staff. Managers, on the other hand, have voiced consistent complaints that too little account is being taken of the effect of staff reductions on the quality of services, and that these reductions – often resulting from the chance effects of staff turnover rather than any planned system – are placing intolerable burdens on the service and on the managers responsible for maintaining standards. Complaint has also been made of the tendency of the axe to cut most deeply into important activities which are not directly in the public eye, and which are not susceptible to very direct quantification in terms of standards or output. For example, public reaction against any fall in educational standards, and the widespread use of the simple, easily understood pupil-teacher ratios, have enabled some education departments to maintain levels of teaching staff, while activities out of the direct public eye such as financial and legal departments have had to accept staff cuts of 10 per cent or more. There can be obvious resentment, too, when a chief officer has to prove his need to fill each vacancy that may arise, both to a vetting officer from a central management services unit, and possibly to an elected members' panel. He may well feel that the whole approach indicates the authority's lack of confidence in his ability to assess the resources he needs to meet his operational objectives, or a lack of trust in his motives. Any system of establishment control which appears to the officers concerned as having been imposed by the elected members must carry these psychological overtones of mistrust between members and officers, and smack of the type of struggle for control between these two groups which is paralleled by the well-publicized views of national politicians about their difficulties in controlling the Civil Service.

From an officer's viewpoint it would be all too easy to develop a theme in this chapter that the arbitrary control of manpower levels by the means outlined above represents a wholly unsatisfactory approach which is the very antithesis of scientific management. Manpower levels, it can be argued, should be the end product of a rational system of corporate planning, the setting of objectives, and the determination of the resource levels necessary to achieve these objectives. But there are practical flaws in this theoretical line of argument. A perfectly respectable economic, not political, case can be made that if the effect of a multiplicity of what might in themselves be wholly rational decisons about manpower in various services has the net effect of a continuing expansion of public sector employment, this net result – with its concomitant shrinkage of the private, manufacturing sector – is economically unsatisfactory. On a more detailed level, few managers would claim that the determination of the scale of administrative, professional and managerial manpower is susceptible to entirely objective assessment. In practice, too, the absence of an emphasis on manpower control has seemed to coincide with fairly rapid growth in numbers, while the staff reductions of recent years have not yet led to many disastrous failures in service. By and large, departments have grumbled – but coped. But the scale of reductions which some authorities found it necessary to make in 1979/80, resulting from central government's policies to reduce public sector expenditure and to reduce rate support grant began to have a direct impact on service standards – particularly in the fields of education, highway maintenance and social services. There is an assumption, too, that manpower control in the sense objected to by many local government managers is a feature of personnel work unique to local (and central) government: that financial disciplines in industry and commerce exercise a form of control absent in the public sector, and that in local government the formal establishment function takes the place of these commercial constraints. This is an over-simple view, and many personnel managers in industry carry out advisory or control functions on manning levels which are, in essence, the same as those of their local government colleagues. The nomenclature is different – 'manpower budgets' are used rather than 'authorized staffing levels' – and the financial bases vary. But in the end, the problems are the same. For a targeted output (of goods or services) how large an input (of manpower) is necessary, and how is such manpower constituted (in terms of skills, organizational groupings, costs and so on)? The industrial manager, planning for a 10 per cent expansion in output, is in exactly the same position as the local government housing administrator faced with a 10 per cent increase in council housing. How much extra work is involved? How many extra staff, and of what types, are necessary to get this work done? Both can bring the same techniques to bear in achieving satisfactory answers, but at the end of the day it may still be necessary for both organizations to take a global view of their overall manpower levels – and decide to reverse the apparently rational process by setting the manpower totals first, and working backwards from those totals to their effect on their operations.

Work measurement techniques (work study, and office work measurement) can supply some answers for manual and clerical work. Staff ratios or yardsticks can be used to translate various forms of work measures (eg capital value of building work, casework loads) into numbers of professional and administrative staff. O and M is a

207

tried and trusted technique for assessing the efficiency of working systems and procedures, and for planning effectively grouped and linked work activities.

Organizational development theory can assist in deciding the most effective organizational structure for new or changed activities. But it may still be argued that one major difference exists. At the extremes, it is held that industrial managers try to keep their staff numbers down to an irreducible minimum in order to lower costs and increase profits, while local government managers empire build in order to enhance their own, and their department's status. Like most generalizations, this has some truth and some falsehood in it. Certainly some industrial managers, particularly in small firms, act in this way. When labour costs form a high proportion of total costs and where, in a small company, an increase of, say, five staff represents a rise of 20 per cent in the wage bill, these financial pressures are highly effective in limiting manpower inflation. But size weakens these disciplines. The individual manager in a multi-million pound company knows that five more staff in his department represents no more than, say 0.01 per cent of his company's pay bill and even less of its total product cost. Large commercial organizations find it exceedingly difficult to maintain a fierce, entrepreneurial cutting edge throughout their extensive management hierarchies, and the pervasive feeling that size and status go hand in hand can result in just as much unnecessary staffing and personal empire building as in the non-commercial world. Indeed, there is some evidence that large companies either have to subject themselves to cyclical blood-letting in order to maintain a financially satisfactory silhouette, or become so organizationally obese that they eventually fail.

Numerous examples also exist of companies which have introduced precisely those very general methods of manpower control which have caused so much adverse comment among local government managers in recent years. Moreover, staff economy campaigns in the private sector rarely include the degree of staff protection guaranteed in most local authority campaigns. This author has had personal experience of undertaking an economy campaign in the private sector, necessitated by low company profitability, which resulted in some 30 per cent of a managerial work-force being declared redundant within one week.

Many managerial incentives operate to reward sheer size, rather than cost-effectiveness. In the industrial world, the business factor which correlates most directly with management salaries is company size, not profitability. In both industry and local government, size, measured by the number of employees supervised, is a standard job evaluation factor: the more employees, the higher the rating, the higher the salary. And in industry as in local government it would not be unknown for the chief officer with the largest department to take the view that he should receive the highest salary. How often, too, when considering candidates for promotion, is the disparaging remark made of an otherwise satisfactory candidate, that 'he's only managing a small section' – or words to that effect.

The personnel manager who wants to break new ground in establishment control would do well to ponder on this question of the underlying influences on management attitudes towards staffing levels. Size and growth are powerful motivators. They carry status and power. They provide opportunities for the indolent manager to delegate the hard, front-line elements in his work. Growth generates more growth. The sub-division of an expanding section into two units will be followed by arguments for a third, to co-ordinate and mediate between the two. Growth provides promotion opportunities and creates cases for up-grading.

Can opposing motivations be created? Can managers gain personal kudos from *not* expanding, from coping with new work within existing manpower levels, from volunteering reductions in their establishments? Within top management salary and reward systems, is cost-effectiveness and cost reduction given a primary position in assessing management performance with a related impact on salary changes? Do managers operate in a climate in which expansion is felt to be personally dangerous (unless demonstrably related to cost-effectiveness), and in which the efficient deployment of manpower is seen and felt to be a desired and applauded objective? In other words, is establishment control to be seen by managers as an unpleasant, negative and external restriction; or can it be built into the management system as a normal internal element, maintained by a complementary motivational climate?

Until questions of this type are answered, personnel managers will have to continue to rely on the existing weapons of O and M staffing yardsticks, Office Work Measurement (OWM) and Organization Development (OD), and a brief discussion of each of these is now given. They will also have to be prepared to operate the more ruthless, less nicely calculated, type of control discussed earlier in this chapter, whenever the more rational approach fails to result in generally acceptable overall levels of local authority employment.

Organization and methods (O and M)

O and M is, perhaps, the most generally applicable technique or process for use in achieving not only optimum manning levels but also a sound pattern or system of work. O and M in the UK originated in the Civil Service as early as 1919 when the Treasury Investigation Section was established to undertake reviews of office methods and equipment. Manpower shortages after the second world war led to an increasing interest in local government in methods of securing maximum manpower effectiveness, and some of the early O and M work was thus more concerned with how to achieve more and better work from inadequate manning levels than in the more contemporary problems of avoiding overmanning.

Two developments in the early 1950s put O and M firmly on the local government map. These were a Treasury-aided O and M review of Coventry Corporation and the formation of the first joint O and M unit in London (now broadened to become the London Boroughs' Management Services Unit).

Broad-based O and M goes well beyond manpower control and is outside the scope of this chapter. What is stressed here, however, is that an important element in securing economic and effective manning levels is the prior factual analysis of the work situation, and the systematic assessment of working procedures, methods and equipment. The O and M officer is not a narrow specialist: he does not use one particular technique. Indeed, one of the problems of O and M is to find a definition which is more specific than the Treasury's: 'a review of work with the object of producing greater efficiency'. The value of O and M lies as much in the concept of a comprehensive, independent review of a department or section as it does in any of the minutiae of the techniques used in the review. The O and M analyst looks systematically and analytically for a whole range of possible causes of inefficiency or waste, such as:

skilled staff spending time on less skilled activities – such as the professional engineer spending significant parts of his time on recording or filing drawings
under or over supervision, inlcuding unclear lines of authority
duplication or overlapping of work, such as two sections both recording the same data without knowledge of each other's records
inessential activities, such as the typing of unimportant internal memos, unnecessarily complex forms and the like
the use of out-dated and low output office machinery
unnecessarily thorough checking, where only sample inspection would suffice.

Effective work and office systems should, by definition, employ manpower with economy and efficiency, and the personnel manager faced with the task of vetting a department's bid for a significant increase in staff would do well to call in O and M assistance. Better still, departments should use internal advisory O and M services in producing their plans for coping with new work, so that O and M does not have to be used in too direct a 'head-cutting' role.

It is a view of this author that one area of local government organization which merits particular O and M (and OD) attention is that of supervisory and management hierarchies. There seems to be a tradition or convention of tall, narrow-based pyramids of control, with each manager supervising only a very few subordinates. The result, of course, is a large number of levels of management and a large number of managerial staff relative to the employees 'at the coal-face'.

The top hierarchy of:

Chief Officer
Deputy Chief Officer
Assistant Chief Officer
Deputy Assistant Chief Officer

is, perhaps, an extreme or out-dated example; but departments with eight or more levels above the lowest grade are not uncommon. Examined statistically, these types of organization seem very odd. Assuming that at each level, each manager or supervisor has only three subordinates, then eight levels will cover over 3,000 staff, and 10 levels some 23,000. If the number of subordinates is increased to five (surely an entirely satisfactory 'span of control') then eight levels cope with 97,000 and 10 levels with nearly 2½ million! Put another way, a medium-sized authority employing 5,000 staff, organized on a span of control of five subordinates per supervisor/manager, should need only seven levels including the base or shop floor level.

Staffing yardsticks

In the absence of thorough O and M studies, yardsticks or ratios can be used to relate some form of quantification of work to the numbers and types of staff required to do it. In principle, this is the same as work measurement on a work study or OWM basis: the difference is its application to areas not susceptible to detailed measurement and in its broader, less precise approach. It is not capable, either, of 'scientific' proof. In theory at least, physical work measurement can be broken down into the most minute analysis of body, hand and eye movements, and the time measurements for these can be tested in laboratory conditions. A yardstick which says, for example, that one housing welfare officer can cope with a work load averaging 20 cases per week cannot be so accurately tested. But if it is based on a study of working methods and of the case output of officers known, on the basis of experience, to be efficient in both organizational and welfare terms, then it can be used as an indicator for determining staff levels against known or estimated casework levels.

There is considerable scope in local government for the production of yardsticks or ratios of this kind.

In the housing construction field, the numbers of architects, draughtsmen, building supervisors, clerks of works and other similar jobs can be related to indices of contract value for different types of construction or of units of production, eg number of houses per year. Conveyancing and planning work can be related to indices of the number, scale and type of cases.

In library establishments, ratios of qualified staff per 10,000 of the general population have been suggested, though within a particular service, formulae which take into account the volume of book stock, book issues, and extent of opening hours can be used to give more precise staffing ratios.

The number of technicians in large colleges may similarly be determined by formulae based on student hours, types of course, volume of research or project work, and so on.

In some cases, staffing levels relative to work load may be laid down or implied by statute or required as policy or regulation by central government. Police establishments and standards of fire cover are examples.

The more difficult area is that of administrative and managerial work – work that is at least one stage removed from operational activities. How much administrative backing dose a team of six architects require? What is the supervisory work load in a stores depot? It is often useful to chart the changes over a period in these staffing relationships. They almost always show an increase in proportion of 'indirect' to 'direct' staff (of clerical and administrative work to operational work). Each increase was justified at the time by a projection of staffing needs in the light of additional work. New legislation, for example, is frequently used to justify additional staff to cope with an expected increase in work loads. Actual increases in work loads are best assessed by examining the effect on operational staff. For indirect staff, the test is then whether their increase has kept within that of the front line troops: and examination of the record will often show it has not, and these unjustified increases in indirects will give the watchful personnel officer a clue as to where tighter staffing yardsticks would be desirable.

A wary eye must be kept too on self-generating ratios. In public relations work, for example, it might seem sensible to relate the number of press enquiries, and the volume of press coverage of the council's activities (say in column inches per annum), to the number of press or public relations staff employed. But there is a danger here. The more press releases and stories generated by the press officer, the more press enquiries there will be for explanations, comments, more stories. The local broadcasting station will expect to be able to ring up and get up-to-date comment in the evenings and at week-ends. Members will be invited to give press conferences, to be interviewed on radio and TV. The public relations section will soon require more staff and, on a yardsticks basis, this will be justified. But there comes a point at which someone may have to say that the solution is not more staff but less work.

The whole area of social work, too, carries this problem of where to draw the line on work load. The more effective the social worker, and the wider the social work coverage, the more cases come to light. The use of indices will ensure only that for the the known and accepted work load, the staff levels are right. The extent of expansion in the area of social work may be a matter of social not personnel policy.

Office Work Measurement (OWM)

The application of work measurement techniques, used in work study and developed in a manual work context, to office and administrative work has spawned a variety of techniques with their associated jargon and initials.

OWM is also known as Clerical Work Measurement (CWM). Techniques of assembling standard or pre-determined times for common clerical tasks and actions abound. Clerical Standard Data (CSD), Universal Office Controls (UOC), Clerical Milli-minute Data (CMMD), Office Staffing Standards (OSS) are only some of the various techniques available.

Consultants have had a field day in developing these techniques into complete systems of clerical work control and management, some of the better known systems being:

Group Capacity Assessment (GCA)
Variable Factor Programming (VFP)
Clerical Work Improvment Programme (CWIP)
Clerical Work Evaluation (CWE)
Master Activity Programming (MAP)

The details of these systems are not the concern of this book. In a manpower control context, however, their importance is that they all provide detailed, quantified methods of assessing the work content of clerical and other relatively simple office tasks, and so of determining proper manning levels.

As with work study, the personnel manager may need to assure himself that too enthusiastic an application of mechanistic methods – attractive to the management scientist because they reduce complex work situations to quantifiable and manipulable data – does not create an unsatisfactory work environment from a social or psychological viewpoint.

Organization Development (OD)

The introduction of OD into a discussion of establishment control may seem unusual – an attempt to marry the esoteric to the mundane. OD is a relatively new set of concepts with a strong behavioural science base, which has grown out of intensive research and development in management studies, particularly in the USA. OD has been defined by Richard Beckhard of the Massachusetts Institute of Technology as:

an effort, planned organization-wide and managed from the top, to increase organizational effectiveness and health through planned interventions in the organization's processes, using behavioural science knowledge.*

It therefore means viewing an organization not only as a total operational system (in terms of interlocking work processes) but as a social organism. It assesses organizational effectiveness not merely in mechanistic process, or financial, terms, but in terms of the quality of social relationships and the attitudes of the people who constitute it. Beckhard sets out the goals of an OD effort along the following paraphrased lines:

To create an organizational system which adapts itself quickly and effectively to new tasks and to changes in external pressures. This involves 'loosening up' the organization so that it re-shapes itself differently to match the differing nature of different tasks. The concept here is that structure follows function – the reverse of the Bains approach which sets out one fixed structure for all tasks

To build in 'continuous improvement mechanisms' to both permanent and temporary management systems by effective analysis of tasks and resources, and feed back of results

To work for high collaboration and low competition between interdependent organizational units: that is, to eliminate the rivalry and competition for power and status between departments and sections

To create a climate in which conflict is accepted as a natural and necessary part of the management process and in which conflict resolution is a creative process, not merely one of compromise

To create a situation in which decisions are made when and where the best information is available, and not on the basis of a static view of defined authority in pre-determined roles.

Now all this seems very far from the conventional establishment task of vetting staffing levels, and OD offers no particular techniques to help in this limited process. What is being suggested here is that conventional establishment work, which is concerned with the quality

*Beckhard R, *Organization Development: Strategies and Models*, Addison Wesley, 1969

214

and volume of manpower resources, can provide a recognized base for the extension of personnel management into the much more exciting and dynamic role of assisting in fundamental organizational change. A flexible, adaptable organization; staffed by committed and enthusiastic employees, harnessing natural rivalries to the agreed objectives of the organization as a whole; making its decisions and taking action on the basis of the best information at the best point in the structure – an organization of this kind will not allow itself to become over-staffed. A trend may already be discerned in the review work of some authorities' management services units towards placing a high emphasis on getting the organization structure right before clawing over in too much detail, the precise numbers of staff in each existing section.

The most ideal contribution a personnel manager can make to the manpower control function is to make the function unnecessary by helping to create a self-disciplined organization. OD provides him with some of the concepts needed (if not the tools) to work towards this end.

Manpower budgeting

The ideal position suggested above would not imply the abandonment of any form of control. It would put the emphasis in manpower control on individual departments rather than on a centralized, and to an extent imposed, system. Like any ideal, reality is likely to fall short of it, and in any event, even a self-controlled department will need to plan and control its manpower in a systematic manner. The growth in recent years of the concept of a manpower budget for the authority as a whole illustrates one broad-based approach which can cope both with detailed systems of building up manpower totals from unit, section and departmental resource analyses, and with the 'fix-the-numbers-first' approach. The concept itself is very simple. By whatever means are appropriate or acceptable, estimates are produced of the numbers of employees each department is expected to need and permitted to employ during the subsequent year. This constitutes the department's manpower budgets, and their combined total is the authority's manpower budget. Regular counts of actual numbers employed are then made during the year, and variations from budget (either in surplus or deficit) examined and if necessary explained. Action may be decided to correct either the budget, if experience shows the initial figures to be impracticable; or the shortfall or surplus if no satisfactory explanation exists for these variations. A manpower budget differs from an establishment in that the latter provides for a schedule of *posts*, while the former is concerned with actual numbers of *employees* in posts. Given that staff turnover is likely to result in, say, two per cent of posts being vacant at any one time (the 'vacancy gap'), a manpower budget would normally be at least that amount less than the establishment from which it is derived. Alternatively, the establishment concept may be dropped and the budget substituted.

This may well depend on the degree of detail built into the manpower budget. At its very simplest, the budget may consist of no more than a total of 'live' employees for the authority, or for each main service or department, which may not be exceeded. In that case, an underlying establishment which specifies each post and its grade will almost certainly be necessary. Without it, a departmental budget total may well be adhered to, but conceal massive changes in the grading distribution of the employees within it. A more effective form of budgeting, now being practised by some authorities, is to break down the totals into numbers or percentages of each grade or group of grades, for example:

5 per cent at PO 1 and above
10 per cent at SO 1 and 2
60 per cent at AP grades
25 per cent at Clerical grades

and each group of grades can, of course, be expressed in much more detail if required. It is sensible and wholly practicable for manual workers, firemen and teachers to be brought within this form of budgeting, though most authorities (largely influenced by convention) have tended to pay more attention to the often smaller APT and C group. The budget will, however, always stop short of listing every post: it is a schedule, by grade, of numbers employed, not a rigid establishment.

Monthly returns of actuals against budget can provide a useful management control tool at departmental level, giving early warning of recruitment difficulties where shortfalls show a failure to meet expected requirements; and possible over-staffing where numbers begin marginally to exceed the budget figures. At committee and council level, a quarterly return with comments on any significant variances is as useful a form of manpower information – and basis for policy decisions to effect change – as the parallel form of financial budgeting and returns. One advantage of this type of system is, in fact, the need it produces for the personnel and finance departments to maintain close liaison to ensure compatibility between the financial and manpower budgets. The grading distributions inherent in any but the very simplest budgeting systems also provide a useful tool for both internal and external comparisons. A major difference between two largely administrative departments in their percentages of managerial (or basic clerical) grades may trigger a necessary enquiry into whether work is being effectively organized. External comparisons may also be made, using APT and C grading data collected and disseminated by LACSAB.

As with any other management system, manpower budgeting and its related aspects such as comparative grading studies will work effectively only if managers become committed to it. Personnel officers are used to a reaction of chief officers to comparative statistics which follows this pattern:

the figures are wrong
if they are not wrong, then the comparisons are invalid because the organizations under comparison differ too much
if they do not differ, then if our figures are higher it shows our standards must be better: or if lower, that we are more efficient.

All this really means is: keep out of my patch!

We come back, then, to the basic problem in all kinds of establishment control – the need to build into organization and management systems the incentives and motivations for a large element of self-control – or in their absence, to accept the validity and inevitability of harsher methods introduced by elected members who have, at the end of the day, the ultimate responsibility for justifying the extent to which local government utilizes the economy's manpower resources.

14 Legal aspects: ultra vires: The contract of employment: Individual rights

It was noted in an earlier chapter that the rapid growth in employment legislation since 1965 has been one factor which has stimulated the general development of personnel management. There is little significant employment law specific to local government and this book does not attempt to explain or discuss the whole gamut of legal constraints and requirements which apply to all employers. That is the subject of other, more general legal textbooks.

At the same time, it cannot be overlooked that certain aspects of local government employment practice have caused particular legal problems to many authorities in recent years. The relationship between the Secretary of State's power to declare a teacher unfit for teaching employment, and the unfair dismissal duties of an education authority as an employer, is one example. In this and the succeeding chapter, therefore, the impact of employment legislation in the specific local government world is examined, mainly by looking at particular issues and at cases which have gone through the industrial tribunals and the courts. This chapter also deals with the general legal powers of a local authority insofar as this affects employment decisons and with the legal rights and duties of the individual employee.

The doctrine of ultra vires

As public bodies established by statute, local authorities are subject at law to one important and over-riding principle – that they can make decisions and take actions only insofar as they are permitted or required by statute. This priniciple applies just as much to an employment decision – say, to introduce a medical insurance scheme for chief officers; or to negotiate a closed shop agreement – as it does to financial or operational matters. Given some projected new decision to assess, a local government lawyer will always want to know from whence the power is derived to make it. If this derivation cannot be shown and if the authority is thus acting beyond its statutorily defined powers, then it is acting *ultra vires*, and stands to be ordered by the courts to desist.

This apparently simple position is in practice less easy to define because relevant statutes do not attempt to list every individual issue or type of decision which might be made: they permit discretion to be used, and introduce the concept of 'reasonableness'. Two such areas of discretion are of particular relevance to employment matters.

The first is very general and applies to all an authority's activities. It is the power given by Section 111 of the Local Government Act, 1972, for local authorities 'to do anything . . . which is calculated to facilitate, or is conducive or incidental to, the discharge of any of their functions'.

The second, in Section 112 of the Act, is specific to employment. A local authority may appoint such officers as it thinks necessary for the proper discharge of its functions, and such officers 'shall hold office on such reasonable terms and conditions, including conditions as to remuneration, as the appointing authority . . . thinks fit'. Note that the first discretion, 'to do anything . . .' is limited by the thing done having to be related to the discharge of the authority's functions. These functions (eg the provision of education services) are, of course, set out in other parts of the legislation, so placing a control over capricious decisions, or attempts to extend an authority's activities into new functions. Note, too, the word 'reasonable' in the Section 112 provisions.

Any employment decision or action is consequently open to two forms of challenge. If it can be shown not to be calcualted to facilitate the discharge of a legitimate function (or not to be conducive or incidental to such discharge) it may be challenged as *ultra vires*. The aggrieved party, who might be no more (or less) involved than an ordinary ratepayer, could then seek a declaration in the courts to that effect. If he won such a case, then the authority concerned would be in contempt of court if the act complained of, and ordered to be stopped, was continued.

Alternatively, it might be argued that while the act or decision complained of was incidental to the discharge of a legitimate function, it was an unreasonable act. Specifically in the employment field, it might be argued, for example, that to provide chief officers with free private medical treatment would go beyond the 'reasonable terms and conditions' permitted by Section 112 of the Local Government Act.

Particularly where alleged unreasonable expenditure is involved, the role of the independent auditor (generally the District Auditor, appointed by central government) is of key importance. Any local government elector may question an item of local government expenditure by complaint to the District Auditor who may, on enquiry, determine whether such expenditure was contrary to law. (The Auditor, of course, has full auditing powers to conduct his own enquiries, whether or not an elector complains). Should the Auditor consider that an item is contrary to law – whether as lying outside the area of statutory powers, or as the unreasonable use of those powers – he may apply to the courts for a declaration to that effect and the persons responsible (normally the councillors) may be 'surcharged'. This means that they have to pay out of their own pockets: further, if the unlawful expenditure is beyond £2,000 they may be disqualified from local authority membership.

It is by no means unknown for irate ratepayers to complain about items of employment expenditure to the District Auditor, and the outcome of most of these cases hinges on the Auditor's assessment of 'reasonableness'.

The incidence of such complaints is greatest when an authority goes beyond the normal set of nationally negotiated pay and conditions of service and pioneers the local application of some new provision – say, the introduction of paternity leave. A ratepayer may consider such an innovation as involving a wholly unacceptable use of public monies. The District Auditor must then take a view as to whether this can be said to constitute a reasonable employee benefit. There are no formally published guidelines on which such decisions are made: it is all a matter of judgement in which, however, comparisons with other employers must certainly play a a part. Indeed, it can be suggested with a fair measure of confidence that the test to apply is that of 'the good employer'. Auditors recognize that local authorities, as large-scale employers, act reasonably if they adopt an approach to employment matters broadly consistent with that of other large employers, and that pay and conditions of service among large employers are generally towards the good, or better, end of the spectrum. On this test, the provision of a free medical insurance scheme for chief officers would be in line with the practice among other large, 'good' employers and would not be unreasonable. Only an actual case, however, could establish this without doubt.

A few real cases may be used to illustrate the approach of the courts in practice.

An extreme, and therefore atypical, case in recent times was that of the Clay Cross councillors who, acting in open defiance of government pay policy, introduced new manual worker wage levels which were eventually judged to be unlawful within the meaning of the statutes. The councillors were surcharged, and disqualified from local authority membership (the subsequent political furore being thankfully beyond the purview of this book).

A considerably older case – Roberts v Hopwood, 1925 – had already set an important precedent in this field. It involved the Poplar Borough Council who, relying on the pre-1972 statute which permitted a local authority to pay such wages 'as they think fit', set their wage levels well above those generally obtaining. The District Auditor disallowed the extra costs involved, and the councillors were surcharged. The case eventually went on appeal to the House of Lords where the auditor's view was upheld, the Law Lords stating that any discretion permitted to a council by statute 'must be exercised reasonably' and that 'reasonably' involved consideration of what was in the interests of the ratepayers*. The 1972 Act, as we have seen, actually uses the word 'reasonable', but most lawyers would agree that the concept of reasonableness is so well established as hardly to require statutory inclusion. The final case selected for comment is worth a slightly longer description in view of its link with recent employment legislation on the controversial issue of the closed shop.

Regina v GLC ex parte Burgess, 1978
Mr Burgess, a London elector, sought an order from the Court (Queens Bench Division, Divisional Court) that the GLC should cease to require employees to retain trade union membership under the terms of a recently concluded 'closed shop' agreement. The argument made on Mr Burgess' behalf was based on the view that union membership involved, *inter alia*, a requirement to go on strike – and a strike would result in the GLC ceasing to provide services to ratepayers. As the GLC had statutory powers (and obligations) to *provide* services, an arrangement which might result in their cessation amounted to the GLC denying itself the use of powers which it had a duty to exercise. In another important local government case not connected with employment (Birkdale District Electric Supply Company v Southport Corporation 1926), it had been stated that if a public body 'is entrusted by the Legislature with certain powers and duties' it could not enter into any contract 'or take any action incompatible with the due exercise of their powers . . .' The Lord Chief Justice, who took this GLC case, stated that if the GLC was in fact, by adopting a closed shop agreement, denying itself the exercise of powers inherent in its situation as a local authority, then 'it would be logical enough to say that this Court should restore such deficiency . . .'

In considering this case, the Court first established that the post-entry union membership agreement concluded by the GLC with its various manual trade unions was itself lawful within the relevant employment legislation. The agreement was, said the LCJ 'perfectly

*See also: Carr v District Auditor, 1952: salaries paid above standard rates are not *ultra vires*, but must be 'reasonable'.

221

respectable'. But on Mr Burgess' behalf it was argued that the agreement was outside the scope of Section 111 of the Local Government Act; that is, it did not facilitate the discharge of the GLC's duties, and was not conducive or incidental to such discharge. The GLC's memorandum, which set out the details of the negotiation of the union membership agreement, explained the introduction of the agreement as being consistent with the orderly conduct of industrial relations.

The Court eventually concluded that:

> it was quite impossible to reach a conclusion that a closed shop agreement on these lines is in some way something which is not conducive or incidental to the discharge of the local authority's functions . . . In the state of understanding of trade unions and their functions no-one is in a position to say that this type of closed shop agreement does not facilitate the carrying out of the GLC functions . . . It is at the very least a matter of debate, and if it is a matter of debate then the local authority must surely be entitled to please itself unless and until it can be shown to be wrong.

Comment: Two aspects of the Court's decision are worth noting. First, the onus of proving that the authority was acting *ultra vires* lay with the complainant – the authority could 'please itself until it can be shown to be wrong'. Secondly, the decision cannot be taken as unreservedly linking a closed shop agreement with the exercise of an authority's proper functions. It merely said that in this particular case, at this particular time, the converse could not be proved. It should be noted, too, that this was not a complaint which could readily have been processed through the District Audit procedure as no extra, identifiable expenditure was involved. The case, generally, is a useful reminder that apparently wholly domestic employment decisions within an authority are potentially open to challenge by individual electors or ratepayers; and that personnel officers must consequently consider both the legitimacy and reasonableness of innovations in the personnel field in relation to their authorities' statutory functions and powers (direct and discretionary).

The contract of employment

Problems arising from the Contracts of Employment Act and its later amendments in the Employment Protection Act* have been relatively few in local government, where general administrative practice has for many years resulted in a greater degree of documentation than in parts of the industrial world. There, the Act resulted in the issue of written

---

*Note that legislation concerning individual rights, including the contracts of Employment Act, has been consolidated into one statute – The Employment Protection (Consolidated) Act, 1978.

letters of appointment with supporting contract documents for the first time in the recruitment of many manual workers. Hiring (and firing) solely by word of mouth was common, for example, in the construction industry. Most local authorities were used to issuing letters or other appointment *pro-forma*. But some problems relating to teachers' contracts of employment and conditions of service have emerged in recent years. Most of these problems have stemmed from the existence of legislation specific to the employment and remuneration of teachers, which pre-dates general employment legislation. The first of these issues concerns the legal status of the pay agreements reached in the Burnham negotiating committees, and of agreements on conditions of service other than pay. The arrangements for determining teachers' remuneration are prescribed by statute – the Remuneration of Teachers Act, 1976. This Act required the Secretary of State to establish committees 'for the purpose of considering the remuneration payable to teachers' by local education authorities. The committees had to have independent chairmen and to include representatives of the Secretary of State (Education and Science), the employers and the teaching staff organizations (trade unions and associations). The Committees' agreements are legally 'recommendations' to the Secretary of State who has then to draft statutory orders setting out the resultant pay scales and, after consulting the Burnham Committees on the details of the draft orders, publish them in the form of directives to local education authorities as to what salaries they must pay to their teaching staff. This system covers only remuneration – not other conditions of service.

In 1973, the two local authority associations involved in education (the ACC and AMA) formed a joint body, the Council of Local Education Authorities (CLEA) to act as a forum for all educational matters. Since 1973, CLEA has negotiated agreements with the teaching trade unions on conditions of service other than remuneration, acting as a national employers' association. The legal status of CLEA and of these non-pay agreements was not formally resolved, and in 1976 questions began to be asked. Was CLEA an employer (or an employers' association) as defined by employment legislation? Were individual local authorities bound to implement CLEA/trade union agreements? Were individual teachers bound by contract to accept the terms of these agreements? Could individual teachers enforce the implementation of these agreements on a contractual basis if their employing authorities failed to apply newly negotiated conditions?

The answer to all these questions was, no. Legally, CLEA was not an employer or an employers' association – it had never applied for certification as such. Its agreements were not enforced by government order, as Burnham pay agreements were. In the absence of any reference to CLEA agreements in individual contracts of employment, individual teachers could not enforce their implementation, and could presumably object to their imposition. The agreements constituted no more than recommendations to local authorities which the latter could apply, modify, or ignore as they thought fit. At the same time, if most authorities applied the agreements, those which did not might have had the unions making a case under Schedule 11 of the Employment Protection Act for the enforcement of conditions not less favourable than those obtaining generally.

The ACC and AMA discussed the problem and agreed a long term aim of securing the repeal of the Remuneration of Teachers' Act, the withdrawal of the Department of Education and Science from pay negotiations, and the establishment of a single authoritative forum for the negotiation of both pay and other conditions of service. Shorter term action was still necessary, and the immediate solution to making CLEA/trade union agreements enforceable was through the individual contract of employment.

The Associations asked local education authorities to do two things. First, to pass resolutions to the effect that they would apply CLEA agreements. Secondly, and from a legal employment viewpoint more important, to include in each teacher's contract of employment a statement along the following lines:

Your salary will be determinded according to Orders made from time to time under the Remuneration of Teachers Act, 1965. Your other conditions of employment will be determined by collective agreements negotiated from time to time between CLEA and the recognized trade unions and by supplementary agreements negotiated between the local education authority and such trade union or unions as are recognized by the LEA for local collective bargaining purposes for the employment group to which you belong.

This formula – which follows the general practice for all other local government employees – thus provides a contractual guarantee to each employee that the local education authority will apply the terms of collective agreements. Were the authority to fail in this, the teacher could sue for breach of contract. This is the standard method of importing the terms of collective agreements into individual contracts of employment regardless of the non-legally binding nature of the agreement on the actual parties to it.

The next problem had some similarities in that it originated in the statutory powers of the Secretary of State – this time in Schedule 2 of the Schools Regulations, 1959. Under these statutory regulations, the Secretary of State has the power to determine that a probationary teacher is unsuitable for further employment, and that any teacher who 'on grounds of misconduct or conviction of a criminal offence' is determined by the Secretary of State to be unsuitable as a teacher shall not be so employed.

It had not unnaturally been assumed that such a determination by the Secretary of State automatically justified dismissal (ie termination of the employment contract) by the employing authority. This view was challenged under unfair dismissals legislation by a London teacher in a case which went on appeal from an industrial tribunal to the Employment Appeals Tribunal.

Sandhu v London Borough of Hillingdon, EAT 1978
Sandhu was a probationary teacher, dismissed after a determination by the Secretary of State that he was unsuitable for further employment as a teacher. He went to a tribunal, alleging that his dismissal came about because of racial discrimination. The tribunal accepted the employers' argument that it would be wrong to enquire into the events leading up to the dismissal, or into the reasons which led the Department of Education and Science to reach the conclusion that Sandhu was unsuitable. The reason for dismissal, the tribunal concluded, was the operation of the statutory bar to employment involved in the Schedule 2 provisions of the School Regulations. And unfair dismissals legislation recognizes the force of statutory bars. But on appeal, the EAT reversed this view. They asked, had the employer acted reasonably? The EAT thought not. 'What a reasonable employer would have done would have been to discuss the matter with him (Sandhu), with the Department of Education and Science (DES), and see whether what had gone wrong could be put right . . .' So the force of a Schedule 2 determination was subject to an examination of the circumstances leading up to it, and could not automatically justify dismissal.

This case was followed by a contract of employment case in the County Court, in which the immediate termination of employment (without contractual notice) on receipt of a DES determination was held to be a breach of contract. The court held that these determinations did not provide that a teacher should cease to be employed on the effective date of a determination – the contract of employment remained in existence and had to be honoured.

These cases led the Association of County Councils to suggest that the position of employing authorities would be strengthened if teachers' contracts of employment incorporated the Schedule 2 provisions. A clause might be inserted to the effect that:

Your employment will be subject to the provisions of Schedule 2 of the Schools Regulations (1959) and in the event that the Secretary of State determines that you are unsuitable for further employment as a teacher, or are suitable only to a limited extent, your employment will be terminated on the date of such determination, or will

225

be limited from that date to the extent so determined by the Secretary of State.

A clause of this kind will not, however, wholly protect the employer from an unfair dismissal claim, because although it clearly establishes a contractual reason for dismissal, the employer will still need to show that he acted reasonably in treating it as a *sufficient* reason for dismissal.

Hours of work
The length of an employee's working week has not normally been a subject of much dispute, and is usually considered to be as set out in the contract of employment. A case involving a part-time teacher, together with another concerning a retained fireman, has complicated the previously simple position.

Lake v Essex County Council (CA 1979)
In this case the authority was defending an unfair dismissal claim on the grounds that Mrs Lake, the teacher concerned, worked less than 21 hours weekly. At that time, part-timers under 21 hours could not pursue unfair dismissal claims. Her letter of appointment specified her weekly hours as 19 hours 25 minutes. Duties outside the classroom (eg preparing class work, marking etc) were catered for by three hours 40 minutes of free time within the contractual hours. The tribunal accepted this explanation and rejected the claim. Mrs Lake appealed on the grounds that the three hours 40 minutes was insufficient to cover the preparation of lessons and marking, and that it was custom and practice that such work was necessary and was undertaken outide the contractual school hours. The EAT agreed. They pointed out that the written contract did not necessarily exclude the possibility of the existence of other unwritten contractual requirements. 'In our judgement', they said 'Mrs Lake was under a contractual obligation to the Council to do as much work outside the school hours specified in her contract as was reasonably necessary for the proper performance of her teaching duties'. Consequently, she might well have been able to show that in total she was working more than 21 hours. However, the Court of Appeal eventually reversed this EAT decision, holding that Mrs Lake's leisure hour working was voluntary.

In the fire service case – *Bullock v Merseyside County Council, EAT, 1977* – a similar problem arose. Was a period on 'standby' to be classified as employment, and all the hours involved counted towards a contractual total. The authority argued that Bullock's duties as a retained fireman involved only attendance at a fire station for two hours weekly, plus response to fire calls while on standby which averaged 8½ hours weekly. Standby involved no more than carrying

226

on his private life while being available to report immediately for duty if summoned. The EAT disagreed. They looked at the degree of control exercised by the employer during the standby period and noted that there was a requirement for the fireman to remain within four minutes' travelling time from the fire station during this period. Further, he was potentially at the beck and call of the fire officer for the whole of this period. His 'employment' was therefore held to include the whole period, whether or not he was actually working, giving him a week of 102 hours! In 1978, the Court of Appeal upheld the EAT decision.

The full implications of these two cases have not yet been established and in any event, too detailed a general rule should not be drawn from the different facts of different cases. The Lake case opened the door, at EAT level, to discussion as to the extent that work done at home was 'reasonably necessary' to the contractual performance of a job; while Denning's judgement might assist teachers (and other staff) in arguing that the employer cannot expect work to be done other than in normal working hours.

Retiring age
A teacher's contract of employment normally includes a statement that employment will finally terminate at the end of the term during which he or she reaches the age of 65.

Unfair dismissal legislation excludes employees who, at the date of dismissal, have attained the 'normal retiring age . . . or if a man, attained the age of 65, or if a woman, attained the age of 60'. Could a woman teacher, dismissed at the age of 61, pursue a case of unfair dismissal? An important Court of Appeal case was necessary to resolve this issue.

Northman v London Borough of Barnet, Court of Appeal, 1977
Miss Northman was dismissed at the age of 61 on the grounds that she was unable satisfactorily to carry out her duties. She considered this unfair and pursued a claim for compensation. Barnet Borough Council defended the case on the preliminary grounds that, as a woman of over 60 she was barred by statute from pursuing an unfair dismissals claim. Both the tribunal and the EAT agreed that the 'normal retiring age' for teachers was 65 and that under this heading Miss Northman could have pursued her case. But they noted that the statute went beyond this. It said, in effect, normal retiring age *or* age 60 for a woman. The EAT considered that the 'or age 60' provision over-rode the normal retiring age. Miss Northman was therefore excluded from pursuing an unfair dismissal claim, even though a man of the same age, in the same circumstances, would not be excluded. On appeal to the Court of Appeal, Lord Denning, the Master of the Rolls, would

have none of this. The EAT ruling, he said, was 'the voice of those who adopt the strict literal and grammatical construction of the words, heedless of the consequences'. In a typical Denning judgement – one of the type that still makes some lawyers' (and politicians') blood run cold – he went on:

> it is no longer necessary for the judges to wring their hands and say there is nothing we can do about it. When the strict interpretation of a statute gives rise to an absurd and unjust situation, the judges can and should use their good sense to remedy it – by reading words in if necessary – so as to do what Parliament would have done had they the situation in mind.

In this case, therefore, the age limitation provisions could be given sense and justice by reading in some extra words thus:

> normal retiring age, *or where there is no normal retiring age*, age 65 if a man, or age 60 if a woman.

Miss Northman could, therefore, pursue a claim for unfair dismissal. Lord Denning's two fellow judges reached the same conclusion by a less revolutionary path. They concluded that the word 'or' (normal retiring age *or* age 60) could be interpreted in two ways – one way linking the two phrases and so making one conditional on the other, the other way separating the two phrases and so enabling them to be applied independently to appropriate cases.

By whatever path chosen, however, this judgement has made it clear that women over 60 throughout almost all local government service can pursue unfair dismissal claims, as the normal retirement age for local government officers – teachers, APT and C or whatever – is clearly the single age of 65 for both men and women, even though the State retirement age for women is 60. The local government superannuation scheme, however, does not discriminate between the sexes and is designed around a normal retirement age of 65.

Contractual duties

Most of the cases discussed so far in this chapter have been concerned with the rights of the employee and the duties of the employer. The other side of this coin is the definition of what duties the employee is obliged to undertake within the terms of the employment contract. Another teaching case is of some importance, particularly in the light of a continuing dialogue between the teaching trade unions and education authorities as to just what duties can legally be expected from a teacher. Industrial action consisting of refusals to undertake playground or mealroom supervision is interpreted by the unions as merely an opting-out of voluntary, not contractual, duties. While the particular case does not deal with non-teaching activities, it does bring out a need to import the concept of 'reasonableness' into the strict letter of the contract.

Fishman v London Borough of Redbridge, EAT, 1978
Mrs Fishman was appointed by Redbridge to a post described in her letter of appointment as a 'full-time permanent teacher in charge of the Resources Centre', a post initially involving no regular teaching commitments though requiring the services of a teacher, and with an unwritten understanding that the appointee would undertake a limited amount of teaching in order to maintain her teaching skills and keep her in touch with classroom realities. After two years, a new head teacher was appointed to the school and things began to change. Mrs Fishman was first asked to teach 12 lessons a week of English, in addition to heading the resource centre, and agreed. Eighteen months later she was asked to increase this to 18 lessons weekly (about three-quarters of a normal teaching workload) and refused. She said that at this level of teaching she would not be able to do justice to her resource centre appointment. Following discussions and correspondence, the head teacher eventually instructed Mrs Fishman to undertake the 18 teaching periods; Mrs Fishman refused, and was eventually dismissed for refusing to obey this instruction. She claimed unfair dismissal compensation and won her case at the tribunal. Redbridge appealed to the EAT, basing the argument on the contractual position. They pointed out that the job was in the assistant master category, and that under the conditions of service for assistant masters/mistresses (which formed part of the contract) a teacher agreed to 'serve under the immediate directions of the Head' and that no formal job descriptions are ever issued. Teachers are employed just as teachers and can be drafted to whatever job the head teacher, or the authority, thinks fit. Mrs Fishman's letter of appointment was a standard letter for teachers, and indeed included a requirement to work 'at such school as may be determined by the Authority' – as well as specifying the initial appointment. She just happened to be engaged at first in the resources centre, but she was under an obligation, said Redbridge, to do whatever job which they or the head teacher might later require. Redbridge's Counsel, pressed by the EAT, developed this theme. While a teacher might initially accept an appointment following the advertisement of a particular post, Counsel claimed that as a matter of contract such a teacher may be required to teach any subject at any time. The EAT found this odd. Their judgement commented that Counsel did not 'shrink from the proposition put to him in argument that if this submission is right, the teacher engaged to teach the violin to the upper school may be drafted to teaching woodwork to the junior school, and *vice versa*. We have found this a startling proposition', the EAT commented, 'and one which we would have expected to be more

229

acceptable in Dotheboys Hall than in the more progressive London Borough of Redbridge'.

Consequently, the EAT rejected the Redbridge view. In their view, the head teacher is entitled to require teachers to do work other than that for which they have been engaged, 'provided that the request is reasonable'. In the particular case, the EAT concluded that in reality Mrs Fishman had not been engaged as a general teacher, but had been offered and accepted a more specialized post. For such a post, a requirement to teach 18 periods of English was unreasonable. Therefore, Mrs Fishman's case for unfair dismissal was upheld. The EAT noted, however, that if Redbridge's operational requirements had changed, so that the resource centre post was no longer needed and an English teacher was, and if Mrs Fishman refused an offer of employment as an English teacher, then a dismissal not for misconduct but on the grounds that the initial post had been abolished and she had refused a reasonable alternative, might not be seen as unfair.

The general point, however, remained. The courts will not uphold an unreasonable contractual duty, or an unreasonable interpretation of a contract.

Fixed term contracts

The extensive employment of teachers and lecturers on a temporary basis has given rise to a number of tribunal and court cases about the nature of the contracts involved. These cases have in the main originated from the provisions of unfair dismissal legislation which states, *inter alia*, that the expiry and non-renewal of a fixed term contract is a dismissal. (The only exception is a contract for a period of a year or more which expressly includes a waiver clause contracting out of the unfair dismissal rights.)

A number of teachers who have been recruited for periods of, say, one term or one school year at a time have consequently instituted unfair dismissal claims when their authorities have decided not to renew their contracts. Two matters have been at issue in these cases; first, have the contracts been of a fixed term nature? Secondly, are non-renewals of such contracts automatically 'fair'?

The first complication arose when, in a BBC case *(BBC v Ioannou, Court of Appeal, 1975)* it was held that the inclusion of a notice period within a fixed term contract destroyed its fixed term nature. The court held that if a contract, stated to be for, say, two years, could be terminated by either party giving three months' notice at any time within the two year period, then it was not in reality for a fixed term. Initially, this case led to the odd conclusion that if a fixed term contract which included notice periods was not a fixed term contract, then its non-renewal was not a dismissal and the employee was wholly excluded from any unfair dismissal rights. But is was eventually held by the EAT that non-renewal at the end of a fixed period *did* constitute dismissal under the normal expiry of contract rules, as by that time any notice period in the contract would be inoperable, and the only reason for the cessation of employment was the contract's expiry and non-renewal.

A different issue was raised by a teaching case – *Wiltshire County Council v NATFHE and Guy, EAT, 1978*. Mrs Guy had been working as a part-time teacher since 1969, though she entered into a fresh contract each year. This provided that she would teach certain classes on certain days, until notified by the college that the course was concluded. No actual finishing date was specified. Her contract was not renewed in 1977, and she brought a case of unfair dismissal based on non-renewal. The authority argued that the contract was not a fixed term contract because it had no specified terminal date – so its non-renewal did not at law equate to dismissal. The EAT disagreed. They held that a fixed term contract could exist without a terminal date being specified, provided the terms were fixed by some specified external event. The Court of Appeal overturned this view. They held that a contract with no defined termination date could not be for a fixed term. Such contracts were 'discharged by perfomance' – they come to an end with dismissal. But the Court also held that Mrs Guy was really contracted to work a whole academic year at a time – and therefore was on a fixed term contract.

Legal battles of the kinds just described do no more than establish that many non-renewals of temporary teachers' contracts constitute dismissals. Education authorities need to be alarmed at this only if such dismissals can be shown to be unfair, and at this hurdle, most of the teachers' cases have fallen.

The point is illustrated in *Terry v E Sussex County Council, EAT, 1976*. Terry was a senior lecturer, engaged on a temporary basis for one year. When this contract expired and was not renewed he claimed unfair dismissal compensation. Under unfair dismissal legislation, the employer has to show that dismissal resulted from conduct, capability or 'some other substantial reason of a kind such as to justify the dismissal'. Terry argued that the expiry and non-renewal of a fixed term contract could in no circumstances constitute 'some other substantial reason'. The education authority argued the contrary. The EAT pointed to two dangers in reaching a conclusion. First, if they agreed with Terry, then there would be thousands of cases in which compensation might have to be paid for no other reason than that a contract could not be renewed. But if they gave *carte blanche* to non-renewal as being automatically 'fair', then fixed term contracts could become a widespread method of evading unfair dismissals legislation.

The EAT concluded that the non-renewal of a fixed term contract *could* be 'some other substantial reason' for dismissal. That is, that in genuine cases where the employer had good reason to offer employment for only a fixed term, and good reason not to renew that contract, non-renewal should constitute a fair dismissal. 'On the other hand, employees have to be protected against being deprived of their rights through ordinary employment being dressed up in the form of temporary fixed term contracts'. Terry's case was consequently remitted back to a tribunal to assess whether, solely on grounds of fact, the temporary nature of his employment had been 'genuine'.

In a later case – *Benge v Salford City Council, EAT 1978* – a lecturer claimed unfair dismissal when his temporary appointment was terminated. The college had decided to disband his temporary lectureship in printmaking, and establish a new, enlarged, permanent lectureship in printmaking, drawing and painting. Benge argued that the college could not rely solely on non-renewal as a reason for fair dismissal. They had failed to give him any priority in filling the new permanent post and had consequently acted unfairly. The tribunal, and later the EAT, did not agree. They found that there was no requirement for an employer to give a relatively short-service employee whose temporary contract had not been renewed, some form of priority of appointment to other posts over and above other suitable candidates.

All these cases leave the whole question of temporary and fixed term contracts on a common-sense basis. If there are good operational reasons for hiring staff term-by-term, or year-by-year, or for the duration of particular courses, then the non-renewal of their contracts because of a relevant change in requirements for their services, though constituting dismissal, will be fair. But if short-term contracts are used for normal, permanent work, or are terminated for other reasons than those which justified their use, then non-renewal may be shown to be unfair.

Individual liability

In most cases in which a remedy is sought in the tribunals or courts against an alleged wrong by an employer, the employer is the body corporate, eg the district or county council in local government terms. Thus unfair dismissal claims are made against the authority as a whole, not against chief officers as individuals. There are two exceptions to this which open the door to proceedings being taken against named officers as well as (or instead of) their employing authorities and cases have been lost by chief officers who have attempted to escape from these provisions. The two fields in which individual liability can arise are health and safety, and sex and race discrimination. Under the Health and Safety at Work Act, 1974, the Health and Safety Inspectorate can initiate prosecution of any manager (or other

232

responsible officer) if an offence can be shown to have been committed with his or her 'consent or connivance', or to have been attributable to such an officer's neglect. In such cases, the individual may be proceeded against as well as the body corporate. Some alarmed local government managers have sought form of indemnification against such proceedings from their authorities, but this cannot be provided. The ultimate sanction against an individual under this legislation is imprisonment, and there is no way by which an authority can protect an officer against criminal prosecution and a consequent gaol sentence. Could an authority pay an officer's fines under this legislation? Such a question needs to be seen in the light of the opening discussion in this chapter of the doctrine of *ultra vires*, and the reasonableness of local government expenditure.

The question has not been tested in the courts, but a case could certainly be made that any general indemnity would be either *ultra vires*, or would constitute an unreasonable use of public funds. Would it not be contrary to the public interest for an authority to guarantee to protect its employees from the financial penalties of their criminal wrong doings? A decision to reimburse a fine after the event, on an individual basis in the light of the particular circumstances, might not, however, be so risky a proceeding. It is worth noting, however, that the Inland Revenue refuses to accept such payments as the reimbursement of expenses wholly and *necessarily* incurred in the course of work, and will consequently tax them!

An alternative approach has therefore been to argue in court that the individual charge is inappropriate, as the following case illustrates.

Armour v Skeen (Procurator Fiscal, Glasgow), High Court of Justiciary, 1976
Armour was the Director of Roads of the Strathclyde Regional Council. He was charged with six offences under the Health and Safety at Work Act and convicted in five of these charges. At the heart of the case was his alleged 'neglect' in failing to issue a safety policy for his department, the various charges all being linked to this issue. Armour's appeal was on two bases. First, that he personally was not under a statutory duty to prepare a departmental safety policy. Secondly, that he did not fall within the class of 'manager, secretary or other similar officer', specified by the Act (Section 37 (i)) as carrying potential personal liability.

The Scottish High Court found on the first point that 'neglect' could not be limited to neglect of a particular statutory duty. True, Strathclyde had issued the authority-wide policy statement required by law. But the council had gone on to issue instructions to all chief officers to prepare supplementary policies for each department, and this Armour had failed to do. Neglect meant the personal neglect of any matter to which the contravention of safety provisions was attributable. The neglect to produce a departmental policy statement meant that safe working systems had not been prescribed, and the absence of such prescriptions could lead to accidents at work.

On the second point, the Lord Justice-Clerk was even shorter:

> Having regard to the position of the appellant in the organization of the council and the duty which was imposed on him in connection with the provision of a general safety policy in respect of the work of his department, I have no difficulty in holding that he came within the ambit of the class of persons referred to in section 37 (i).

So on both counts Armour lost his appeal and remained personally liable, and his fine by the lower court stood.

In the Sex Discrimination Act, 1975, the question of personal liability is not so clearly set out, and this lack of clarity provided the basis for argument in a local government case in which a preliminary hearing was held to determine whether an applicant could join a chief officer as a second respondent to an application involving a district council.

Read v Tiverton District Council, Exeter Tribunal, 1977
Mrs Read was an assistant in the Land Charges Section of the Solicitor's Department. The post of Chief Land Charges Clerk became vacant, but Mrs Read was not appointed to it. She complained to a tribunal that she had been discriminated against on grounds of sex, naming the Council's Solicitor as her employer. He suggested that Mrs Read might wish to substitute Tiverton District Council as the respondent. The council, not he, was Mrs Read's employer. But she considered him to be personally involved, and joined him with the council in her action. Tiverton argued that this could not be done as the Act made no specific reference to the liability of manager or other officers.

Mrs Read's solicitor argued that by inference, the Act did permit this. The Act used the expression 'it is unlawful for a *person*, in relation to employment by him to discriminate against a woman . . .' It goes on to say that anything done by a person in the course of his employment shall be treated as done also by his employer. Further, it says that an employee or agent for whose act the employer is liable shall be deemed to aid the doing of the act by the employer.

Putting all this together, the tribunal chairman decided that it was open to Mrs Read to accuse Mr Bull, acting on behalf of the council, of committing an act of discrimination against her. That act (if eventually proved) would be direct discrimination for which the council would be responsible because the law provides that Mr Bull's act be

234

treated as an act of the council. But Mr Bull could also be personally liable because he aided the Council to commit that unlawful act and the law requires that he be treated as doing that same act.

As the hearing was limited to this preliminary point, no evidence was heard about the act complained of. But Mrs Read was given permission to proceed against Mr Bull as well as against the Tiverton Council.

Unfair dismissal
Perhaps the most important single right for the individual employee in employment legislation is the right not to be unfairly dismissed. Several of the earlier cases in this chapter have been concerned with the removal of restrictions on that right, while there have undoubtedly been more articles, books, seminars and training courses written for managers on this one element of employment law than on any other single aspect. As this chapter is not a general exposition of unfair dismissals legislation, but is restricted to issues with particular local government elements, no attempt is made here to explain the whole legal concept of unfair dismissal. It is sufficient to say that the heart of the concept is simple. Once it is shown that dismissal occurred, then two questions arise:

What was the reason for dismissal?
Having regard to the particular circumstances – to equity and to the merits of the case – did the employer act reasonably in treating the reason as sufficient to justify dismissal?

The onus of proof of the reason and reasonableness of the dismissal used to fall on the employer. Recent legislation has lifted this onus, and left it to the tribunal to determine each case on the evidence.

In assessing reasonableness, account must be taken of the ACAS Code of Practice on disciplinary procedures, as well as of the legislation itself. Equity and the Code, require as key principles that:

except in cases of serious or gross misconduct, dismissal should not normally follow a first offence
the employee should know what he is to be dismissed for, and should be given an opportunity to explain and defend himself before dismissal is effected.

In assessing the sufficiency of a reason for dismissal, a tribunal will have a general regard to contemporary standards of employment practice. An act that might have justified instant dismissal in 1890 or 1950 will not necessarily so justify today. Because of the emphasis in the legislation on 'fairness' and 'reasonableness', and the regard tribunals pay to current employment standards, the successful defence of unfair dismissal cases requires the knowledge and skills of the professional personnel manager just as much, if not more, than those of the pure lawyer. The Fishman-Redbridge case, outlined earlier, illustrates the lack of sympathy of the modern labour law court (the EAT) for a purely legal argument (*viz* the reference to Dotheboys Hall!). Tribunals and the EAT look for an up-to-date employment approach by the employer – particularly large public sector employers as local authorities are.

The following short selection of unfair dismissal cases illustrates the types of problem that may be involved within local government, and points up the value of such cases being argued on the basis of employment as well as legal criteria.

Boyten v East Herts. District Council, EAT, 1977

In this EAT case, East Herts appealed against an industrial tribunal decision that their dismissal of Boyten, a refuse collector, for being involved in a fight with another employee, was unfair.

Boyten and a temporary employee (a student) had initially been suspended for fighting, pending the outcome of an investigation. The student produced a signed statement by two other refuse collectors to the effect that Boyten had made an unprovoked attack on him. The senior officer involved decided that Boyten should be dismissed. Boyten appealed, using the agreed appeals procedure. His appeal was finally heard by the authority's appeals committee – an elected member body. The committee upheld the dismissal.

At the appeal committee hearing Boyten and his senior officer made statements, but neither the student nor the two other refuse collectors were called. Their letters were produced instead and Boyten was given the opportunity of commenting on them.

The tribunal found that the dismissal was unfair on the grounds that the appeals committee should have 'insisted upon those witnesses giving verbal evidence in front of the committee'.

East Herts appealed against this decision. The EAT took a different view from the tribunal. They confirmed that the appeals procedure had been properly followed, and noted that this procedure was, in effect, a collective agreement. The procedure did not require the physical presence of all witnesses. The EAT went on: 'it is not for an industrial tribunal or for that matter this Appeals Tribunal to rewrite an agreed code of that kind which has been hammered out by both sides of industry'. Consequently, had the tribunal directed their minds to the correct point – ie did the employer act reasonably – 'they could not possibly have come to any other conclusion than that the employer was acting reasonably in this case'. The EAT consequently allowed the appeal, finding that Boyten was dismissed fairly.

Comment: This fairly simple case illustrates several important points. First, it shows the value of sticking to agreed procedures. Secondly, it shows that tribunals err if they go beyond asking the simple question as to whether the employer was acting reasonably. It also shows that a domestic appeals hearing need not follow tribunal or court procedures – by calling all witnesses, for example – though the procedure must be inherently fair. Finally, the case shows the value of appealing to the EAT if it is felt that a tribunal finding is perverse.

Bowly v Nottinghamshire County Council, EAT, 1978

Bowly was a school-teacher who was convicted by a magistrates court of an offence of gross indecency with a man in a public lavatory (a matter outside the purview of the school). He was eventually dismissed by the decision of the education authority's Disciplinary Sub-Committee – a member-level body. An industrial tribunal found the dismissal unfair by a majority, not a unanimous decision – the legal chairman dissenting. The majority view was that the disciplinary sub-committee had no satisfactory evidence of any incident suggesting a risk to pupils, and should also have made efforts to find Bowly another job, 'probably administrative'.

The EAT, when the county appealed, disagreed with the tribunal's approach. 'We have to warn ourselves', they said, 'that we must not fall into the same error as tribunals sometimes do' of remaking the employer's decision. 'The test was not whether we might have done the same ourselves faced with the same problem, but whether the respondents were acting reasonably'. So – 'what would the ordinary, sensible, reasonable disciplinary sub-committee have done in this case?' The EAT thought that there were some cases where the answer was obvious. This was not such a case.

> The facts in this case lie within that grey area where, provided they approach the matter fairly and properly and direct themselves correctly, the Disciplinary Sub-Committee cannot be faulted in doing what in their judgement, being the responsible body, is the just and proper thing to do.

And the EAT commended the view of the chairman of the tribunal who pointed to the entitlement of education authorities to expect certain standards of their teachers and expect them to set examples to the children under them. The EAT concluded that the county's appeal should be allowed, and the decision of the tribunal set aside.

Comment: This case reinforces all the points illustrated in the Boyten case. Beyond that, it also throws useful light on the extent to which criminal offences committed outside work can fairly be taken into account in a dismissal. The general rule is that some adverse effect must be involved within the work situation before the outside offence can be used to justify dismissal. This general rule, however, must be interpreted sensibly (and sensitively) in the particular context of each case. The EAT certainly accepts that higher standards can justifiably be required of a teacher – someone who has a responsibility for the moral welfare of children – than of a worker in a job in which an offence of the Bowly variety could not be held to damage any necessary confidence required within the job. A tribunal case follows which throws further light on this point.

Richardson v City of Bradford Council: Leeds Tribunal: 1975
Richardson was a senior meat inspector in the environmental health department. He was charged with the theft of money from his Rugby Club till and confessed to the police to taking upwards of £200 over a period of several months. He was eventually dismissed after a hearing by an elected member appeals panel. In a dismissal letter from his chief officer he was told that:

> the job of any inspector requires the highest standard of integrity, and your conduct, albeit that it was outside working hours, seriously detracts from the public confidence and from my confidence in you, both of which are essential for you to carry out your duties.

The tribunal, finding the dismissal fair, commended Bradford for 'seizing the nettle' and reaching a necessary and firm decision. 'Some councils,' said the Chairman, 'might have refused to grasp the nettle, might have taken refuge in equivocation or found an excuse for not carrying out what was its clear duty in this case, to dismiss the applicant from its service'. The tribunal concluded:

> the honesty and integrity of public servants throughout this country has been questioned in the past few years. It is only right that when the integrity of a public servant who is employed in a position where integrity is of prime importance is found to be wanting, the local authority which employs him should take the necessary steps to remove him from public service.

Comment: Some commentators might feel that this tribunal was expecting very high standards indeed from local government officers at relatively junior levels, and one tribunal judgement cannot be taken as giving *carte blanche* to dismiss any APT and C employee for any out-of-hours offence. Nevertheless, the firm views of the tribunal on the higher standards expected of public servants may encourage some local government managers who (without, perhaps, the experience to justify it) talk about the failure of current legislation to support their attempts to maintain high standards. Once again, the value of a proper disciplinary and appeals procedure, properly and responsibly followed, is demonstrated in this case. An instant dismissal was apparently considered initially in this case, but in the event, the longer

238

process of disciplinary interviews and an appeal hearing was followed, a course of action which undoubtedly strengthened Bradford's position at the tribunal hearing.

Daubney v E Lindsey District Council, EAT, 1977
Daubney, a 57 year old building surveyor, was dismissed by the district council on grounds of ill health. His termination letter described this as 'action to enable you to retire immediately', but it was accepted that this constituted dismissal.

Daubney had been absent on certificated sickness for several months. The council's director of personnel consequently asked the district community physician for a report on Daubney's health, and an indication as to whether he should be retired on grounds of permanent ill health. The community physician's reply was:

Thank you for your letter of 27.6.76 regarding the above named employee.

I asked Dr O'Hagen to examine Mr Daubney and have now received his report. Because of his remarks, I feel that Mr Daubney is unfit to carry out the duties of his post and should be retired on the grounds of permanent ill-health.

Five days later, Daubney was sent the termination letter already referred to. There was no communication between the district council and Daubney during this five days. The council did not ask for or see Dr O'Hagen's report. There was no evidence given to the EAT that Daubney knew that his future employment was in jeopardy when he was seen by Dr O'Hagen.

The tribunal which first heard the case decided the dismissal was unfair for two reasons. First, they said the district council failed to obtain and consider a full medical report before dimissing Daubney. Secondly, they said the council should have given Daubney 'the elementary right either to contend against dismissal or at least to seek an independent medical opinion'.

The district council appealed to the EAT, expressing particular alarm at the first of these two points. On this issue, the EAT agreed with the council. 'It is not', they said, 'the function of employers (or tribunals) to turn themselves into some sort of medical appeal tribunal to review the opinions and advice received from their medical advisers'. Employers must not be expected to be medical experts. On balance, therefore, the EAT felt the council was being reasonable in accepting the community physician's report – although they thought this very short letter was 'verging on the inadequate'.

On the second point, however, the EAT came down strongly against the council.

Unless there are wholly exceptional circumstances before an employee is dismissed on the grounds of ill health it is necessary that he should be consulted and the matter discussed with him . . . the employee may then wish to seek medical advice on his own account which, brought to the notice of the employer's medical advisers will cause them to change their opinion . . . One thing is certain, and that is that if the employee is not consulted and given an opportunity to state his case, an injustice may be done.

E. Lindsey lost their appeal.

Comment: This is an important case for local government, where ill-health retirements, based on the formula of permanent unfitness and handled within the provisions of superannuation regulations, are not infrequent. The use of a busy community physician to give advice on these cases is an arrangement stemming from the 1974 transfer of medical officer of health functions from local government to the area and district health authorities. It is often difficult to obtain as full a medical report as is perhaps, desirable. The absence of any form of medical appeal has not been an uncommon feature of ill-health retirement procedures. The emphasis on 'retirement', because of the superannuation involvement, has tended to obscure the fact that unless the employee is wholly co-operative about leaving, what is occurring is a dismissal. One consequence of this case – which follows the standard disciplinary code in requiring an appeals mechanism – is that a number of authorities have fundamentally revised their whole ill-health retirement procedures to ensure three things take place:

the employee is made fully aware that the purpose of the medical examination is to consider fitness for continued employment

that on receiving the medical adviser's view that the employee is permanently unfit for continued employment in the present job, this view is discussed with the employee and the possibility of more suitable alternative work is examined

that if this fails, and enforced retirement (ie dismissal) is necessary, the employee is given the opportunity of seeking additional medical advice before dismissal is effected.

Redundancy
Despite the 'cuts' in recent years, there has been considerably more security of employment in local government than in the private sector, and the statutory redundancy provisions have not been a source of major problems to local authorities. Improved superannuation provisions for the over 50s have assisted in achieving small-scale voluntary redundancies in some slimming operations; the major legal point here being the need to document the terminations in such a way as to ensure their formal redundancy status – rather than allowing the euphemism of voluntary early retirement to prevent justifiable claims

240

by the employer on the national redundancy fund. There has sometimes been confusion, too, between retirements 'in the interests of the efficiency of the service' as the superannuation regulations put it, and redundancies. It is worth emphasizing that to qualify for a statutory redundancy grant (and its offsetting refund to the employer from the national fund) redundancy as defined in the legislation must be capable of proof. This formula requires the dismissal to result from the cessation or diminution of the employer's requirement for employees to carry out work of a particular kind. Voluntary leavers who are replaced – directly or indirectly – cannot be classified as redundant. Three cases, all dealt with on appeal, illustrate other potential difficulties in handling redundancy legislation.

Kyte v GLC, NIRC, 1973

Kyte was a painter who, after breaking his leg at work, was employed only on ground floor work. It became increasingly difficult to find sufficient work of this type for him and he was asked to take on other work which sometimes involved standing on low trestles. Although certified fit for this work, he refused to do it. He was then compulsorily retired on the grounds of permanent incapacity to carry out the work of a painter. He claimed redundancy, using the argument that he had been employed for seven years as a ground-floor painter and that the employer's requirement for work of that kind had now ceased – causing his dismissal.

The NIRC (the predecessor of the EAT) confirmed a tribunal's view that although he had been employed on a restricted range of work for some years, his contract of employment had not been altered and he was paid as a fully able-bodied painter. There was no diminution in the GLC's requirement for able-bodied painters, so there was no redundancy. Kyte still had a contractual obligation to work a full range of duties; the employers had merely chosen to waive their entitlement to a full discharge of his duties. When medical evidence was given that he would be permanently unfit, they were not unreasonable in deciding they could not permanently waive their contractual requirements. So the dismissal was not only not redundancy, it was also not unfair.

Comment: Redundancy legislation tends to lean more heavily on strict legal definitions and concepts than unfair dismissal law which leaves doors wide open for interpretations of 'reasonableness' and 'fairness'. Altering an employee's work is always a danger area under contract and redundancy law. In the Kyte case, the court decided no contractual change had been made. The next case illustrates the converse.

Taylor v Kent County Council, Division Court, 1969

Taylor was the headmaster of a school which was eventually merged

241

with another. He was unsuccessful in obtaining the headmastership of the new school. Instead, Kent offered him employment as a supply headmaster in the mobile teachers' pool, with a protected salary. Clearly he was redundant insofar as his post had been eliminated. But the Redundancy Payments Act provides that entitlement to a redundancy grant can be extinguished if a new contract is offered which 'as to the capacity and place in which he would be employed and as to the other terms and conditions of his employment would differ from the corresponding provisions' of the original contract. The employee must not unreasonably refuse such an alternative if he is to establish redundancy rights.

So was the supply job a reasonable alternative? Taylor thought not, and the court upheld his views. The new job, said the court, must be substantially equivalent to the old. In this case, even though salary was protected, there would be a loss of status and the new post's peripatetic nature also had disadvantages over the old job. So Taylor, not being unreasonable in refusing the alternative offered was redundant and entitled to a grant.

Comment: There is a wealth of case law on what is or is not a reasonable alternative. Each case must be judged in the light of its own circumstances – including the personal and domestic circumstances of the individual if the new job involves a geographical move, or longer daily travelling.

Rights of the individual employee
The rights not to be unfairly dismissed, and to receive redundancy payments, do not of course exhaust the whole gamut of individual rights incorporated in employment legislation, even if they account for over 90 per cent of the cases going to the tribunals. Few of these numerous other rights, however, have given rise to specifically local government problems and are not therefore discussed in detail in this book, except for those relating to trade union activities which are dealt with in the next chapter.

There is one other exception – the question of 'positive discrimination' within the terms of the Race Relations Act. Individual employees have a right not to be discriminated against on grounds of colour, race, nationality of ethnic origins. (Or, of course, on grounds of sex or marital status). The Act permits discrimination in favour of a particular racial group in regard to education and training – though not in regard to recruitment or promotion. Local authorities have been additionally urged by the Secretary of State to take positive steps to make facilities available which would encourage ethnic minorities to take advantage of training opportunities for areas of work in which the proportion of persons of a particular ethnic group is small in relation to the proportion of persons of that group within the local or national population. Preferential selection of blacks into training schemes for, say, social work or architecture might be examples. Few authorities have stepped into this highly controversial arena, most preferring to follow a policy of impartiality or equality – rather than actively opening training doors to ethnic minorities. Where positive steps have been taken, as in Camden in 1977 or Lewisham in 1978, the spotlight of not always accurate publicity has tended to generate the very sensitivity to race which equal opportunity policies are intended to reduce. Nevertheless, the continued under-representation of blacks in white collar occupations and the evidence of continued adverse discrimination, particularly against the professionally qualified black, produced by bodies such as PEP and the Runnymede Trust, cannot be wholly ignored. It is to be hoped that the establishment of sound personnel management practice generally in local government will of itself create an employment environment in which genuine equality of opportunity is really achieved. If not, public bodies are likely to continue to experience pressure from government, and from particular interest groups in race relations, to demonstrate their high level of public responsibility by doing more than merely not dissue bland policy statements.

Reverting to individual rights, this chapter concludes with the following check list of what these rights are. Detailed guidance on these matters may be sought in the booklets produced by the Department of Employment, and in the LACSAB Employee Relations Handbook, listed in the bibliography at the end of this book.

An employee has a right:

to a written statement of particulars, setting out the terms and conditions of his employment

to receive an itemized pay statement

to receive designated minimum periods of notice, related to length of service

to receive a 'guarantee payment' of a minimum daily sum if work is not available

to receive normal pay for up to 26 weeks if suspended on medical grounds because of the specific requirements of health and safety regulations

if a woman, to receive maternity pay . . . and to be reinstated after maternity absence within defined length of service and absence criteria . . . and not to be dismissed for pregnancy

to time off to look for work, or arrange for training, when under impending redundancy

not to be unfairly selected for redundancy

to time off to undertake scheduled public duties

to time off as a safety representative or trade union official

not to be unfairly dismissed

to claim that constructive dismissal occurred, if the employer's action justifies 'walking out'

not to be dismissed for taking part in trade union activities

to request written reasons for dismissal

to be given a four week trial period in an alternative job to redundancy before formally accepting it as a suitable alternative

not to be discriminated against on grounds of race, colour, ethnic origin or sex

to receive equal pay for equal work – as between men and women employees

to expect the employer to ensure his health, safety and welfare at work (so far as is 'reasonably practicable').

All these rights impose their resultant mirror-image duties on the employer, ie a duty to dismiss fairly, to provide reinstatement to the woman returning from maternity absence, to ensure the safety of employees, and so on. Taken together, these rights and duties form the very core of employment principles and practice. Their interpretation and practical application cannot be seen in wholly legal terms, or left to lawyers for implementation. It has become a major function of personnel officers to monitor legislative developments – including rapidly changing case law – and ensure that their authorities' personnel policies and procedures not only comply with the law, but, so far as is possible, also use the legal framework constructively to form a consistent set of personnel activities which serve the employers' purpose of securing an efficient and effective workforce.

15 Employment legislation: Trade union and collective rights: industrial democracy

The previous chapter concentrated on the rights of the employee as an individual. This chapter looks more at collective rights. While some of the rights connected with trade union activities are individual – the right to become a shop steward, for example – the general setting and emphasis of the legislation in which such rights are incorporated is very much that of promoting collective representation and collective bargaining. Politically, of course, much of this legislation has been described as heavily biased towards promoting the role and interest of the TUC and its constituent unions, though that debate is avoided here, and the chapter concentrates on the more specifically local government aspects or implications of the legislation.

The chapter concludes with an outline of the discussion in the mid 1970s about the prescription of some form of industrial democracy in local government. In that no legislation has yet emerged on this issue, it might be considered premature to go into as much detail as will be found in the latter part of this chapter. It seems likely, however, that the subject will re-emerge as a live political issue, and a knowledge of its historical background should be a useful aid to understanding and coping with whatever legislative or other developments may eventually emerge.

Trade union rights for the individual employee
It has been commented in the chapter on industrial relations that local government is one of the most highly unionized sectors of employment in the UK. To that extent, authorities have been used to working in coexistence with powerful trade unions, and with employees at all levels being active in union affairs. Practices in relation to time off and other facilities for trade union members have been built up over the years and a good deal of the new provisions in recent

legislation do little more than require other employers to bring their practices up to existing local government levels. There are, nevertheless, several issues which have caused problems to local authorities, and a summary of the individual's trade union rights can usefully open a discussion of these issues. The most significant of these individual rights are:

not to be prevented or deterred from joining an independent trade union, or penalized for so doing, or for not joining

not to be prevented or deterred from taking part at an appropriate time in the activities of an independent trade union, or penalized for so doing

as a union official (eg shop steward) of a recognized trade union to have 'reasonable' time off with pay during working hours to carry out official union duties which are concerned with industrial relations between the union and the employer, and to undergo such training in industrial relations as is approved by the TUC or the union concerned. Similar paid time off rights are also given to safety representatives

as a union member to have reasonable time off (the legislation is silent as to pay) to take part in union activities.

Closed shop agreements are permitted, provided employees can opt out on grounds of conscience or deeply held personal conviction (80% of those eligible must also vote in favour of a closed shop agreement). The provisions about no penalization or deterrence of joining or being active in a union apply to any independent trade union; that is, a union which has been formally certificated by the Certification Officer (a statutory appointment) as being independent of employer control or influence. Authorities must avoid, therefore, making it difficult for employees to join unions unrecognized in local government, such as ASTMS, the British Firefighters' Federation, or the Association of Polytechnic Teachers – however much the recognized unions such as NALGO, the FBU, and NATFHE may dislike this.

The time off provisions, however, apply only to recognized trade unions and it is not, therefore, unlawful while granting a NATFHE representative time off for a union training course, to refuse a member of APT. Note, too, the difference in time off provisions between the ordinary union member and the shop steward. The latter can claim time off with pay; the former cannot claim *paid* time off – unless, of course, local agreements beyond the statutory provisions provide for this. The restriction of a right to the member of *any* independent trade union to take part in union activities *at an appropriate time* is consistent with the provisions just outlined. 'Appropriate' is defined in the statute as being outside working hours unless other arrangements are agreed by the employer. A member of the independent but unrecognized British Firefighters' Federation could not, therefore, claim the right to collect union dues during working hours (unless his Fire Authority so agreed) but could most likely establish a right to enter his own fire station for this purpose when off shift. Tribunal cases are so far rare, though an attempt in 1978 by the Firefighters to secure extensive facilities in Cornwall, using these particular provisions, failed at a tribunal. (More modest facilities were later agreed on an out of court basis). Local authorities generally are now finding it necessary or desirable to standardize and codify their practice in granting time off, by negotiating facilities agreements with the recognized trade unions. Trade union response varies. Some use such negotiations as an opportunity for extending their local rights. Others (and NALGO has been among them) sometimes prefer a less defined situation. The existence of a local agreement is certainly of major assistance in preventing claims to tribunals. One case involving alleged unlawful discrimination against an active trade unionist is of interest.

Beyer v City of Birmingham District Council, EAT, 1977
Beyer was a bricklayer and a member of the building union, UCATT. He was described by the EAT as having views of 'a militant progressive nature' and motives which 'may be admirable, but his methods over the last few years have in certain quarters earned criticism and even hostility'. He had what was described as an interesting and stormy career in the building industry in the Birmingham area, so that by 1975 no large employer who recognized him would give him a job. In that year he applied for a job with Birmingham, allegedly giving a false name and a bogus reference. He was engaged, but within an hour of starting work was recognized and summarily dismissed. In 1976, as an inconspicuous member of a three man gang, he was again engaged by the council at a site where his face and name were unknown to the site agent. But within a couple of hours he was again recognized, and again dismissed instantly. He claimed unfair dismissal.

Normally, an employee has to have six months service before being able to use the unfair dismissal machinery. But if the reason for dismissal is that the employee 'had taken, or proposed to take part at any appropriate time, in the activities of an independent trade union', then no length of service requirements apply. Beyer claimed that his dismissal was due to his known role as a trade union activist, and was therefore unfair. Birmingham said he had been dismissed because of his alleged gross deceit in obtaining employment in 1975.

The tribunal supported Beyer. They concluded that the deceit he had practised in 1975 to obtain a job was, in effect, a trade union activity which had been necessitated by the discrimination employers

247

had practised against him because of his known trade union militancy. On appeal by Birmingham the EAT would have none of this. They found it 'surprising that the tribunal could have erred and misdirected themselves to the extent that they did'. Trade union activity as defined by statute, said the EAT, could obviously refer only to activity after employment had commenced. It could not conceivably refer to activities outside and before employment began. The tribunal's decision was consequently set aside. The EAT commented at some length on this case and in particular stressed that '. . . there is nothing in the legislation which lays down that an employer may not refuse to employ a man unless he has reasonable grounds for refusing'.

Collective (trade union) rights
Legislation after 1974 created new rights for workers collectively – or more specifically for trade unions – in five main areas:
   the right to process claims for recognition through a statutorily defined procedure
   the right to receive information from the employer to assist in effective collective bargaining
   the right to advance consultation about impending redundancies
   the right to establish parity of pay and conditions of service with comparable groups (within defined limits)
   the right to appoint safety representatives.

It is beyond doubt that the Government's (and TUC's) intention in introducing most of this legislation was to strengthen collective bargaining, and trade union membership and influence, in sectors in which trade union organization was weak. Retailing, the hotel and catering trade, and some areas of industrial and commercial white collar employment are typical of these sectors. This approach is emphasized by the statutory duty, laid on ACAS by the Employment Protection Act, to promote the improvement of industrial relations, and encourage the extension of collective bargaining. It did not originally appear likely that a sector such as local government, in which a comprehensive system of industrial relations already existed, would or should be significantly affected by the new legal provisions. In the event, things have turned out differently. Of the five sets of trade union rights just listed, only one has so far made little impact in local government – the right to receive information.
   That right was clearly designed to assist unions in the private sector to obtain facts and figures about the financial standing of companies, in order to assist in assessments of what the firms could afford to pay in the context of wage bargaining. In local government, almost all significant financial information is actually or potentially publicly available, and the unions are not inhibited in collective bargaining by any dearth of data. At national level, it is noticeable that union pay
248

claims tend to be very simply presented, and to be based on general aspirations rather than on any closely argued economic argument. Indeed, the impression sometimes arises that the submission of pay claims for 40 per cent increases (as in 1978) is assisted by an *absence* of information about the financial effects. The national trade unions have certainly shown no marked enthusiasm for examining the realities of average earnings and similar information which the employers produce in the course of national negotiations. At local level, shop stewards may occasionally attempt to use the information provisions of the Employment Protection Act to obtain information on confidential items, but no real difficulties seem to have emerged to date.

In the other fields – union recognition and so on – the position is different. Here, legal provisions designed to strengthen weak industrial relations systems, and to extend collective bargaining into hitherto untouched areas, have been used in attempts to weaken or change existing systems and challenge the entrenched position of powerful trade unions.

Recognition rights*

An independent trade union which sought recognition by an employer was able, if refused, to seek the assistance of ACAS. ACAS could not refuse to act on such an approach. If its conciliation efforts failed it had to examine the issue more formally, consult all affected parties, and in due course issue a report. In the course of its examination, ACAS had to 'ascertain the opinions of workers to whom the issue relates' and, if it thought fit, conduct a ballot. It was not bound to accept the ballot's results, and in reaching a conclusion had to take into account its twin duties of improving industrial relations and extending collective bargaining. In its final report, ACAS had either to make a recommendation, specifying the extent of recognition to be accorded to a specified union for a defined group or description of workers; or make no recommendation – the formula for turning down a recognition claim.

If an employer failed to implement a recommendation, the trade union applied to the Central Arbitration Committee (CAC). There is a curious twist in the statutory processes at this point. The CAC had no powers to order recognition as such. What it did, if it considered the union's claim well-founded, was to make an award that the employer should observe such terms and conditions of employment as it may

*The 1980 Employment Act has deleted the recognition procedures described in this section, which should consequently be read as an historical commentary. In the absence of a statutory procedure, recognition issues lie to be resolved wholly by voluntary or negotiated processes.

specify. These terms (eg a specified level of wages) then had effect as part of the employees' individual contracts of employment. If the employer then failed to apply them, employees sued for breach of contract. This indirect method of enforcing recognition – through enforcement of the pay and conditions that a union claim it wished to achieve were it to be granted recognition – is one of the aspects of this legislation which the TUC wished to see changed.

In local government, the recognition cases which have occurred so far are concerned with the earlier stage of an unrecognized union seeking an ACAS recommendation that it should be accorded employer recognition for collective bargaining purposes. The two arenas are in the education and fire services, and the two unrecognized unions involved have been the Association of Polytechnic Teachers (APT), and the Retained Firefighters' Union (RFU).

The first major difficulty (for both unions and employers) has been that to achieve real involvement in collective bargaining a union needs to seek national, not local, recognition. Local government's industrial relations systems are based firmly on the principle of national collective bargaining, with local authorities recognizing at local level those trade unions which are parties to the various NJCs (including Burnham). But the Act refers only to recognition by an employer (or by associated employers). The official side of an NJC is not, in legal terms, an employer. So the APT and RFU have had to make separate approaches to a range of individual local authorities, and to name these authorities – rather than the employers' side of Burnham and the Fire Brigade NJC – as the employers from whom they seek recognition.

In both cases, the national employers' and LACSAB's advice has been against granting recognition, on the basis of the principle of recognizing locally only nationally recognized unions; and of avoiding the disruption of well-functioning industrial relations systems. In both cases, the unions have gone to ACAS, and the procedure already outlined has been followed. The process can be illustrated by following the ACAS reports on the APT claims which, although made separately to four different local authorities, were described by ACAS as identical.

All the claims were for limited negotiating rights, ie recognition for the purpose of bargaining on local, rather than national, issues.

APT and the polytechnics at Portsmouth, Lanchester, N London and the City of London: ACAS, 1978
ACAS decided that the other parties concerned were NATFHE (the main trade union for college lecturers), the National Society for Art Education, the Association of Principals of Colleges, CLEA (the employers' body), LACSAB, the two local authority associations

(AMA and ACC), the Department of Education and Science, and the Committee of Directors of Polytechnics. All were consulted by ACAS.

The employers' bodies generally opposed recognition (though with considerable reluctance in some cases), as did the other trade unions. They were concerned with the possible fragmentation of existing negotiating machinery. DES agreed that in principle it was open to a local authority to grant purely local recognition, but pointed to the very limited scope for local negotiations in the light of the high degree of prescription of pay and conditions through Burnham and CLEA agreements. The Committee of Directors of Polytechnics – a purely advisory body – argued that polytechnics should be recognized as a distinctly separate element in education from the general 'Further and Higher' category in which they were now placed, and which the national industrial relations system reflected.

ACAS issued questionnaries to the Polytechnic teaching staff. At Portsmouth (Hampshire County Council) 40 per cent of those replying were APT members, and 39 per cent belonged to NATFHE. Asked which union they would prefer to represent them in future, 64 per cent chose APT and 35 per cent NATFHE.

In ACAS' words: 'The central issue raised by this reference is whether a union should be allowed to negotiate locally in an area where other unions hold negotiating rights, particularly when the matters to be resolved flow directly from nationally agreed recommendations to which the recognized unions are party'. ACAS felt they had to balance the views of the 65 per cent majority of lecturers against a number of other considerations – particularly 'the desirability of achieving a broad national similarity in the basic conditions of service of all teachers in the whole field of further education'. ACAS concluded that these objectives 'would be frustrated by the introduction into local collective bargaining of a union which has, at present, no responsibility for the agreements made at national level'. Although some scope existed for local negotiation on purely local issues, ACAS felt the recognition of APT would fragment the existing collective bargaining machinery 'and would not be helpful to the development of good industrial relations'. APT consequently failed in their claim.

Comment: It would be misleading to leave this case without commenting on the political overtones involved. ACAS has come under growing Conservative and employer criticism for allegedly leaning towards the TUC's views, and TUC affiliated unions. APT have seen ACAS in the same light. APT is not TUC-affiliated.

A concurrent private sector case involving the United Kingdom Association of Professional Engineers (UKAPE) in which an ACAS report was declared null and void by the High Court (UKAPE v

ACAS, 1978) seemed to APT to add weight to this view. There were differences of fact, however, between this UKAPE case and APT's claims. It was possible for UKAPE to argue that ACAS had failed to pay sufficent attention to their statutory duty to extend collective bargaining, and had considered only the improvement of industrial relations. Recognition of UKAPE would have introduced collective bargaining into a wider white-collar area. APT could not so argue, as all Polytechnic staff are already fully within the purview of the Burnham (and CLEA) systems.

Conservative authorities, however, found ACAS' slamming of the door on APT far from satisfactory; and discussions were continued at local level in at least some of the authorities concerned about the possibility of agreeing some form of purely local recognition.

Similar procedural and political problems have occurred in the RFU claims in which even more authorities have been named by the union. The potential difficulties of introducing a new union into the highly organized and sometimes militant world of an opposing Fire Brigades' Union are obvious. The employers' initial rejection of RFU claims reflects not so much an opposition to that union as such, but a preference for a consistent, national approach which a set of ACAS recommendations might achieve. Were ACAS to recommend recognition across all the authorities involved, it is speculated that the FBU would find it more difficult to react than if authorities agreed recognition individually and wholly of their own volition. Taken together, the FBU and RFU cases do give some indication that the existence of statutory machinery for pursuing recognition claims has encouraged, rather than discouraged, breakaway unions in attempting to establish a bridgehead in the nationally entrenched positions of the main, recognized trade unions in local government.

Redundancy consultation rights
The relative infrequency of significant redundancies, and the absence of detailed, formal redundancy agreements, have already been commented on. The Employment Protection Act's provisions for consulting trade unions in advance of impending redundancies have consequently caused some difficulties for authorities unused to this degree of formality.

The provisions require an employer to consult the recognized trade unions concerned about any proposal to declare redundancies. Where 100 or more redundancies are foreseen, consultation must begin at least 60 days before the first dismissal occurs; where 10 to 99 redundancies are expected, consultations must begin at least 30 days before dismissal. The form of consultation is also specified. It must be by telling the unions in writing of the reasons for redundancy, the numbers and types of employees involved, and the proposed methods
252

of selection for redundancy and of effecting the dismissals. The Act also requires the employer to 'consider any representations' made by the unions and to reply to them, giving reasons if any such representations are rejected. Notifications also have to be given to the Secretary of State (in practice, the local Department of Employment Office) within identical time scales.

A failure to meet these time periods can carry two forms of financial penalty. First, a trade union can obtain a 'protective award' under which the employees concerned have to be paid remuneration for such 'protected period' as a tribunal may decide – normally, the missing period of notice. Secondly, the Department of Employment may refuse to pay the employer's rebate from the central redundancy fund. An education department case illustrates the type of procedural difficulty which can arise, and shows, too, the need to consider the intentions behind legislation as well as the precise words of a statute.

NUT v Avon County Council, EAT, 1977
Avon's Education Committee decided, in October, 1976, to make a number of teachers redundant. Letters giving notice of termination of appointment were sent to the teachers concerned on 28 October, the effective date of termination being 31 December. On 29 October a letter was sent to the National Union of Teachers as the first formal step in the statutory consultation process. The NUT complained to a tribunal that Avon had failed to submit this notification within the then 60 day rule (for between 10 and 99 employees). The tribunal decided in Avon's favour. They thought that it was the date of actual dismissal – ie the date employment ceased – which constituted the date before which 60 days notification must be given to the trade union.

On the NUT appeal, the EAT reversed the tribunal's decision. EAT commented:

. . . though 'dismiss' may be ambiguous and mean either the giving of a notice, or the effective bringing into effect of that notice by its expiry, it seems to us that in the context it is the former which is in contemplation . . . The beginning of consultation must precede the giving of notice.

If this gave rise to particular problems in particular cases, EAT pointed out the existence of an escape clause in Section 101 by which the employer could argue that it was not 'reasonably practicable' to give the statutory notice period to the trade union. But in this case, that had not been argued and the EAT remitted the case back to the tribunal so that Avon might have the opportunity of stating why earlier consultation (or presumably the later issue of termination letters) was not practicable.

253

Comment: The EAT's approach is fairly typical of their (and the Court of Appeal's) approach to the small print of employment legislation. What, they ask, is the intention behind the actual words in the Act? In this instance, to ensure that meaningful consultation occurs before irrevocable decisions are made. It follows that consultation after the issue of termination letters does not accord with the intentions of the statute, and the words of the Act must be construed to serve that intention.

Parity rights: Schedule 11*
Schedule 11 became one of the private sector's *bêtes noire* among the many provisions of the Employment Protection Act. It is a provision which, while apparently designed to improve pockets of low pay, was in practice exploited by legally skilled and ingenious unions such as ASTMS to raise earnings of groups of employees in very different circumstances from those envisaged by the Act's draftsmen. Its particular attraction during the 1976-78 pay period was that pay and conditions awards under this schedule were not subject to pay policy restrictions.

Claims could be made to ACAS, by an employer or by an independent trade union, that a worker or group of workers had less favourable terms and conditions of service than either:

the 'recognized terms and conditions' – meaning the terms and conditions of comparable employees in the same industry which have been settled by a collective agreement: or – if no such agreements apply

the 'general level of terms and conditions' – meaning the terms and conditions generally observed by employers in the same industry for comparable workers in similar circumstances.

On receiving a claim, ACAS attempted to settle it through conciliation but, failing settlement, referred it to the CAC. The CAC (constituted like an industrial tribunal with an independent chairman sitting with an employer's and a trade union representative) then heard each side's case and gave a ruling. CAC's awards are given the effect of being incorporated into employees' individual contracts of employment, and are therefore enforceable at law. The great bulk of CAC Schedule 11 cases have been in the private sector, where many employers consider the whole process destructive of the independence of individual employers to fix their own pay rates in direct, local negotiations; and inflationary in that the implication is that no-one should be paid less than average! This book is not the place to develop those

*The 1980 Employment Act has deleted the Schedule 11 provisions. This section should therefore be read as an historical commentary.

themes.

In local government, relatively few cases arose in the early years after the Act. One or two minor cases were brought jointly by an authority with a trade union in circumstances in which a pay or grading increase had been agreed in principle, but pay policy prevented implementation. The GLC, for example, went along with a case involving a small group of Festival Hall manual workers who fell outside the general local government manual categories and could, instead, have their wage rates pegged to those in London's theatre trade.

Later, however, claims far less acceptable to the employers began to be made. Some were constructed on the 'recognized terms' argument – particularly where the union felt it could establish a case that an individual employee was incorrectly paid within the purple book terms, or was not receiving some locally negotiated benefit to which entitlement could be established.

Other cases were made on the 'general level' basis, mainly where a particular occupation was not specifically listed in the national or provincial manual worker or APT and C grading schedules. In such cases, the general level of payment in neighbouring authorities was quoted as establishing a benchmark – and a statutory right under Schedule 11.*

LACSAB's approach has been to attempt to achieve a settlement of claims 'out of court' (not in CAC) by assisting in re-opening local discussion and negotiation.

Schedule 11 will not have been in existence long enough to make a major impact on the status of national, provincial and local level agreements. But one or two cases, won by the unions at the CAC, could have opened a door to highly unwelcome pressure to standardize grades and local conditions across whole provincial areas.

A list of some of the occupations for whom, in late 1978, the major unions were using Schedule 11, illustrates these potential difficulties:

occupational therapists (a claim for National Health Service, not local government, rates)

roadworkers (a local application of standby payments)

school caretakers (a claim for standard accommodation charges to be applied)

*See NALGO v Dudley Metropolitan District, CAC Report 78/543, November 1977, decided by CAC as a 'general level' case on the grounds that the Purple Book technician grades are only absolute minima, that the 'recognized terms' are for local discretion to be exercised, and that comparisons can therefore be made to assess the extent to which that discretion is in line with the general grading levels in neighbouring authorities.

museum attendants (a claim in one authority, quoting neighbouring rates)
part-time FE teachers (a claim for inter-county parity).

Safety rights
Most safety legislation is concerned with protecting the individual and so lies outside the scope of this chapter. In one particular respect, however, the Health and Safety at Work Act of 1974 entered the collective rights arena and resulted in a successful revolt by local government against the introduction of statutory regulations.

The Act provides[1] for the Secretary of State to make regulations for the appointment by recognized trade unions of safety representatives, and for the definition of these representatives' functions. When the consequent regulations[2] were produced in draft in 1976, it was seen that no restriction was to be placed on the number of representatives a union could appoint, there appeared no way in which an employer could object to such appointments however unrealistic the scale of such an exercise might be. Further, the regulations provided that any two safety representatives are entitled to ask for the formation of a safety committee.

Given local government's complete unionization, and the fact that at most establishments several recognized unions would have members, the situation could be envisaged of the sudden appointment of tens of thousands of safety representatives. Taking these representatives' individual rights into account – and particularly the right to paid time off for their functions and for safety training – it was calculated that the annual cost to local government could well reach £80 million annually. The local authority associations consequently made a stand against the early introduction of the regulations and the government deferred their activation for 18 months until October, 1978 – despite strong TUC objections. The TUC thought the cost would be no more than two million pounds. The government eventually compromised on an estimate of £40 million, and agreed to add £20 million to the 1978/1979 rate support grant settlement to recognize the cost for the half-year, October 1978 to March 1979.

This delay, and the shock it gave the TUC, had one constructive result. The TUC's local government committee faced the problem of the unco-ordinated appointment of a multiplicity of representatives in multi-union establishments, and issued guidance and advice to the constituent trade unions. They urged moderate, sensible, and co-ordinated action between trade unions; confirmed their acceptance of a safety representative from one union looking after the safety

[1]Health and Safety at Work Act, 1974, Section 2
[2]Safety representatives and Safety Committee Regulations, 1977

interests of another union's members in the same location, and accepted the value of working out an agreed approach to the establishment of new safety committees through discussions with each local authority.

During the 18 months breathing space which the associations had achieved, most authorities sat down with their local trade union officials and hammered out procedures for the notification of appointment of representatives, for agreed hazard reporting systems and safety inspection procedures, and for safety committee constitutions and functions. In consequence, no significant legal difficulties seem to have arisen. At least two potential sources of trouble can, however, be identified.

First, there are signs in some authorities that some unions are less than enthusiastic about cooperating in shared representation in multi-union establishments. UCATT, the building union, has often tended to act independently from other unions in general industrial relations matters, and would not consider itself bound by the guidance issued by the TUC's local government committee. A refusal by an authority to recognize the *bona fides* of a safety representative appointed by such a union, in breach of local agreements about the numbers and constituencies of representatives could clearly cause legal – as well as industrial relations – problems.

Secondly, some safety representatives may have difficulty in reconciling their statutory function as a representative of employees' interests, with their contractual role as a supervisor or manager and the statutory duties which go with a position of managerial responsibility. The extreme example of this role confusion has arisen in some schools where, under agreements between the unions for a single representative to cover all employees at a school, the head teacher has been nominated by the NUT as the school's safety representative. Yet the inspectorate of the Health and Safety Executive (and the law) would consider the head teacher to be the senior manager at the school, responsible as a manager for the health and safety of the school's staff. It is difficult to resist commenting that this type of nomination may be symptomatic of the rudimentary nature of many teachers' understanding of the concept of a mangerial role. It certainly creates a potential source of legal difficulty when the interests of the two roles conflict.

Industrial democracy
No industrial democracy legislation yet exists, and to that extent, a discussion of the concept as it might apply to local government may seem somewhat premature. On the other hand, the topic has been one of intense national debate, and the subject of a highly controversial committee of enquiry and of a subsequent government white paper.

Local government trade unions have become increasingly involved in the TUC campaign for legislation, while the local authority associations have resisted any suggestions which might weaken the concept of full elected member control of local authority decision-making. One consequence of elected member resistance to any union involvement in councils or council committees is that union interest may turn towards involvement in management (officer level) committees and management decision-making systems.

An outline of how trade unions' and authorities' views have developed over the past few years may help to set the scene against which future legislative or other developments may occur.

Developments prior to 1975

Any discussion of industrial democracy needs to include a definition, not least because other terms, particularly 'worker participation' were in more common usage in the early days of public and political debate on this subject, and carry a somewhat different emphasis.

Industrial democracy, as currently discussed, is taken primarily to apply to forms of employee participation in an organization's formal decison-making process, particularly at the policy level. That the emphasis has changed over the years from a rather general concept of employee involvement in formal and informal decision-making at all levels, to a much more specific concentration on employee representation on policy-making bodies, is illustrated by tracing the development of Labour Party and trade union thinking since 1965.

Following a Labour Party Conference decision in 1965, the Labour Party set up a working party with a remit to 'fundamentally reconsider earlier attitudes of the labour movement to the extent and forms of worker participation'.* The working party took five years to report, eventually suggesting the development of five forms of worker participation:

more extensive collective bargaining.
joint management/union action (eg in administering pension schemes)
direct worker control.
the extension of joint regulatory bodies such as the industrial training boards on which trade unions and employers were represented.
worker representation on company boards.

The report suggested that the public sector should take take the lead in these developments, but made no reference to local government. The report, as a whole, represented a significant change of approach

*Industrial Democracy: information paper no 27, Labour Party, 1972

away from the traditional view of trade unions as working class bodies opposing the capitalist system, to a new view of labour organizations sharing power in a mixed economy. The TUC had concluded in 1944 that worker-directors would jeopardize union independence. In 1971, however, Congress called on the government to legislate for worker representation on directorial boards, and set up a study group to develop its industrial democracy policies. A TUC report was eventually published in 1974,[1] proposing 50 per cent trade union membership on supervisory (policy-making) boards. The TUC's local government Committee discussed this report in draft in 1973 and NALGO in particular criticized the absence of references within it to industrial democracy in central and local government. The only comment in the report was: 'workers in the public services should not be totally excluded from the decision-making process'.

Developments from 1975
Reaction from public sector unions to the weakness of this statement continued and in 1975, largely due to pressure from the local government trade unions, the TUC General Council published proposals for local government, involving 20 per cent voting membership for employee representatives on council committees. Congress approved these proposals later that year. The full recommendations[2] endorsed by the TUC were:

employees of all kinds (not just teachers) should be represented on bodies such as the governing bodies of schools
employee representatives, elected by trade union members, should form 20 per cent of the membership of all council committees, and have full voting rights
membership of committees covering only single departments should be drawn from employees in those departments
committees, such as policy and resources, covering all departments should have employee members elected by all the authority's union members.

The TUC commented that employee membership of committees would contribute 'expertise and specialist knowledge' to the committee's deliberations – a view which chief officers felt overlooked their advisory role as the professional heads of their services.
The TUC also commented that 'teachers had been sitting on education committees with full voting rights for the past 70 years'.

[1]Industrial Democracy: a statement of policy: TUC, 1974
[2]Report of Congress: TUC, 1975

The TUC's reference to teachers was a somewhat over-simplified view of the special position of teachers in relation to the membership of Education Committees. This membership dates back to the Education Act of 1902, which abolished the former school boards. The Act, supplemented later by legislation in 1933, permitted the appointment to committee membership of persons 'holding office in a school or college, aided, provided or maintained by the council'. The purpose of this provision was not to provide for employee representation, but to ensure that committees would not be deprived of the services of educationists.

By 1975 a Labour government was in office, and progress towards industrial democracy legislation became part of the 'social contract' between the government and the TUC. In 1975, the Bullock Committee was set up with terms of reference which specified the acceptance of 'a radical extension of industrial democracy by means of representation on boards of directors'. Bullock was asked how, not whether, to establish worker directorships. The Committee was concerned only with the private sector and its report*, published in 1977, did not therefore impinge on local government. The report, proposing that trade union nominated representatives should form one third of the boards of companies (with one third shareholder representatives and one third independents) raised such a storm of protest from industry and commerce that progress towards legislation was halted in its tracks.

Before the Bullock report was published, the government had, in 1976, set up three separate studies under Civil Service sponsorship, of the possible extension of industrial democracy into the nationalized industries, central, and local government. The local government associations were invited to submit their views and in late 1976 reached the unanimous conclusion that the direct participation of staff as members of councils and committees was wholly unacceptable. The then Labour-controlled AMA thus differed in its view from a Labour Party/TUC *concordat* in 1977 to support 20 per cent *non-voting* employee membership of council committees. It will be noted that the TUC thus dropped its 1975 claim for full voting membership.

In 1978 the government produced two White Papers on the subject. One dealt with the private sector, and adopted a less prescriptive approach than Bullock. The other dealt with the nationalized industries and again, dealt with general principles, rather than laying down detailed systems. The government even recognized that while the Post Office had independently begun an experiment in worker representation at board level, in other industries the unions had stated a

*Industrial Democracy: Report of the Committee of Inquiry: HMSO: 1977
260

preference for an extension of joint consultation and collective bargaining as an alternative to board membership.

Government statements in 1978 also referred to studies of how representatives of the Civil Service trade unions might participate in top level management boards with civil service departments. No formal report from these sources ever emerged giving proposals for local government. Some trade union agitation at the lack of progress occurred, at national if not local level, and in 1978 NALGO appeared to turn their attention away from committee membership and towards possible trade union involvement in departmental and corporate management bodies in local government.

Meanwhile, a handful of Labour authorities took unilateral action in the heady atmosphere of 1976 to 1977 to introduce some form of non-voting employee participation in council committees. This was done relatively quietly in one or two districts, and was the subject of a very lengthy and detailed study in the GLC, culminating in a resolution of the council to invite trade union nominations for one-third employee membership of council committees on a non-voting basis*. Passed in December, 1976, this decision was overtaken by the electoral events of May, 1977, which returned a Conservative administration to County Hall, one of whose first decisions was not to proceed with the previous administration's policy on industrial democracy. It is worthy of note that this reversal engendered no significant trade union reaction. The GLC trade unions had been invited to nominate their committee representatives immediately after the Council's resolution, but by early May, over four months later, had failed totally to respond. Despite the formal policies of unions at national level, no great enthusiasm for committee membership is evidenced at local level by the GLC's experience, and the actions of the one or two districts who actually instituted such membership has not been followed generally.

The legal position
It might be questioned as to how the GLC and others could contemplate accepting employees as committee members within existing local government law.

Section 80 of the 1974 Local Government Act disqualifies a person from election to, or membership of, a local authority if he or she holds any paid office or employment with that authority. This disqualification applies to Council, rather than Committee, membership. But Section 104 of the Act applies to committee membership, the disqualification that Section 80 applies to the council itself. Thus, while

*Other authorities with employee representatives attending committees include Slough, Basildon and Hereford and Worcester

Section 102 enables a council to appoint to a council committee up to one third of members who are not members of council (ie co-opted membership), Section 104 bars employees from such co-options. Teachers, as noted earlier, are the only exception.

The general disqualification is not removed by the use of non-voting membership. The disqualification is of membership *per se*, whether of a voting nature or not. It follows that it is currently unlawful for a council formally to appoint an employee as a member of a committee and some other device would therefore have been necessary if the GLC had gone ahead with its proposals.

The device chosen was simplicity itself. There is no legal bar on any persons being invited to attend a committee and speak (by invitation of the committee) on matters in which they have an interest. The GLC's proposal to the trade unions was, therefore, that they be given a standing invitation to attend and speak at committee meetings, the number of representatives to be not more than one-third of the current number of committee members. In the longer term, the GLC wished to campaign for legislation to remove the disqualification bar to membership. Two possible complications might arise were legislation ever to clear the way to full employee membership of committees. First, there is the question of members' liability to surcharge in the event of a committee exceeding its statutory powers and incurring unjustified expenditure. In that event, an employee member would be as liable as any elected councillor – unless special statutory safeguards were created.

Secondly, there is the matter of members' pecuniary interests. Section 94 of the Local Government Act requires a member to declare such an interest in any matter under discussion, and thereafter to take no further part in the proceedings. It is difficult to see how an employee member of a personnel committee could avoid being in the position of having a pecuniary interest in a considerable proportion of such a committee's business, and consequently have his membership rendered almost useless.

A personnel management comment

From a personnel management viewpoint it is disappointing that so much of the industrial democracy debate has been conducted on a political, rather than employment, basis. There has been little real analysis of the principles involved, and one consequence seems to be that staff – as distinct from trade union hierarchies – have not felt proposals such as committee membership to be of any particular relevance to the realities of daily work. The debate in local government also reveals a failure to analyse the real nature of the decision-making process and the different roles of officers and members in this process.

262

If a clearer view is to be taken of the subject, a better starting point may be to examine the concept of 'staff-involvement' rather than 'industrial democracy', using 'staff involvement' to cover any form of employee or trade union association with the decision-making process.

All forms of staff involvement are intended to influence managerial decisions in some way. The extent of this influence depends on the form and purpose of involvement and on where, within the decision-making process, the involvement occurs. It is necessary, therefore, to examine the decision-making process itself, to comment on the different forms and places of staff involvement within this process and discuss the various objectives the unions may have in trying to achieve a greater involvement in the work of the council committees.

The unique and most important single feature of decision-making in local government is the involvement in the total management process of both elected Members and officials. The simple concept is that decisions are taken by Members in committees and Council: and what might be described as 'implementary decisions' are taken by officers to put these policies into effect. In practice, the process is more complex.

First, in the political arena, the evolution of ideas leading to decisions about new policies often takes place mainly within the party mechanisms rather than in public committee, particularly where a minority party has a significant proportion of the total council membership.

It is difficult to envisage effective staff involvement in committees unless the staff also has some form of access to, or influence on, the development of ideas and positions which precedes the formal adoption of recommendations by committees. Members, however, obviously wish to retain their freedom to discuss a wide range of policy options privately and in advance of any pressures or submissions by particular interest groups.

Trade unions, on the other hand, not infrequently hear of subjects being under discussion within the party groups and urge that they should be given an opportunity of expressing their views at this early stage before political views begin to crystalize.

Secondly, it is useful to distinguish between four forms of member decision-making:

the evolution of policies initiated within the party mechanisms
the decisions taken by Members on proposals initiated by officers
a combination of these when a broad policy is decided initially within the majority party and officers are then asked to work up detailed, and sometimes alternative, implementation plans

the approval (often by committee chairman) of sometimes quite minor operational or executive matters on which Member authorization (eg of expenditure) is required by standing orders.

A feature of many of these processes is the informal nature of much of the discussion which precedes the formulation of formal recommendations. Apart from discussion between officers there is often informal contact between officers and Members. A chief officer who is considering a possible restructuring of his department may well discuss his ideas with his Chairman before formulating a detailed set of proposals, and the options eventually put to Members for formal decision will be significantly influenced by these earlier, informal soundings.

Members, in calling for inplementation plans for a Member-initiated policy change, may well seek preliminary information and ideas from officers, and these contacts will influence the range and nature of the plans eventually submitted for formal committee approval.

Informal Member/Officer discussion on 'chairman's action' items is similarly a very normal and useful feature of the whole management process.

Staff are, of course, aware that the realities of decision-making involve informal Member/officer contact; and that a chairman's working relationship with a chief officer may be very influential in influencing actual decisions. There is no effective method, however, of introducing formal staff involvement into this day-to-day pattern of informal discussion. Indeed, one of the major problems in industrial democracy is that the larger and more formal the forum in which staff involvement is provided, the greater the likelihood that the real decision-making process will occur elsewhere, and less formally. This is a difficulty which is not peculiar to local government.

Managerial decision-making at officer level also takes place in both formal and informal settings. Major issues are discussed, and a common view evolved within the Chief Officers' Group. Within departments, chief and senior officers use a variety of regular meetings to discuss problems, hammer out solutions, and monitor progress. To support and supplement these more formal contacts the effective manager will undertake a whole range of informal discussions by which he acquires information, assesses attitudes, tries out his own preliminary ideas, and seeks alternatives.

Staff involvement within these management processes at officer level may also be both formal and informal. Formally, joint management/union committees may be used to provide an opportunity for staff views to be expressed. There are similar problems of timing here as for Members. Senior Officers may well need to have a considerable amount of preliminary discussion before reaching an agreed departmental view which can be put on to the table for discussion with the unions. Staff, on the other hand, will press for involvement at the early, formative stage.

Informally, the effective manager will try out his own ideas on his own subordinate staff and so extend the range of involvement in the individual, as distinct from collective, sense. On some issues he may well go further and, if he has established a good relationship with the trade unions, talk informally to the relevant union representatives about possible developments which might affect the staff.

It is worth noting that decision-making extends throughout the whole spectrum of management. The foreman or office supervisor within his area of responsibility makes decisions about the allocation of work, work methods, standards and priorities, just as senior managers do at their level. There are therefore opportunites for staff views to be taken into account in decision-making throughout the whole management process and not merely at its more formal summits.

At least four kinds of formal staff involvement can be distinguished – consultation, joint study of specific issues, negotiation and co-determination.

Joint consultation is the conventional form of obtaining staff views on matters of concern to them. The basic pattern of consultation in relation to the decision-making process is:

management proposals are prepared
proposals are put to the staff, who then comment on them
management proposals are then possibly (though not necessarily) modified in the light of staff views

Staff sides often have two criticisms of this approach. First, consultation is often limited to reports which are held to have staff implications ie proposals which change working methods, staff numbers or grades, organization structures and the like. No consultation may occur on broader policy papers or on many technical or financial proposals. Secondly, by the time a draft report has been prepared, a great deal of preparatory work has already taken place, and departmental management views have been defined. Staff sides would prefer to be consulted at a much earlier point in the whole process.

Joint studies of specified issues are sometimes used to prepare proposals for Member level decision. A working party of senior officers and staff representatives is set up, with defined terms of reference, to study a particular problem and report. Departmental reorganizations are sometimes studied in this way, or the evolution of new work systems.

These joint study groups do not usually make decisions: they produce proposals and these sometimes include alternatives which

265

reflect differing officer and union views. They do, however, provide a mechanism for staff involvement at the formative stage in the whole decision-making process.

Negotiation on pay and conditions is another conventional form of staff involvement. In recent years there has been a tendency for a wider range of issues to be treated as negotiable. Working methods, staff numbers, equipment, accommodation – matters of this kind tend to be the subject of potential disputes and consequent collective bargaining. London Fire Brigade experience has shown that if joint study groups are treated (by either side) not as problem-solving bodies which produce proposals, but as negotiating bodies which have to bargain for a single decision, then the whole arena of management action can become an industrial relations battleground.

Co-determination – that is, joint decision-making, is the primary issue in the national debate on industrial democracy and no working examples can be seen in local government. If unions think that committee membership would equate to co-determination, the views set out above would suggest that committee membership may provide the shadow of shared power, rather than the substance.

In considering the various forms of staff involvement, the purpose of such involvement is often overlooked. At least three very different emphases can be given to staff involvement:

the protection of staff interests
the contribution of staff expertise
power-sharing.

The protection of staff interests is the most obvious reason for staff involvement. Management proposals are vetted by the staff to ensure that they have no deleterious effect on pay, status or security, and alternative proposals are put foward by staff to protect these interests. The normal system of staff side consultation on committee reports encourages this fairly narrow view. It is an approach, too, which tends to encourage a defensive or exploitive negotiating stance from the unions.

The contribution of staff expertise to the study and solution of work problems is a more constructive ideal in staff involvement. Who better to advise the top decision-makers as to the practicalities of various plans and policies than the workers who have to put them into effect? Joint study groups are based very much on this idea. Two problems arise. First, joint discussions usually involve senior management and trade union representatives but omit supervisory staff and junior management. Yet one *raison d'être* for supervisory and lower management ranks is for them to build up a body of collective practical wisdom about a department's operational problems.

266

Secondly, unless there is acceptance of this joint problem-solving role by managers and staff representatives, this form of staff involvement can easily degenerate into attempts by staff to extend the negotiating area for purely sectional interests, and by managers to defend any encroachment into their traditional managerial preserves.

Power-sharing is the more political view of staff involvement, inherent in much of the current national debate. It is a significant feature in some unions' policies (eg TGWU). It cannot be satisfactorily resolved without a clear view of the evolving role of trade unions in British society. Are they to remain in their traditional role of protective organizations for their members, outside the formal institutions and structure of power; or are they to develop more recent trends of being incorporated into the formal, established system? It is difficult to see how a co-determinist, power-sharing role can be combined with the independence of a free collective bargaining stance.

Within local (and national) government, there is the additional problem of resolving the principle of election solely through the ballot box, with that of the interest-group representation of employees. Any weakening of a council's accountability to, and representation of, the local electorate can be seen as a fundamental breach of the democratic basis of local government.

From a personnel management viewpoint, more emphasis on ways – formal and informal – of involving employees in decision-making within the day-to-day realities of their own jobs seems a more constructive approach to raising employee motivation and commitment, than discussion about the legal and political complications of employee membership of committees.

16 The role of the elected member

Official guidance about the relationship between council members and council employees is provided in the national Code of Conduct for Members, and this merits quotation here:

Councillors and officers

    (a) Both councillors and officers are servants of the public, and they are indispensable to one another. But their responsibilities are distinct. Councillors are responsible to the electorate and serve only so long as their term of office lasts. Officers are responsible to the council and are permanently appointed. An officer's job is to give advice to councillors and the council, and to carry out the council's work under the direction and control of the council and its committees.

    (b) Mutual respect between councillors and officers is essential to good local government. Close personal familiarity between individual councillor and officer can damage this relationship and prove embarrassing to other councillors and officers.

    (c) If you are called upon to take part in appointing an officer, the only question you should consider is which candidate would best serve the whole council. You should not let your personal or political preference influence your judgement. You should not canvass the support of colleagues for any candidate and you should resist any attempt by others to canvass yours.

For the councillor with an active interest in his authority's employment activities, this guide, unexceptional as it is, does not go very far. If he is appointed to the personnel committee or if, through trade union contacts for example, approaches are made to him by employee groups, this code will be of limited practical use in guiding his activities. In 1978, LACSAB produced a 'Guide for Members on Employee Relations in Local Government' which provided much more relevant information, though biased heavily towards industrial relations matters.

    Councillors do not enter local government, of course, with the primary ambition to oversee their council's personnel activities. The motives for standing for local elections are various: a social conscience, a sense of public service, political ambition, the promotion of community democracy, the reduction of council spending – all these can be primary reasons for a councillor's presence in the council chamber. Yet by becoming a councillor, the elected member also becomes, in one sense, an employer and acquires a responsibility for the well-being and effectiveness of the council's staff. This responsibility is a collective one: it pertains to the council as a whole and not to any individual member. But collective responsibilities have finally to be effected by individuals and councils have to establish systems by which their employment responsibilities and activities can be undertaken by designated councillors. So the new councillor, hoping for a seat on the housing or education committee, may instead find himself gently pressed on to the personnel committee because, perhaps, of his working experience in staff management, or as a trade unionist. What is the purpose of this committee? To what extent should it become involved in the authority's day to day employment problems and activities?

The Mallaby and Maud reports of 1967 cast doubts on the desirability of any real member involvement in employment matters. Factually, the reports noted that a number of authorities had set up establishment committees to deal with employment matters. No doubt many of these committees had been set up in line with the pre-war recommendations of the 1934 Hadow report. But the Maud report said:

> establishment work is basically a management function and as such falls into the category of staff work to be done by officers. We do not see a special co-ordinative role for an establishment committee which, in so far as it is retained, should be an advisory body having particular responsibility for considering key officer appointments.

Existing establishment committees were seen as concerned primarily with the reconciliation of conflicting departmental pressures for expansion. But in that the availability of finance is the ultimate limit on the size of the establishment, establishment committees were seen as 'inevitably subordinate' to finance committees.

The Bains report, concentrating within its terms of reference on management rather than council structures, nevertheless sketched in a role for a personnel committee.

Resource availability and management, suggested Bains, was a matter of primary concern for a council. A local authority needed to bring into one key committee the co-ordination of planning for the effective use of the three primary resources of land, finance and manpower. A policy and resources committee was proposed for this purpose. But Bains thought that this committee should deal only with matters of major importance. 'The more routine matters requiring member participation should be dealt with by three resource sub-committees each dealing with one of the three main resources'. Bains thus suggested that a manpower or personnel sub-committee should operate under the policy and resources committee and many authorities have followed this pattern. But there is little advice in Bains about this sub-committee's real functions, or about the nature of manpower matters with which the policy and resources committee itself should be concerned.

It is useful, therefore, to review the employment activities in which members have normally been involved in practice, either through membership of a personnel or establishment committee, or through other formal or informal channels. At the same time some suggestions can be made as to how members might ensure real effectiveness in these roles. Six main types of involvement can be distinguished:

individual case enquiries and contacts
membership of grievance and appeals panels
membership of joint consultative committees
participation in negotiations with trade unions
membership of staff selection panels
membership of personnel or establishment committees.

Each is examined in more detail below.

Individual contact

Councillors can become involved in individual employee problems in a number of ways. Constituency case-work will sometimes throw up an employment problem as a subsidiary factor in some other issue. Thus a council employee may approach his local councillor for help in a housing problem apparently quite unconnected with his job. On investigation, it may appear that the housing problem has been exacerbated by a recent job transfer from one part of the district to another, and that a simpler solution than re-housing would be to reverse the recent transfer of job location. What should the councillor do in this situation? Should he use his council position to put pressure on the departmental management? The simple answer is that he should take the same steps *vis-à-vis* the council as an employer as he would have done had his constituent been employed elsewhere. But this may be an over-simple solution. The plain fact is that he is likely to be able to obtain more information about the case through council channels than he would had the constituent been working elsewhere. So the first step would be for him to write either to the chief officer of the department concerned, or to the chairman of the personnel (or employing) committee, describing the case and asking for information and assistance. (Authorities have their own rules or traditions as to the 'correct' channels of communications: some encourage direct member/chief officer contact, others prefer contacts, at least initially, to be through chairmen). If the explanation of the employment position is acceptable to him then his problem is a normal councillor-to-constituent one of explaining the outcome of his enquiries. If it is not acceptable, he is back in the employment arena and again must decide to what extent he pursues the matter through official channels.

If he is genuinely unconvinced by the explanation he has been given, and further channels are open, he is failing in his responsibility to his constituent if he does not take the matter further through follow-up discussions with the committee chairman involved.

Two other forms of individual councillor/employee contact are worth noting: the member visit to a council work location and the direct approach by an employee to a member about an employment problem.

Visits of council members to the authority's offices, depots and other work sites are a necessary and useful way for members to keep in touch with council activities. Visits are also appreciated by employees and can help to break down the sense of distance and impersonality that often exists between the workforce and 'them' – the council. Should the visits be arranged or unannounced? Should the chief officer concerned always know about them – or even be present? Local style, size and precedent will usually determine the answers, and any new councillor would be well advised to check the drill with his more experienced colleagues and with the chief executive. Nevertheless, one or two general points are worth considering. Councillors who prefer the freedom and informality of the individual, spur of the moment visit need to be aware of how inconvenient the unexpected visitor may be to a busy manager with a full appointments diary. They should be prepared to be shown round by quite junior members of the staff – whoever happens to be sufficiently free of pressing duties to spare the time – and that being so, should be a little wary of accepting everything that may be said as giving a complete picture of the points discussed. Senior officers, on the other hand would, it is hoped, welcome the interest of individual councillors and if they are unavoidably engaged when the councillor 'drops in', would be well advised to relay a message regretting their inability to meet and offering an appointment for a later discussion.

When visits are arranged in advance, councillors might sometimes gain a better impression of the work of the unit if they make it clear that they would like to be shown round by the local manager and his staff, rather than by a more senior officer who comes down from the head office merely for the visit. Senior officers, when advised of requests for visits, might also contact the councillors in advance to see if there is any particular aspect of the work which they would like to see or discuss.

Returning more specifically to the employment field, one particular problem of visits is that the councillor who encourages employees to talk, not so much about their work as about their employment conditions, is likely to collect a number of complaints. Firemen may press on him the view that they should have free messing. Refuse incineration operatives may aver that they had wage parity with sewage workers until the Water Authorities took over the latter and increased various allowances. An electrician on a bonus scheme may allege that bonus pressures force him to take safety risks. Clerks in an air-conditioned office may complain that the dry air is resulting in an increase in sickness absences. What should the councillor's response be?

He is correct, of course, to tell them that he is not in a position to comment and that they should take up their complaints with their local management. But as coldly proper a response as this will hardly improve the staffs' opinion of councillors. At the other extreme, he can express sympathy with their views and promise 'to do something about it'. This runs the very real risk of prejudicing negotiations which may well be proceeding between the trade unions and management on some of the issues, or of raising false hopes. It will also rile the managers, who will feel that their side of the story has been ignored and that, by inference, they have been judged wrong. There are therefore, two standard and useful queries in response to complaints. 'Have you taken this up with your manager?' – and if the answer is yes, but without results – 'Have you taken it up with your union?'. Alternatively, where the complaint is clearly an individual one, in an authority which has a grievance procedure, the question can be 'Are you taking it through the grievance procedure?'. Disputes and grievance procedures and negotiating systems work effectively only if they are positively promoted and used. Councillors can help their authorities considerably by being aware of the existence and general nature of these procedures, and by referring employment problems to them when the occasion arises. A brief description of these procedures might well be included in the member's handbook which many authorities issue to new councillors.

Informally, there is room for rather more direct action. The councillor may be able to bring the local manager immediately into his conversation with the complaining employee, or he may be able to say 'Look, this isn't really according to the book, but I'll have a word with your manager and ask him to see you about this'. It is understandable that many local managers and senior officers are happy only with the planned and organized visit, and are worried when councillors insist on speaking to employees with no managers directly present. It is this author's view that over-sensitivity on this issue is usually unfounded. Provided councillors are prepared to listen to the manager's view as well as the employee's, and not wilfully to undercut established procedures for dealing with grievances and complaints, direct councillor/employee contact should improve mutual understanding and benefit employee morale. Councillors have responsibilities for personnel policies. The occasional informal visit, with direct conversations with employees at workshop and office level, is a useful way of assessing the general mood of employees, their attitudes to the council, and the extent to which policy actually gets translated into practice. Managers who find themselves resenting such visits would do well to examine their reaction for traces of over or under confidence in the state of their units, or of somewhat outdated concepts of absolute managerial authority.

Individual councillors are also sometimes approached directly by individual employees, shop stewards or trade union officials for help in dealing with employment problems. Many authorities have for years had standing instructions prohibiting such approaches by employees, and breaches can and have led to disciplinary action. There are several reasons for this. It is in everyone's interest that employee grievances and problems are dealt with fairly and effectively through the normal employment channels. The by-passing of these channels by the direct approach to members weakens the management system, and opens the door to differential treatment between employees who keep to the procedural rules and those with the nerve to break them. Moreover, a councillor as an individual cannot speak for the council as an employer and can therefore do little more than pass any employment problems put to him back into the proper management or grievance procedure, which is where they should have been in the first place. Most councillors have quite enough constituency casework to deal with, without acquiring extra cases by acting as an unofficial court of appeal for employees. Employees, too, should normally look to their trade unions to help them in grievance situations, not to councillors. The non-unionist, who appeals to a councillor on the ground that he has no-one to assist him, has an obvious alternative solution (though if he is a constituent he has a right to a more sympathetic reply than 'join a union!').

All this having been said, this author would be hesitant to enforce, by disciplinary action, an absolute ban of the kind implied by conventional staff rules. In any large workforce, there is the likelihood of having one or two irritating but not necessarily inefficient eccentrics who will fall foul of the employment system at some stage in their career, and who will fight their cases all the way up the proper procedures – and lose. With a burning sense of injustice, they will then write impassioned letters to the leader of the council or to their constituency councillor, asking for aid. It is too easy to deal with this by refusing to answer and by taking disciplinary action. People are more important than rules, and any real sense of injustice (however unjustified) is worth an attempt to resolve. Local government, with its tradition of service to people in the community, should surely not behave internally in an impersonal or autocratic manner. The leader or councillor who asks the appropriate chief officer or chairman for the full facts on this sort of case, and who (if necessary with advice from the personnel officer) sends an informal reply is promoting a sense of internal justice and sympathy; though he must also be prepared to be included in the enemy camp by the really dedicated and possibly unbalanced employee maverick.

Approaches to councillors by shop stewards and trade union officials are rarely so innocent. Active trade unionists are always well aware of the proper disputes and grievance procedures and of the accepted patterns of discussion and negotiation. The quiet, back-door approach to a councillor is usually a conscious attempt to achieve a bargaining advantage outside the proper channels. Shop stewards should normally be firmly and pleasantly directed back into the system.

The trade union official's contacts, particularly with trade union or Labour Party colleagues who are council members, have to be looked at in a different light. To the politically naive manager they are just as unacceptable and dangerous to the system as any other by-passing of procedures. But it is more realistic to accept the likelihood of such contacts and to think of them as no more than normal, quasi-political, lobbying. From the councillor's viewpoint, his handling of this lobbying is very much a matter of judgement rather than principle. He is in the position of having a responsibility for supporting the role of the council as an employer. He also has his non-council connections and obligations to honour and maintain. Two extreme examples illustrate the problem.

Consider first the trade union official who is involved in negotiation with the chairman of the personnel committee about the dismissal of an employee who happens to be a shop steward. He may contact a councillor, a member of the same trade union, and try to enlist this councillor's help in finding out, covertly, the extent to which the chairman is committed to his current line of action. It would not seem unreasonable to expect the councillor's reply to be 'Sorry, but I can't play a double game. I'm very willing to talk to the chairman about your problem in this case but I can't get information out of him to feed to you, on a false basis'.

As a different example, take a case in which the trade union official is engaged in a campaign for the council to provide new canteen facilities. He may approach his councillor colleague and ask for his assistance in pressing his case on the council. This seems wholly acceptable, however much it might irritate some senior officers. If the councillor agrees with the trade union's case there is no reason why he should not, quite openly, speak to the chairman concerned in support of the case. There are two points for him to watch. First, any pressure he exerts should be on the appropriate committee chairman and not on individual senior officers. Secondly, he should avoid the type of contact with the employee group concerned which might lead to his being quoted (or rather mis-quoted) as implying that the council (as distinct from an individual councillor) supports its case.

Employees may also approach a councillor with a complaint against a trade union. Insofar as this can be dealt with as a constituency problem, the councillor has as much of a duty to pursue it as in any other complaint. But if the appeal is really to the council as an employer, the matter will need very cautious handling. It is a golden rule of industrial relations that the employer should not attempt to interfere with the internal affairs of a trade union. A wholly informal approach on the trade union or Labour Party network may be possible; but it is usually dangerous and unacceptable for the authority as an employer to be seen to be taking sides in either inter-union disputes, or disputes between a union and an individual employee.

Grievance and appeals panels

As noted in the earlier chapter on local level industrial relations, most authorities have set up grievance and appeals procedures. These may follow the models set out in NJC agreements, or may be modified to fit local style and custom. The last stage of most of these procedures enables the aggrieved employee to put his case to a panel consisting wholly, or partly, of council members. The member's role on such a panel is quite different from involvement in joint consultative committees. In the latter, members are speaking for the council and will explain and defend council policies. On an appeals panel, the member's task is to reach a wholly impartial, independent view of the case as it is presented. There is a close similarity to an industrial tribunal. The objective is to see that a just decision is reached, not to uphold council regulations for their own sake nor to act merely as a modifier of management decisions. Two dangers exist. Some members may feel that the priority is to uphold the authority of the managers concerned, and that only an unusually blatant case of faulty management would justify reversing whatever decision the employee is appealing against. Alternatively, other members may feel an almost instinctive sympathy with the individual employee in his lone battle against the whole weight of managerial authority and will look actively for even the most minor reason for reversing the management decision. A middle course between these two extremes is what both managers and individual employees should expect and obtain. The industrial tribunal test of 'fairness', taking rules, regulations and precedents into account, is really what is wanted. The fact that this is extraordinarily difficult to define only emphasizes the importance of sound, unbiased and unemotional judgement.

Before such judgement can be exercised, the facts of the case have to be established. There is obviously an onus on both the employee who is appealing, and the managers who are defending their earlier decisions, to put all the relevant facts before the panel. The onus is greater on the managers to show the rectitude of their position than it is on the employee to prove, as it were, his innocence. The panel's job, by careful questioning of all parties, is to round out the two sides of the case they are presented with, in order to gain as complete a picture as possible.

Questioning of this type demands a fair level of skill. Questions such as 'Do you admit that you went into the stores to see if there was anything worth taking?' tend to generate uninformative and monosyllabic replies. A better form of question would be 'Tell us what you had in mind when you went into the stores?'.

Similarly, questioning the senior officer thus, 'Don't you think that you were rather hasty in suspending Mr X?' will only reinforce the officer's defensiveness. Instead, 'Tell us what factors you took into account before deciding on the suspension' will sound far less aggressive but in fact be far more probing.

In grading appeals, one primary feature will need to be borne in mind – that it is the *job* which is graded, not the individual. Personnel officers often feel that members are too influenced by what they think of the employee making the appeal; and that pleasant, articulate employees tend to win appeals regardless of the real merits of the case as it relates to the impersonal features of the post.

Joint consultative committee

Members' involvement in joint consultative meetings with employee representatives is of an official nature, that is, the member involved represents the Council as the employer, he does not participate as an independent assessor or commentator. There are three aspects to such involvement.

First, members can explain council policies and the reasons for them. A change of policy emphasis, for example, from constructing new houses to renovating old ones will have a major effect on the nature and balance of work in the housing department. While the chief officer should be perfectly capable of explaining this change and its effects to the employees, only members can speak at first hand about the underlying local or political reasons for the change. The word 'political' is used here very deliberately. Many local government employees – at all levels – resent what they see or describe as the intrusion of politics. They complain bitterly about changes in work which they feel have been caused 'just by politics'. The view that politics is not an abstract or detached activity, but is intrinsically all about the nature of, and priorities in, housing, education, and other social and public services is not readily accepted. Whose responsibility is it to explain this political view of public service? Clearly it is for council members. The free and frank exposition of the council's policies and priorities, in the realistic setting of local political activity, can be a most valuable function of the members' role in joint consultative committees.

Secondly, members can listen to what the employees have to say about their work and about the effect of council policy on their jobs and their attitudes. Policy changes which demand too great or sudden a change in work methods or job skills will be ineffective. Through joint consultative committees, members can learn at first hand of employee reaction, and can benefit from the resulting proposals and suggestions.

Thirdly, the explanation and the listening roles taken together can generate the joint evolution of ideas and solutions new to both sides. A productive line of discussion can be 'Here is what the council wants to do, and for these reasons. We've heard your reactions and we can now understand your objections. So we have a bit of a problem. What would *your* solution be?'.

Trade union negotiations

There are several different ways in which members may become involved in trade union negotiations. The chairman of the personnel committee, supported by some of his members, may well be part of the normal negotiation process at local level, particularly to deal with issues where agreement cannot be reached by officers. This may be formalized in a disputes procedure. Members may be involved on a more infrequent basis when a really serious dispute arises and for which an *ad hoc* negotiating group may be set up. Finally, as noted in the chapter on national level industrial relations, a small number of members across the country are elected or nominated to the employers' sides of the various provincial and national joint councils.

Perhaps the biggest problem facing the member who finds himself in a negotiating role is that of ensuring that he is sufficiently well-informed. Industrial relations is becoming an increasingly complex subject. Wage systems are influenced by national, regional and local agreements and are complicated by national pay policies. The mass of new legislation in recent years has created a new and complicated legal dimension to many negotiating issues. Trade unions themselves have formed new alliances and are changing their internal power and authority structures. These are dangerous waters for the amateur. More than one London borough, faced with strike action in the 1974-75 period of difficulty with dustmen, found that apparently single-issue problems such as banning totting, or using outside contractors, or disciplining an employee convicted of a criminal offence, rapidly developed into multi-issue disputes including such factors as the extent to which weekly pay is guaranteed, the maze of the law regarding picketing, the interpretation of the social contract and the role of ACAS in relation to NJC disputes procedures.

Most councillors need expert advice on the issues which can arise in disputes and in consequent negotiations. If the personnel officer does not, or cannot, offer it they should find out why, and press for the necessary action.

Two other pitfalls may be mentioned. First, any dispute over one issue carries with it the danger of a secondary dispute over some other issue. For example, during the electricians' national industrial action in 1975 some authorities, without discussion with their local electricians, brought in outside contractors to carry out urgent repairs. Within a week the national action had been called off but the local men blacked the sites where contractors had worked. A national wage dispute had been converted into a secondary and local 'strike-breaking' issue. In at least one case the decision to call in contractors was taken by a service committee chairman in the absence of any information or advice about possible employee reaction from either the personnel officer or the personnel committee chairman.

Secondly, there is a strong tendency for any negotiator to become emotionally committed to a particular viewpoint. Changing this view then becomes not a matter of commonsense and practical compromise but one of personal dignity almost regardless of the facts. A member at one employers' side meeting of the NJC is alleged to have opened the proceedings by declaring that 'I've come here today to oppose any suggestion that there should be any compromise and I hope other members won't waste my time and their's trying to change my mind'.

The keynotes of successful negotiation are flexibility, ingenuity and an absence of passion. Members who are nominated by their Councils or local authority associations to membership of Provincial Councils or NJCs also require intelligent briefing. Formally, this is given by the employers' secretariat (provincial secretary or LACSAB) of each body. But without a knowledge of the local background to the issues discussed at provincial or national level, the elected member may find it difficult to do other than accept the secretariat's formal advice. This

278

may be perfectly sound advice – but if members are always to endorse it one might well query the need for their involvement. What a member can bring to provincial or national negotiations is information and ideas from local level, and a feel for how a particular line would affect his own authority and its employees. Many such members consequently discuss provincial council and NJC agendas and their formal briefing notes with their local personnel officers – and expect informed and perceptive comment from these officers to assist their deliberations.

Staff selection panels

Authorities' practice varies in the nature and extent of member involvement in the selection and promotion of staff: but all authorities select officers to some posts by some form of member committee. At one extreme is the whole council, meeting to interview applicants for chief officer appointments. At the other extreme is the chairman of the personnel committee, or of a special staff appointments board, interviewing applicants on his own. More normal is some form of panel with three to eight members.

The larger the size of the panel, the more formal and the more tense is the interviewing situation. It is difficult to the point of impossibility to get candidates to talk freely and in a relaxed manner when confronted by a phalanx of interviewers. On the other hand, members may wish to see how a candidate does behave in this fairly formal and stressful situation. The size and procedure adopted for a panel should therefore be decided in the light of the objects of the interview. If the intention is to conduct a lengthy and in-depth study of the candidate's knowledge and attitudes, a 20 minute interview before a large panel is quite useless. On the other hand, the panel may wish mainly to observe the candidate's reaction to a formal, committee-type situation, and to make its own, almost intuitive assessment of his personality. Personality, as distinct from technical competence, is an important factor in selection and one on which councillors may wish particularly to be assured – especially when appointments are being made to posts involving a high degree of contact with the public (the constituents).

The conventional, fairly short, panel interview has been heavily criticized by many selection experts as being superficial and misleading. They point out that it is quite impossible to find out the real extent of a candidate's knowledge, and to determine the whole range of his abilities, on so short and formal an occasion. If the panel interview constitutes the whole of the selection process, this is clearly true. But more normally, the members' panel will be interviewing a short list of candidates prepared after a thorough selection process by senior officers and this, it may be hoped, will have included at least one in-depth interview by the personnel officer. With this preliminary and thorough screening, what purpose does the final members' panel serve? There are two primary answers:

Where senior officers are concerned, in posts which may involve them in frequent contact with members, members need to feel confident that the candidates will 'fit-in'; that the authority will acquire and promote senior staff who can work well with the members.

Senior officers, again, will usually have to attend and advise committees. They need to have an ability to think on their feet, to speak explicitly and intelligently to laymen about their particular specialisms. The panel interview is quite a good analogue of the committee situation.

Additionally, when external as well as internal candidates are involved, members are able to check that the quality of internal staff is generally matching external standards.

In effect, however, the main factors being assessed are personality and communicating skill. The problem with panels is that the self-confident and articulate candidate will put up a much more impressive performance than the quieter, more introspective candidate. And not all jobs require on-the-spot articulation as a primary characteristic. It is not difficult to envisage, say, a senior fire officer who is highly competent and decisive in the rigours of a command situation 'on the fireground', but who is nervous or uncommunicative in front of a selection panel. The skills of the fireground, and those required to perform well at formal interview, are almost completely dissimilar. The danger is that the glib, but ineffective, extrovert will impress the panel with his ready response to questioning while the highly capable, quietly analytical but somewhat reserved introvert will pass almost unnoticed. It is a responsibility of the officers concerned with short-listing to eliminate the merely glib.

One other common practice of members' selection panels merits comment, that of using questions prepared by officers. There seem to be two reasons for this. First, an attempt to ensure absolute fairness by asking all candidates precisely the same questions. Secondly, a feeling that members need help in framing questions to test professionals' knowledge. On the first point, the fairness of equal treatment needs to be balanced against the advantages obtained from a more natural and informal approach: and the need to get each candidate to talk about his own particular experience. The second point – the use of prepared 'professional' questions – is open to serious criticism. If members are not *au fait* with the details of the profession of or specialism of the candidate they are interviewing, asking questions designed by experts is quite useless. Professional answers need to be judged by professional assessors. What the lay member needs to know is whether the professional can explain his specialism to laymen; for this, intelligent but lay questions are needed. An example illustrates the dangers. A personnel officer was asked to prepare questions for a members' panel to ask of an applicant for a senior management services job. One of his questions, used by a members' panel which was not expert in management theory, was 'What contribution do you think organizational development can make to the concept of corporate management?' Most of the answers were unintelligible except to a fellow expert. A better, lay question would have been 'Tell us how you think management services might be used to get a better team approach to top management'.

Finally, a panel which has the task of final selection must decide to what extent it makes this decision solely on the basis of the interview. There is a view that all other factors except interview performance should be put aside. Speaking of a promotion board, a councillor said to a county personnel officer that while, from several years of personal knowledge, he was sure that Mr Y was the better man, he had to plump for Mr X because 'he interviewed so much better'. Other panels deliberately exclude considerationof senior officers' previous interview records and career assessments and, again, rely almost entirely on interview performance.

If the interview is regarded as the last test, the last hurdle to overcome, this line can be justified. But if the limitations of the panel interview are accepted, it would seem wiser to consider interview performance as the last piece of the whole jigsaw of relevant information, and for the panel to take into account all available information. This would include employment history, references, career history and performance appraisals where internal candidates are concerned, and the interview assessment of officers concerned with the preparation of the short list.

Personnel and establishment committees

Most authorities now seem to have established personnel committees. Some are full committees, reporting direct to the council, perhaps most follow the Bains pattern of sub-committees of the policy and resources committee.

The functions often include staff selection and the oversight of the joint consultative, grievance, disciplinary, appeals and negotiating systems which have been discussed above. Other common responsibilities are:

setting the authority's manpower resourcing policy; deciding whether total employee mumbers and/or numbers in particular services are to be permitted to rise, or are to be kept static or reduced – in general terms, setting the authority's manpower budget and monitoring it

vetting and giving approval to departments' requests for additional staff or for variations in the deployment of posts; this is the traditional establishments (or staff numbers) function

approving any significant grade changes, ie the transfer of a job or jobs from one grade to another; again, part of the traditional staffing control function

approving changes in employment regulations or conditions, including ratification of significant negotiations with trade unions on pay and conditions issues

approving improvements in and plans for employee welfare and amenities, such as canteens, sports clubs, rest rooms, welfare service

approving expenditure on individual cases such as *ex gratia* injury payments, enhanced retirement benefits compensation payments, special study leave

considering reports on individual employees such as serious disciplinary cases, examples of outstanding merit, unusually long service

receiving reports on the employment implications of new legislation and of new national agreements, and reviewing possible action thereon.

This type of practical action list tends to conceal the underlying nature of the role of a personnel committee. It is useful to look at this in a very different way, that is, to consider the committee as having a three-part purpose:

to establish and maintain personnel or employment *policy*

to ensure that *procedures* exist to put policies into effect

to *monitor* the effectiveness of these policies and procedures as effected.

Policies – guidelines of principle and action – are necessary across the whole employment field if the authority's management of its manpower is to be positive, effective, consistent and constructive. Two examples illustrate this:

First, in the industrial relations field, managers require a policy decision about the extent to which employee involvement in joint committees of various kinds is to be limited to trade union members. Some authorities may feel that all employees, whether union members or not, should have the opportunity to serve on safety, canteen and other consultative committees. Other authorities may consider that all collective employee involvement should be through the recognized collective channel of trade union membership. Managers need to know what the official line is, and should certainly not be left to make

282

up their individual minds on the issue. The personnel committee can easily clarify the principle by issuing a policy statement that, for example, 'This council believes that all employee involvement in joint committees of all kinds should be through normal trade union channels, by existing employee representatives such as shop stewards'.

Secondly, in the field of promotion, departments should all operate the same degree of preference for internal candidates. Employees will feel a sense of injustice about inconsistencies in this matter. An authority might therefore, through its personnel committee, approve a policy statement that 'When a promotion opportunity occurs, no external candidates shall be considered until it has been determined that no suitable internal candidate is available'. Another authority may take a significantly different line: what is being stressed here is the value of a formal policy being defined, whatever that policy is.

Policy guidelines are valuable across the whole range of personnel management. Some of the most important areas in which policy needs definition are:

manpower planning, where policies are needed to determine the mix of skills, qualifications and age groups required in the workforce, and to decide to what extent various sources of manpower (school-leavers, graduates etc) are to be used

manpower budgeting, where policy decisions can set global limits on the numbers to be employed, and endorse a variety of staff ratios to determine manning levels (eg the number of manual workers per foreman, the median span of control of managers at various levels)

wages and salary systems, where policy guidance is needed as to the use of bonus schemes, the extent of shared savings, the use of techniques such as OWM, work study, and job evaluation

other conditions of employment, in which policies are required about the use of overtime, the granting of special leave, the degree of flexibility in working hours etc

career development, where policies are needed to determine the nature and extent of performance appraisals, the approach to the identification and development of 'high-flyers', the degree of openness of career development information

training, an area in which major policy decisions are needed as to the purpose and extent of training generally; and the balance between internal and external training

industrial relations, a field for a range of policy statements on such issues as the closed shop, facilities for shop stewards and the respective roles of line managers, the personnel officer and members in negotiations

equal opportunities, where policies may be needed to confirm and expand on legal requirements – such as a policy to take positive

283

action to promote equality of treatment

health, safety and welfare, where policies will be necessary about such matters as the structure of safety committees and safety consultation; and the standards to be aimed for in various aspects of accident prevention work, and in the provision of employee amenities.

It would be a useful exercise for any personnel committee to review the extent to which policy statements have already been issued, and to identify the areas in which they are missing.

Procedures – policy statements are ineffective unless procedures are introduced to ensure they are put into effect. The promotion policy example, given above, illustrates this. This policy requires a systematic promotion procedure: a timetable for internal advertising and interviewing; a method of approving the issue of external advertisements. The joint committee membership policy, too, needs a procedural drill for notifying trade unions of vacancies, ratifying new appointments and so on.

The personnel committee's job here is to check that each new policy statement is given the necessary procedural teeth. It will be concerned less with the details of these procedures (which are matters for the personnel and administrative experts) than with their existence.

Among the more obvious procedures which all authorities need are those for:

Internal promotion
Selection methods
Staff advertising
Individual grievances
Collective disputes
Discipline and appeals
Bonus implementation
Job gradings
Staff budgets.

The purpose of procedures is to set out precisely who is responsible for taking what action in what timescale in order to achieve a defined objective or reach a specified type of decision.

Again, personnel committees might call for a schedule of service-wide employment procedures relative to all formal statements in order to assess the extent to which policies are being backed by positive action.

Monitoring – only regular reporting will enable the committee to assess the real extent to which policies and their related procedures are being effective. Most major aspects of personnel work can be fairly easily assessed by some form of regular report. An internal promotion policy, for example, can be assessed by a statistical return showing the proportion of promotion vacancies actually being filled by internal candidates. A short narrative report by the personnel officer can expand and explain the cold figures.

Staff turnover, showing the proportions of voluntary and involuntary losses for different categories of employees, is a useful indicator of many policy aspects, such as employee stability and recruitment capability.

An annual report of industrial disputes showing days lost, duration and cause will, over a period, highlight trends and thus point the way for changes in policies and procedures.

Tables of average earnings per grade will reveal the extent and impact of overtime and bonus payments.

Statistics of staff in post, and vacancies, will indicate shortcomings and successes in forecasting, recruitment and internal promotion. The use of regular monitoring reports of numbers employed has already been discussed in the chapter on establishment control.

There is a danger that the committee will become overloaded with interesting but unused reports and statistics. But if the purpose of these reports is kept to the fore – that is, their use as monitors of performance – the right selection of indices and narrative reports becomes easier. There is considerable scope here for the intelligent layman to suggest new and sharper forms of report. Committees are well advised to challenge the 'professional' indices first offered by the experts. They may be used as much to conceal as to throw real light on the issue.

One example will suffice. A quarterly staff numbers return may give separate totals for, say, main grades, senior officers and principal officers, showing the net pluses and minuses. These net figures can conceal a great deal and a committee may find far more useful a breakdown for each grade of the following movements:

number of resignations
number of retirements, deaths
number of external recruits
number of transfers from lower grades
number of transfers to higher grades

with a further note, relating to numbers of posts as distinct from numbers of staff, showing:

number of extra posts – new positions
number of extra posts – upgraded from lower grade
number of posts completely disbanded
number of posts lost – transferred to higher grade.

A net movement of nil posts for one grade may thus be shown to result from significant changes, say:

two extra positions
four lower grade posts upgraded
three posts transferred to higher grade
three posts disbanded.

Committees also need to be wary of the usual statistical traps such as percentages being used without an indication of the actual numbers concerned eg:

staff turnover at 240 per cent annual rate for tree-pruners (in a monthly return) – meaning only that one of a gang of five resigned that month.

And averages being used without any indication of the range of values eg:

average weekly earnings for a group of 10 heavy vehicle drivers quoted as £70 deriving from seven earning £50 and three £117. (The £70 is arithmetically correct but will not explain why the majority of the men are taking militant action for a guaranteed £60.)

Skills are also required in interpreting some of the more subtle aspects of committee reports. For example, there is one fairly common method of persuading a committee to accept an unpopular proposal for an increase in staff. The formula is to suggest that the proposal be agreed, 'subject to a review and further endorsement in 12 months'. This may be an entirely sensible solution – but councillors should be aware that it is not overwhelmingly difficult to justify the existence of staff once they are in post.

Reading between the lines is a useful art and may indicate areas in which probing for more information may prove fruitful. For example, a report by the Social Services Director for extra staff may have appended an apparently routine concurrent report from the Chief Personnel Officer, saying: 'I have been consulted during the preparation of these proposals and do not raise objections to them in their present form'. Translated, this might read: 'I've had the hell of an argument about these extra staff. I achieved a minor reduction in the director's original proposals and as a result I am now having my arm twisted to drop my objections – but I am still not convinced, though I cannot really put my finger on a serious flaw in his csse. So I think the committee should really probe this whole situation in depth before they agree'. Similarly, a comment by the Director of Finance that 'the committee may wish to be assured of the necessity of these proposals in the light of the expenditure involved', really means 'I think these proposals are a complete waste of money'.

In summary, and taking a broad view, the Personnel Committee's role is to ensure that the authority's needs are met for a competent, economical and effective work force at all levels. The dimensions of this task include the setting of policy guidelines, ensuring that the authority has the procedures and organizational framework necessary to achieve its manpower objectives, and the shrewd monitoring of managerial and manpower performance. To these tasks, and to his day to day contacts with his authority's employees, the individual councillor can contribute the informed amateur's practical common-sense, and the politician's sensitivity for human attitudes and reactions. Qualities of this kind can be a most valuable counterpart to the sometimes more impersonal characteristics of professional management.

17 Trends and conclusions

This book has attempted to set personnel management in its local government environment and particularly to trace its historical development there. At the same time, some ideas have been suggested about future trends. As a post-script, this short, concluding chapter summarizes some aspects of the future which seem to be discernible in the confusion and uncertainty of the late 1970s – though with the certain knowledge that the only wholly predictable feature of the future is its unpredictability.

Over-riding any detailed view of the future of personnel management itself are two particular sets of uncertainties, one specific to local government, the other a national issue. First, there is the question of the direction in which local government as a whole will develop. Will financial and political pressures lead to a further shift of control from local authorities to central government or to new, single-function authorities? Local authorities certainly see this as a danger in 1980. Or will yet another debate on national devolution lead to another major re-organization of local government structures, with a possible amalgamation of present first tier authorities with larger regional assemblies? Alternatively, will growing pressure for the devolution of power to smaller, more community-based units, and for more public participation, begin to swing the pendulum back in the opposite direction along the lines of Peter Shore's 'organic change'? Personnel officers may well feel that in any event, a key emphasis in local government staff training should be the prevention of alienation between councils and public by the improvement of relationships between council staff and the communities and individuals they serve.

Secondly, there is the whole question of central government intervention in employment matters, both through legislation and by concordats with the TUC and employers' organizations. In some ways this is just one more dimension of the broader debate on centralization versus devolution. Other than in the incomes field, we are surely reaching a plateau in legislative intervention. There are few aspects of employment on which there has not been a recent (or impending) definition of statutory obligations and standards. The contrast with the freedom of 10 to 20 years ago is startling. It seems improbable that this degree of legislative control can (let alone should) be continued much further. Perhaps the personnel officer's main task in this field over the next few years is to absorb recent changes and, by the evolution of new policies and procedures, help to create a set of employment norms for many years ahead.

Such a sanguine view cannot be taken of pay. Three conflicting pressures exist here. There is the need, in national economic terms, to determine the proportion of the national cake to be taken out by incomes. There is the pressure for less inequality in earnings. There is also pressure to provide differentials to recognize and reward differences in skill, effort and responsibility. Local government is in a particularly sensitive position on these issues. Its labour-intensity results in employment costs being a major element of total expenditure. Its pay levels come under critical, and often ill-informed, scrutiny by the public and press. It employs a wider range of occupations than almost any other employer and so has to establish multifarious differentials and pay relativities. It also has a convention of long, hierarchical pay scales. Personnel officers may well have to give a great deal of thought to the possibility of producing simpler pay structures which, while reflecting some compression of traditional differentials, are perceived by staff as providing acceptable differences in pay for differences in skill and responsibility, rather than as paying for out-dated concepts of status. A simplification of management structures would be an integral part of such an excercise. It seems likely, too, that local government will have to pay more regard than heretofore to pay comparisons with other parts of the public sector, and in industry and commerce.

Devolutionary pressures and public participation have their reflections in the slow trend towards a greater involvement of employees in the management of the organizations in which they work. Worker participation may become a subject for eventual legislation but developments will (and should) continue, regardless of statutory backing. From the collective angle, pressure will continue from the trade unions. From the viewpoint of the individual employee, a greater degree of understanding, involvement and responsibility in his job is surely to be encouraged. Personnel officers will be expected to make a major contribution to these developments, which will mean changes of attitude to at least as great an extent as changes in patterns of organization. Local government will have some unique problems – the question of employee or trade union membership of councils and their committees being a subject for political as well as organizational debate. On the trade union side, a clearer view will be needed of the role of employee representatives in decision-making machinery. Should they act solely as defenders of employee interests, as a perpetual opposition, as it were, or are they willing to join with managers and councillors in jointly solving problems? This latter role carries the implication of the acceptance by employee representatives of responsibility for decisions jointly reached – even when these decisions may not appear to employees generally to be in their immediate interests.

For managers, worker participation challenges traditional concepts of managerial autonomy, and provides the opportunity for positive action to harness the whole range of talent and experience in the workforce – not merely the narrow, specific, occupational skills for which wages are paid.

This more constructive role for all employees, linked with current pressures for more equality of opportunity, may result in a growing awareness of the last remaining (and major) area of employment inequality: that between manual and non-manual employees. That such large differences as still exist should have gone unchallenged for so long indicates the existence of deep, sociological roots to what may still pass largely unnoticed as 'natural' social phenomena. Two areas of employment practice illustrate the situation.

First, the field of wage and salary systems. White collar staff consider as normal an incremental salary progression within a job, and a steady rise in salary (and status) resulting from promotions from grade to grade within a career. Manual workers are paid one fixed rate for the job; many remain in the same job, and therefore on the same pay point, all their working lives. Secondly, in the related field of career development it is noticeable how formalized systems of staff appraisals, succession planning and the like are evolved and applied almost wholly within the white collar sector. The philosophy behind these, and many other, differences is socially divisive to a degree which must surely become increasingly obvious and increasingly unacceptable. Should a movement towards the harmonization of blue and white collar employment standards get under way, local government will have particular difficulties. Existing differences have become fully institutionalized. There are two powerful and different trade union blocs for blue and white collar staff and the unions would have severe demarcation and membership problems if all employees were on the same terms. The two main sets of employment conditions differ in style and substance and are enshrined in highly detailed national agreements. There is a powerful hangover (in attitudinal terms) of the old distinctions between 'officers' and 'servants'. But the rigidity of existing differences emphasizes the importance of thinking forward to an employment environment with much greater equality of opportunities and rewards. Personnel officers should surely be ready

290

to take a leading part in any movement towards a more socially healthy environment of this kind.

Other trends have been touched on in earlier chapters. The closed shop is likely to continue to be a source of political, if not employment, controversy. The problem of second generation bonus schemes is already with many authorities; in the longer view it may be overtaken by moves towards equality of pay principles between blue and white collar staff. The search for better methods of controlling staff numbers will continue; it may fail unless expansionary attitudes and motivations are given as much attention as methods of work measurement. Selection standards and procedures still have scope for improvement. The problems of manpower planning in an institution with activities as diverse as those of local government, and as subject to sudden changes as the result of national, political decisions, have not yet been solved. Stresses within a centralized collective bargaining system may lead to more pressure for local negotiations: and within the trade union movement, breakaways from the massive general unions – particularly NALGO – may occur as particular occupational groups or professions demand more direct representation at the collective bargaining table.

So the future workload for local government personnel officers is a heavy one. What of the future of the personnel function itself? How is it evolving to cope with the increasingly complex problems of people at work in large organizations? True to local government traditions, it seems to be the function or profession itself, rather than local government as an employer, which is having to promote its own development. One result is the move towards the establishment of new professional bodies within local government, such as the Society of Chief Personnel Officers (SOCPO), which will give the personnel function the same type of institutional identity enjoyed by other professional groups. It is to be hoped that SOCPO will also be recognized formally as a body that should play a key advisory role in national collective bargaining by some form of linkage with LACSAB and the various employers' sides of the NJCs. It is, perhaps, inevitable that personnel management should follow this same path as other, older professions. Is there a danger that the 'departmentalization' of personnel management will reinforce one of the very tendencies which the function was expected to modify? Local government is not a closed environment. Employee attitudes are formed by the whole tenor of society. The personnel officer, more than any of his management colleagues, should be acutely in touch with the shifting expectations and moods of employees and employers at large. He must be 'plugged in' to the whole employment circuit, and not insulated by the walls of the Town Hall or of an introverted professional group. Close contact with his fellow professionals in other parts of the public sector, and in industry and commerce, is at least as important for real work effectiveness as any internal grouping – though the development of internal personnel associations need not be an alternative, but rather supplementary, to active involvement in the profession as a whole.

For the individual personnel officer, his recognition by councillors and other officers as someone with a positive and distinct contribution to make to local government management processes, will depend on his own personal and proven expertise. It is hoped that this book will stimulate individual personnel staff to expand their own interest, knowledge and critical awareness of the continually changing influences on their work. They will thus equip themselves for the task of developing personnel management beyond its originally narrow, administrative base to that of a major dynamic, positive and truly managerial function.

Appendix A

Table 1
Numbers of Local Government employees (by service)

Service	Non-manual	Manual	Totals
Education:			
lecturers and teachers	705,334	—	705,334
other staff	197,955	519,554	717,509
Construction	16,090	119,819	135,909
Transport services	4,383	18,066	22,449
Social services department	100,418	202,160	302,578
Public libraries and museums	33,229	8,359	41,588
Recreation: parks and baths	18,047	65,896	83,943
Environmental health	14,263	8,687	22,950
Refuse collection and disposal	3,910	45,819	49,729
Housing department	35,784	20,496	56,280
Town and country planning	22,265	407	22,672
Architect	24,217	1,001	25,218
Estates	6,682	1,488	8,170
Consumer protection	3,973	201	4,174
Other administrative departments	9,441	2,243	11,684
Chief Executives and secretaries	36,410	19,519	55,929
Personnel and management services	9,841	87	9,928
Treasurer's and computers	53,438	324	53,762
Engineers and technical	47,216	46,760	93,976
Fire service	37,802	3,343	41,145
Other services	4,351	26,423	30,774
Total	1,384,849	1,110,652	2,495,701

Notes
1. In addition to these totals, the Police Forces employ 113,836 police officers and cadets, 39,301 civilian staff, and 4,592 traffic wardens.

2. The totals shown are actual employees: for costing and other purposes, the part-timers can be converted to a smaller number of full-time equivalents.

Source: Joint Manpower Watch, March 1979

293

Table 2
Numbers of Local Government employees (by types of authority)

Type of Authority (England and Wales)	Figures in thousands			
	Manual	Non-manual	Total	%
Non-Metropolitan counties	490	693	1,183	47.4
Non-Metropolitan districts	163	122	285	11.4
Metropolitan counties	12	22	34	1.4
Metropolitan districts	283	315	598	24.0
London boroughs	126	156	282	11.3
GLC/ILEA	36	77	113	4.5
Total	1,110	1,385	2,495	100

Source: Joint Manpower Watch, March 1979.

Notes These figures exclude police and staff employed in probation, after care and Magistrates' Courts in Inner London.

Appendix B

Table 1

Manual workers' and craftsmen's basic wage rates, August 1980

Employee Group	Job Group	Weekly Rate (£)
Manual Workers (*see* Note 2 below)	A	54.45
	B	55.50
	C	57.20
	D	60.40
	E	62.89
	F	66.11
	G	68.91
	School Caretakers	63.08 to 73.25 (depending on floor area of school)
Building and engineering (*see* Note 3 below)	Engineering Craftsmen	£75 basic

Notes
1. Annual pay settlement date: 1st November.
2. The rates quoted for Manual Workers are as recommended by the Clegg Commission in August 1979, payable in stages between August 1979 and April 1980 and updated by the 1 November 1979 settlement.
3. The rates payable to building craftsmen are subject to the outcome of a pay comparability study, payable in two stages in November 1979, and April 1980.

Table 2
Average weekly earnings,
Local Government and other employment sectors, April 1978

Sector	Full-time manual employees figures in £s	
	Men	Women
Local Government	69.5	46.9
Central Government	71.1	51.7
Public Corporations	87.6	59.3
Private sector	80.5	49.0
All sectors	80.7	49.4

Source: New Earnings Survey: Department of Employment, 1978

Appendix C

Table 1

APT and C salaries as at January 1980

Grade	Minimum £s	Maximum £s	Number of Increments
Clerical 1	1,980	3,990	13
Grades 2	3,990	4,356	3
3	4,476	4,848	3
Administrative, Professional			
and Technical Grades 1	3,408	3,990	5
2	3,990	4,476	4
3	4,581	5,130	4
4	5,268	5,784	3
5	5,973	6,381	2
Senior Officers 1	6,636	7,077	2
2	7,287	7,722	2
Principal Officers 1	7,287	9,330	9
2	9,090	11,250	9
Chief Officers: salaries determined by population of authority:-	Minimum salary calculated between these figures, by relating actual population to population range		
Under 75,000	8,700	11,061	3
75-250,000	11,061	15,042	3
250-600,000	15,042	16,941	3
600-850,000	16,941	17,778	3
850-1,200,000	17,778	18,606	3
1,200-2,000,000	18,606	19,437	3
Over 2,000,000	19,437	20,217	3

Notes:
1. Annual settlement date 1st July.
2. Individual Principal Officer posts are allocated to five consecutive salary points within these ranges, thus giving four increments per post.
3. The minimum salary for an individual chief officer is determined by relating the population of his local authority to the scales set out above. His salary range then consists of three increments above this 'fulcrum point'. A further four increments may be paid for other extra responsibilities and involvement in corporate management. Chief Officers' salary maxima may consequently be some £2,500 above the figures in the table.
4. Technical 1 grade starts, for juniors, at £1,980.

Table 2
Average weekly earnings,
Local Government and other employment sectors, April 1978

Sector	Full-time non-manual employees figures in £s	
	Men	Women
Local Government	100.1	75.6
Central Government	102.8	60.0
Public Corporations	101.9	60.8
Private sector	100.3	51.6
All sectors	100.7	59.1

Source: New Earnings Survey: Department of Employment, 1978

Appendix D

National Negotiating Bodies and the Trade Unions and Staff Associations Represented on them.

National Joint Council for Administrative, Professional, Technical and Clerical Services

National and Local Government Officers' Association
General and Municipal Workers' Union
National Union of Public Employees
Transport and General Workers' Union
Confederation of Health Service Employees

National Joint Council for Manual Workers

General and Municipal Workers' Union
National Union of Public Employees
Transport and General Workers' Union

Joint Negotiating Committee for Chief Executives

Association of Local Government Chief Executives

Joint Negotiating Committee for Chief Officers

Society of Education Officers
Association of Public Service Professional Engineers
Association of Public Service Finance Officers
Association of Passenger Transport Executives and Managers
Association of Planning Officers
Association of Local Authority Chief Architects
National and Local Government Officers' Association
Union of County and District Secretaries
Guild of Directors of Social Services

Joint Negotiating Committee for Justices' Clerks

Justices' Clerks' Society

Joint Negotiating Committee for Justices' Clerks' Assistants

Association of Magisterial Officers

Burnham Further Education Committee

Association of Agricultural Education Staffs

Association of Principals of Colleges
National Association of Teachers in Further and Higher Education
National Society for Art Education

Burnham Primary and Secondary Committee

Incorporated Association of Assistant Masters
Incorporated Association of Assistant Mistresses
Incorporated Association of Headmasters
Incorporated Association of Headmistresses
National Association of School Masters/Union of Women Teachers
National Union of Teachers
National Association of Head Teachers
National Association of Teachers in Further and Higher Education

Joint Negotiating Committee for Youth Workers and Community Centre Wardens

Community and Youth Service Association
National Union of Teachers
National and Local Government Officers' Association
National Association of Teachers in Further and Higher Education

Soulbury Committee

National Union of Teachers
National Association of Inspectors and Educational Advisers
British Association of Advisers and Lecturers in Physical Education
Association of Educational Psychologists
National Association of Youth and Community Education Officers
National Association of School Meals' Organisers of the Hotel, Catering and
    Institutional Management Association

Joint Negotiating Committee (Building and Civil Engineering)

Electrical, Electronic, Telecommunications and Plumbing Trades Union
Union of Construction, Allied Trades and Technicians
General and Municipal Workers' Union
Transport and General Workers' Union

Joint Negotiating Committee (Engineering Craftsmen)

Confederation of Shipbuilding and Engineering Unions and Affiliated
    Organizations

Standing Conference for Heating, Ventilating and Domestic Engineers

National Union of Sheet Metal Workers, Coppersmiths, Heating and Domestic Engineers

Standing Conference for Electricians

Electrical, Electronic, Telecommunications and Plumbing Trades Union

National Joint Council for Workshops for the Blind

National League of the Blind and Disabled

*Joint Negotiating Committee for Former Approved Schools and Remand Homes in
England and Wales*

National Union of Teachers
Association of Community Home Schools
National Association of Heads and Matrons of Assessment Centres
National Association of Schoolmasters/Union of Women Teachers

300

Residential Establishment Officer Committee and Standing Joint Advisory Committee for Staffs of Children's Homes

The Association of Community Home Schools
Association of Hospital and Residential Care Officers
National Association of Heads and Matrons of Assessment Centres
National Association of Probation Homes and Hostels
Confederation of Health Service Employees
Managerial, Administrative, Technical and Supervisory Association (GMWU)
National Union of Public Employees
Association of Clerical, Technical and Supervisory Staff (T & GWU)

Whitley Council for New Towns Staffs

National and Local Government Officers' Association
New Towns' Chief Officers' Association

Whitley Council for the Staffs of the Industrial Estates' Corporation and Development Agencies

National and Local Government Officers' Association

National Joint Council for Local Authorities' Fire Brigades

Fire Brigades Union
National Association of Fire Officers

National Joint Council for Chief Officers of Local Authorities' Fire Brigades

National Association of Fire Officers
Chief and Assistant Chief Fire Officers' Association

Police Council

Association of Chief Police Officers of England, Wales and Northern Ireland
Association of Chief Police Officers (Scotland)
Police Superintendents' Association of England and Wales
Association of Scottish Police Superintendents
The Superintendents' Association of Northern Ireland
Police Federation for England and Wales
Scottish Police Federation
Northern Ireland Police Federation

Joint Negotiating Committee for the Probation Service

National Association of Probation Officers
Standing Conference of Chief Probation Officers

Joint Negotiating Committee for Coroners

Coroners' Society of England and Wales

Joint Negotiating Committee for the Fees of Doctors Assisting Local Authorities

British Medical Association

Source: Employee Relations in Local Government: A Guide for Members, LACSAB, 1978

Appendix E

Abbreviations used in the text

ACAS   Advisory, Conciliation and Arbitration Service
ACC   Association of County Councils
ADC   Association of District Councils
AMA   Association of Municipal Authorities
APEX   Association of Professional and Executive Staffs
APT   Association of Polytechnic Teachers
APT and C Administrative, Professional, Technical and Clerical
ASTMS   Association of Scientific, Technical and Managerial Staffs
ATCDE   Association of Teachers in Colleges and Departments
            of Education
ATTI   Association of Teachers in Technical Institutions
AUEW   Amalgamated Union of Engineering Workers
BSI   British Standards Institution
CAC   Central Arbitration Committee
CCTSW   Certificate of the Council for Training in Social Work
CMA   Certificate in Municipal Administration
COHSE   Confederation of Health Service Employees
DMA   Diploma in Municipal Administration
EAT   Employment Appeals Tribunal
EETPTU Electrical, Electronic, Telecommunications and Plumbing
            Trades Union
FBU   Fire Brigades Union
GLC   Greater London Council
GMWU   General and Municipal Workers Union
HGV   Heavy Goods Vehicle
ILEA   Inner London Education Authority
INLOGOV Institute of Local Government Studies
            (University of Birmingham)
IPM   Institute of Personnel Management
JNC   Joint Negotiating Committee
LACSAB Local Authorities' Conditions of Service Advisory Board
LAMSAC Local Authorities' Management Services and Computer
            Committee

LBMSU	London Boroughs' Management Services Unit
LGEB	Local Government Examination Board
LGTB	Local Government Training Board
MATSA	Managerial and Technical Staffs' Association
NAFO	National Association of Fire Officers
NALGO	National and Local Government Officers' Association
NAS	National Association of Schoolmasters
NATFHE	National Association of Teachers in Further and Higher Education
NIRC	National Industrial Relations Court
NJC	National Joint Council
NUPE	National Union of Public Employees
NUT	National Union of Teachers
OD	Organization Development
O and M	Organization and Methods
OR	Operational Research
OWM	Office Work Measurement
PO	Principal Officer
RIPA	Royal Institute of Public Administration
SO	Senior Officer
SOCPO	Society of Chief Personnel Officers
SOLACE	Society of Local Authority Chief Officers
TASS	Technical and Supervisory Section (of AUEW)
TGWU	Transport and General Workers' Union
TUC	Trades Union Congress
UCATT	Union of Construction, Allied Trades and Technicians
UKAPE	United Kingdom Association of Professional Engineers

Bibliography

Local Government

Bains, M A, *The New Local Authorities; management and structure*, HMSO, 1972

British Standards Institution, *Glossary of Terms used in Work Study*, BSI, 1969

Central Office of Information, *Local Government in Britain*, HMSO, 1975

Greater London Council, *Industrial Democracy in Local Government*, GLC, 1976

Knowles, R S B, *Modern Management in Local Government*, Barry Rose, 1977

LACSAB/LGTB, *Employee Relations in Local Government*, Guides for Members and Chief Officers, LACSAB, 1978

LACSAB, *The LACSAB Employee Relations Handbook*, LACSAB, 1979

LACSAB, *Schemes and Conditions of Service*, (and handbooks of the various NJCs)

LGTB, *Annual Reports*, 1969 to 1979

LGTB, *Industrial Relations Training*, LGTB, 1977

Poole, K P, *The Local Government Service*, George Allen and Unwin, 1978

Shaw and Sons, *The Local Government Superannuation Scheme*, 1974

Sherman, T P, *O and M in Local Government*, Pergamon Press, 1969

Steward, J D, *Management in Local Government*, Charles Knight and Company, 1971

Personnel Management

The reader will also find many of the IPM's publications covering specific aspects of personnel management and related subjects helpful. A catalogue giving details of these is available free from the address on the title page.

Index